The Global Stock Market

The Global Stock Market

Issuers, Investors, and Intermediaries in an Uneven World

Dariusz Wójcik

OXFORD
UNIVERSITY PRESS

This book has been printed digitally and produced in a standard specification in order to ensure its continuing availability

OXFORD
UNIVERSITY PRESS

Great Clarendon Street, Oxford OX2 6DP
United Kingdom

Oxford University Press is a department of the University of Oxford. It furthers the University's objective of excellence in research, scholarship, and education by publishing worldwide. Oxford is a registered trade mark of Oxford University Press in the UK and in certain other countries

Reprinted 2012

British Library Cataloguing in Publication Data
Data available

Library of Congress Cataloging in Publication Data
Data available

ISBN 978-0-19-959218-0

For Ania, Gordon, Maria, and Zbigniew

Contents

Preface

While media's attention devoted to finance is focused on mortgages and banks, corporate equity remains the largest class of financial assets in the world. In 2007, global stock market capitalization exceeded $50 trillion, which according to the Bank of England's estimates was one-third larger than the global value of bank deposits, and twice larger than that of government securities. The years 2003–7 have seen a spectacular boom on stock markets, with record profits of stock exchanges and investment banks. The Dow Jones Global Exchanges Index rose from 100 at the start of 2000 to 1,200 at the end of 2007, and at 650 at the end of 2010 still represents an impressive growth since its inception.

In addition to massive growth, the last decade has witnessed unprecedented qualitative changes on stock markets. Corporate sectors in emerging markets, with China, India, Russia, and Brazil in the lead, have exercised enormous demand for public equity capital, stealing the spotlight hitherto reserved by companies from mature markets. Hundreds of corporations from emerging markets listed their shares and issued equity outside of their home markets, on stock exchanges in London, New York, and other financial centres. The first inter-continental stock exchanges have emerged in the form of the NYSE-Euronext and the NASDAQ-OMX Group. At the same time, alternative trading venues, set up by investment banks, force stock exchanges to redefine their business model.

In 1992, anticipating the impact of financial liberalization and technological advances, a survey of the *Economist* entitled *Financial Centres* predicted that stock markets would divorce financial centres, with exchanges and other stock market agents free to locate anywhere. In the same year, Richard O'Brien (*Global Financial Integration: The End of Geography*, 1992) announced the rise of finance free from geographical constraints. The world, however, is still intrigued and puzzled by the relationship between the fate of stock exchanges and the fate of financial centres. In later special issues, the *Economist* admitted that their predictions were wrong. A special issue of the *Financial Times* in 2007 entitled *Financial Centres and Exchanges* testifies to the continued significance of the spatial organization of stock markets. One of the many questions here is whether the international consolidation of stock exchanges represents a turning point in the history of financial centres or whether it is just a soap opera, relevant to shareholders of the exchanges involved, but not to the balance of power between financial centres.

Major books published on stock markets in the last decade focus on primary markets (*Going Public* by Tim Jenkinson and Alexander Ljungqvist, 2001), trading and market microstructure (*Trading and Exchanges* by Larry Harris, 2003), investors' behaviour (*Irrational Exuberance* by Robert Shiller, 2005), governance (*What is an Exchange?* by Ruben Lee, 1998), historical performance (*Triumph of the Optimists* by Elroy Dimson, Paul Marsh, and Mike Staunton, 2003), historical evolution (*The Global Securities Market: A History* by Ranald Michie, 2006), and political economy (*The Origins of Europe's New Stock Markets* by Elliot Posner, 2009). None of them however pays much attention to the geographical constitution and footprint of stock markets. There is an increasing number of papers concerned with the role of proximity in stock markets, published in the *Journal of Finance* and other leading journals in financial economics, including award-winning papers on home and local bias of investors (by Joshua Coval, Tobias Moskowitz, and Harald Hau among others). Although they talk about geography, they do not engage with any geographical literature, and are far from a comprehensive spatial conceptualization of stock markets.

This monograph intends to fill this void by offering an empirically and theoretically rich, historically informed but forward-looking account of the spatial organization of stock markets. The meaning of the latter goes far beyond the question of the location of stock exchanges. It involves investors, issuers, and intermediaries, of which stock exchanges are only one. At issue is the future of the financial industry, the corporate sector, and cities.

Goals

The book has four related groups of objectives. Empirically, it documents recent trends in global stock markets. These include the cross-listing of companies from emerging markets, with emphasis on Brazil, Russia, India, and China; the reaction of stock market investors in New York, London, and Hong Kong to the global financial crisis of 2007–9; mergers and acquisitions among stock exchanges; and the emergence of alternative trading systems. Empirical evidence covers both mature and emerging stock markets in Americas, Europe, and Asia. Investigation of these trends uncovers that the global integration of stock markets cannot be seen as a simple shift from national to global markets but rather as parallel processes of globalization and localization, with growing competition accompanied by concentration of stock market intermediaries in leading urban centres.

Second, the book develops a theory of a network of stock market centres in order to explain the geographical constitution of stock markets. The theory starts with securitization of corporate ownership as a process enabling institutional and geographical dispersion of ownership. This gives rise to an industry of intermediaries linking issuers with investors, and investors with investors (including brokers, dealers, investment banks, and stock exchanges), as well as an industry of intermediaries addressing the agency and information asymmetry problems arising from the separation of management from control, and increasing distance par excellence between the two (including corporate governance rating and consultancy, investor relations, stock analysts, equity lawyers, accountants, and auditors). This multitude of firms constitutes the stock market industry. They benefit from proximity to each other, and also from proximity to issuers and investors, thus giving rise to stock market centres, functioning in a network underpinned by international operations of stock market intermediaries, with investment banks in the lead.

Third, the book argues that the footprint of stock markets is uneven. Stock market centres benefit from agglomeration economies present in leading urban centres, and are key to their growth. They flourish in legal and institutional environments that promote securitization, such as the United States and the United Kingdom. In addition, the network of stock market centres does not serve all sectors and places equally. Issuers from stock market centres tend to be over-represented on stock markets. There is a core-periphery pattern in stock market development, which persists even in countries with the highest level of securitization.

Finally, with regard to the future, the book suggests that we are far from the end of history of stock markets. While securitization of mortgages got out of control and is likely to be curtailed, there is a lot of room for continued securitization of corporate ownership, as well as cross-listing, cross-border portfolio investment, and consolidation of stock exchanges. While high inflation, and the glut of government securities crowding out equity may threaten the short-term future of stock markets, in contrast to some interpretations of the 1929 great crash, stock markets are not seen as the villains of the current recession, and are likely to be revived, continuing to shape the geography of cities, financial sector, and corporations.

In summary, the book shows how the map of stock markets is being redrawn at the start of the twenty-first century, and how central this map is to understanding the structure and dynamics of the world economy.

Intended readership

The book is written in a manner accessible to mid- and upper-level undergraduate students, graduate students, and academics, and should also be of interest to financial analysts and policymakers. The empirical evidence of the book is presented without the use of advanced mathematics or statistical models.

The student audience would include MBA students as well as students in business and management, economics, geography, sociology, and political science. As the book covers the key components of the stock markets in a systematic manner, it could serve as an introduction explaining how stock markets work in the real world. It could also complement reading lists for courses on globalization, as it presents the tensions between the forces of globalization and localization, as they play out in stock markets.

For academics, the book is a contribution to research in business and economics, as well as social sciences in general. It reviews and extends studies on the role of geography in financial markets found in financial economics, as well as research on the historical, political, and social construction of financial markets in history, geography, sociology, political science, and urban studies. This book both challenges and complements the existing works by offering the first comprehensive account focused on the spatial organization of stock markets, and arguing how crucial geography is to understanding these markets.

Financial analysts and policymakers should find this book attractive not least because they are likely to search for works based on alternatives and complements to mainstream financial economic theory. The book reviews various biases existing in stock markets, makes a strong argument about their uneven development in space, and draws implications for the future of stock markets and financial centres. As such, it should appeal not only to those interested in stock markets but also to those interested in the competition between different financial systems and financial centres.

The theoretical component of the book as well as its rich empirical coverage, including the United Kingdom, Continental Europe, North and South America and Asia, and mature as well as emerging and developing markets, makes it relevant to audiences around the world. Not a single chapter goes unfurnished with diverse and comprehensive data, some of which is presented, not only interpreted, for the first time in an academic publication.

Intellectual agenda

In the wake of the global financial crisis, mainstream financial economics has been criticized for promoting a benign picture of financial markets, derived from the efficient market hypothesis (EMH). The economics editor of the *Daily Telegraph* has even described the EMH as a massive intellectual failure responsible for the crisis (Conway 2009). While the rumours about the death of the EMH may be premature, the least that is required, paraphrasing a recent briefing of the *Economist* on the state of economics, is to re-establish the study of finance as a part of social science of the real world (2009).

Behavioural economics is often anointed as a successor of the EMH, with its success resting largely on a marriage of economics with psychology. This book provides another alternative, rooted in a combination of economic geography and financial economics. In this approach, stock markets are not seen as consisting of anonymous actors interacting in space with no friction of distance or any other significance of geography. They are made of issuers, investors, and intermediaries that have locations and relate to each other in a real space of regions, cities, and countries. Multiple information asymmetries existing in stock markets have fundamental geographical dimensions, as proximity, though to a varying degree, helps to minimize them. Here, I build on the established work of Sanford Grossman and Joseph Stiglitz (1976, 1980) as well as recent research on the role of proximity in stock markets emerging in financial economics.

The analysis of the uneven access to information, combined with agglomeration economies, leads me to propose a theory of stock market centres. This is, however, not a top-down model a la Paul Krugman's new economic geography. Rather, it is a conceptual framework built inductively on empirical material, grounded in the tradition of financial geography, exemplified by the works of Stuart Corbridge, Ron Martin, and Nigel Thrift (*Money, Power and Space*, 1994); Ron Martin (*Money and the Space Economy*, 1999); Gordon L. Clark, Adam Dixon, and Ashby Monk (*Managing Financial Risks*, 2009), as well as my own earlier work with Gordon L. Clark (*The Geography of Finance*, 2007).

The theory of stock market centres advanced in this book is closely related to the theories of Saskia Sassen (*Global City*, 2001) and Peter Taylor (*World City Network*, 2004), as it shows how seemingly abstract market mechanisms translate into a tangible reality of cities. There is, however, one key difference. In the world of global and world cities, business services firms co-locate and form the core of leading urban centres, but proximity to their corporate customers does not matter. In the world of stock market centres, proximity of issuers to intermediaries and investors matters as well.

The analysis of relationships between different stock market actors undertaken in this book highlights the social construction of stock markets, allying it with social studies of finance, including the works of Paul Langley (*The Everyday Life of Global Finance*, 2008), Donald MacKenzie (*An Engine Not a Camera*, 2006), and Karin Knorr Cetina and Alex Preda (*The Sociology of*

Financial Markets, 2005). The bottom–up, fact-rich account of the book allies it also with works in financial history, in particular studies focused on the development of financial centres, such as those by Youssef Cassis (*Capitals of Capital*, 2006) and Daniel Verdier (*Moving Money*, 2002).

In summary, the book takes a multidisciplinary approach building on insights from economic geography, financial economics, financial sociology, financial history, and interdisciplinary studies on globalization. As such, it aims at contributing to the social science of the real world of finance.

Structure

Chapter 1 introduces the map of the global stock market, demonstrating that its development is a quintessential part of economic integration and globalization. It starts with an outline of the history of stock markets, and then focuses on their unprecedented growth in the last two decades. Data and novel measures are used to show that the development of stock markets is highly uneven, and far from finished. There remains a large potential for future growth, even in the most developed markets. Existing explanations of stock market development are shown as insufficient, ignoring the spatial nature of stock market processes, and focusing too narrowly on the national scale of analysis. The chapter finishes with a summary of controversies surrounding the role of stock markets in economy and society, and a roadmap for the rest of the book.

Chapter 2 starts the investigation of the role of proximity in stock market relations, by focusing on issuers entering the market. It shows that firms from leading business centres of their countries are more likely to go public than their provincial counterparts. This bias in listings is analysed for thirty-two countries, including all members of the European Union, the United States, and Japan. It is shown to be particularly strong in countries with underdeveloped stock markets and closed corporate governance regimes, but it is still present in countries with the most developed stock markets and most open corporate governance, such as the United Kingdom and the United States. Potential reasons for the bias are discussed, including the benefits of issuers' proximity to initial public offerings intermediaries and specialized labour markets, corporate governance incentives, as well as national and local institutional factors.

Chapter 3 continues the focus on issuers, but this time in an international context. The analysis is based on the most dynamic part of the foreign listing market in 2000s: issuers from Brazil, Russia, India, and China listing their shares in the United States, the United Kingdom, and Luxembourg. The results show that these issuers are mostly large firms, coming from relatively high-growth, internationally oriented sectors, and headquartered overwhelmingly in the leading business centres of their home countries. Key intermediaries in the foreign listing process are the global investment banks, linking the locations of the cross-listing firms with the financial centres where the host stock exchanges are located. Competition is fierce, with both the host markets and intermediaries specializing in terms of the size, sector, and geographical origin of the issuers they serve.

In Chapter 4, the focus of the book switches from primary to secondary markets. The main argument is that proximity between investors and issuers plays an important part in explaining the behaviour and performance of investors in the trading of stocks. The chapter combines insights from research on home and local bias in financial economics, showing that investors overweigh local and domestic stocks in their portfolios, with economic geographical research on proximity and knowledge in financial markets. There are many types of proximity that matter in secondary stock markets: physical, cognitive, social, organizational, and institutional. Their implications are discussed for investment industry, corporate sectors, communities, and policymakers. The chapter finishes by discussing the limits to the role of proximity, determined mainly by the demand for liquidity and global knowledge.

With continued focus on investors, Chapter 5 investigates the circulation of information on secondary stock markets, using the case study of HSBC shares traded on the exchanges in New York, London, and Hong Kong. The distribution of price discovery is analysed across the three markets, within a twenty-four-hour cycle of trading, and in the period between 2006 and 2009. London, the seat of HSBC headquarters, home to most of its decision-makers and key business relationships, dominates price discovery. Hong Kong, the former home of HSBC and hub of its Asian operations, is second. New York, unable to rival London or Hong Kong's access to private information about HSBC, is last. Its role in price formation was particularly weak during the financial crisis, when confidence in publicly available information was at its lowest.

Chapter 6 switches the focus of the book to stock exchanges, providing a detailed empirical account of the geographical nature of their activities. The analysis focuses on the case study of the Warsaw Stock Exchange (WSE) in Poland, representing one of the most dynamic and successful stock markets in the world in the last decade. The empirical sections investigate the relationships of the WSE with exchange members, issuers, and investors, showing that technology complements rather than substitutes the value of physical proximity, as many stock exchange activities rely on close social contacts. It is argued that the success of the WSE lies in its embeddedness in the Polish economy and long-term developmental perspective. The chapter also suggests that while the international consolidation of exchanges is likely to continue, financial centres and exchanges remain crucially important for each other.

Chapter 7 investigates competition in the stock exchange industry and its relationship with the development of financial centres. In 2000s, regulation in the United States and Europe unleashed competition never before witnessed in the stock exchange industry. By 2010, new exchanges in the United States and Europe proved successful in the battle for liquidity. Essential to their success was the adoption of a simple and efficient business model of two-sided platforms, which contrasts with and threatens the model of diversification and vertical integration embraced by incumbent exchanges. The increased competition and network effects in the industry have been accompanied by its continued concentration in the New York City area in the United States, and emerging dominance of London in Europe. The chapter argues that while their iconic incumbent exchanges may suffer, revolution in the stock exchange industry benefits New York City and London as financial centres.

Chapter 8 summarizes the argument of the book, proposing a theory of stock market centres, understood as concentrations of stock market intermediaries, investors, and issuers' headquarters, operating through a global network. The theory is supported with evidence presented in Chapters 1–7, as well as new empirical evidence on the size and evolution of stock market centres in the six largest economies of the world: the United States, China, Japan, Germany, France, and the United Kingdom. In this way, the book completes the journey from the map of stock markets focused on countries to a more complex, but also truer map on which cities play a key part. The chapter finishes with speculations about the implications of the theory of stock market centres, as well as other theoretical and empirical findings of the book, for the future of the global stock market and cities.

Acknowledgements

Inevitably, a project like this draws upon the resources and materials of a whole range of institutions. Most importantly, I was fortunate to work on this book in a stimulating and supportive environment of the School of Geography and the Environment, Oxford University, and St. Peter's College, Oxford. In addition to these institutions, Jesus College, Oxford, and the British Academy (SG-54019) provided financial support for parts of the project.

I would like to thank those who facilitated access to data. Tyrone Bester from Bureau Van Dijk in London helped with the Amadeus and ORBIS databases; Kanako Toyooka from the Statistics Bureau of Japan helped with data on Japan; Jiazhe Sun with data on China; Rafael Plata with data from the Federation of European Stock Exchanges; Michael Grote with data on Germany; and Artur Kawończyk with data from Factiva.

Beyond data, I benefited from interviews with a large number of stock market experts. In Poland, this was first of all Wiesław Rozłucki, President of the Warsaw Stock Exchange, an economic geographer and the longest serving chief executive in the stock exchange industry in one person. My research in Poland drew upon a long list of interviewees: Lidia Adamska, Raimondo Eggink, Ewa Gajewska-Markiewicz, Krzysztof Grabowski, Łukasz Jagiełło, Beata Kacprzyk, Adam Maciejewski, Andrzej Sopoćko, Iwona Sroka, Piotr Szeliga, Andrzej Szerszeń Fernando Bicho, Jarosław Dominiak, Bartosz Drabikowski, Mirosław Dusza, Waldemar Gębuś, Marcin Hejka, Norbert Jeziołowicz, Mirosław Kachniewski, Adam Kałdus, Stanisław Knaflewski, Alicja Kornasiewicz, Wojciech Kostrzewa, Jarosław H. Kozłowski, Jan Kuźma, Marek Łukaszewski, Krzysztof Opawski, Paweł Orkisz, Jakub Papierski, Wojciech Sadowski, and Ludwik Sobolewski.

In Sweden, those who shared their expertise with me were: Claes-Urban Dackberg, Kerstin Hermansson, David Woods, Kristian Blixt, Thomas Asada, Per-Ola Jansson, Per Högberg, and Olof Neiglick. In Norway: Eivind Hadler-Olsen, Vegard Annweiler, Christopher Møllerløkken, Ottar Ertzeid, Ole G. Stenhagen, Eirik Bunaes, and Johan Solbu Braaten. In Denmark: Klaus Willerslev-Olsen, Søren Gade, Jan Ovesen, Nicolai Wallin Pedersen, Poul Erik Skaaning-Jørgensen, Gorm Praefke, and Claus Silfverberg. In Ireland: Tom

Healy, Deirdre Somers, Tom Hardiman, Ken O'Brien, Derek Moriarty, Deirdre Lyons, Donncha Connolly, Michael Deasy, Caoimhe Scolard, Myles Lee, Enda Twomey, Damian Neylin, Gary Palmer, Pat Wall, Brian Healy, David Dillon, and Michael Walsh. In London: Alasdair Haynes, Mark Hemsley, Peter Randall, and Willy Van Stappen.

Many people offered help throughout the project. Alan Gilbert and Peter Wood provided support at the early stage of my research on stock markets, during my lectureship at the University College London. Najat El Mekkaoui de Freitas and Gunther Capelle-Blancard shared with me their expertise in financial econometrics. Angel Pardo offered supportive comments at the Convention of the Federation of European Stock Exchanges in Brussels, December 2009. I also benefited from presenting parts of the project at conferences and seminars, obtaining valuable comments from Yibiao Chen and Steven Zhou at the Hong Kong Polytechnic University; Ewald Engelen, Manuel Aalbers, and Anna Glasmacher from the University of Amsterdam; and Javier Lezaun and Marc Ventresca from Said Business School, Oxford.

Close to home, I was lucky to test the ideas for the book with my colleagues at the School of Geography and the Environment, including fellow economic geographers Ashby Monk and Adam Dixon, as well as my doctoral students including Atif Ansar and Steve Lew. Olga Thönissen, Kiran Rajashekariah, and Chang Liu provided exceptional research assistance. Csaba Burger helped with both impeccable research assistance and ideas, being a co-author of one of the papers that contributed to the book. I have also tested preliminary findings for the book on a great audience of undergraduate and graduate students. Christopher produced Boote an exemplary dissertation on the geography of the US stock markets, and together with Joanna Wilkin, Christopher Roberts, and Daniel Levene helped with proofreading. Most inspiring of all has been Gordon L. Clark, who has helped me with his great insights and practical advice throughout the project. I would like to dedicate this book to him, in addition to my supportive wife Ania, and my parents Maria and Zbigniew, who nurtured my economic geographical hobby.

The author would like to acknowledge the permission of Oxford University Press to republish portions of 'Financial centre bias in primary equity markets' (2009), *Cambridge Journal of Regions, Economy and Society*, 193–209; and portions of 'The role of proximity in secondary equity markets' in *Managing Financial Risks: From Global to Local*, edited by Gordon L. Clark, Adam D Dixon and Ashby H.B. Monk (2009, 140–62). The author would also like to acknowledge the permission of John Wiley and Sons to republish portions of 'Geography of stock markets' (2009), *Geography Compass*, 1499–514; portions of 'Geography and the future of stock exchanges: Between real and virtual space' (2007), *Growth and Change*, 200–23; and portions of 'Listing BRICs: Stock issuers from Brazil, Russia, India, and China in New York, London, and Luxembourg' (2010), *Economic Geography*, 275–96.

List of Figures

List of Tables

List of Abbreviations

ADR	American Depositary Receipt
AIM	Alternative Investment Market
BNYM	Bank of New York Mellon
BRIC	Brazil, Russia, India, China
CEO	Chief Executive Officer
CITI	Citibank
CS	Credit Suisse
DR	Depositary Receipt
FC	Financial Centre
FESE	Federation of European Securities Exchanges
GDP	Gross Domestic Product
GDR	Global Depositary Receipt
GMT	Greenwich Mean Time
GS	Goldman Sachs
HKEx	Hong Kong Exchanges and Clearing Ltd
IPO	Initial Public Offering
ISD	Investment Services Directive
IT	Information Technology
LSE	London Stock Exchange
M&A	Mergers and Acquisitions
MC	Market Capitalization
MiFID	Markets in Financial Instruments Directive
ML	Merrill Lynch
MPT	Modern Portfolio Theory
MS	Morgan Stanley
MSA	Metropolitan Statistical Area
MTF	Multilateral Trading Facility
NYSE	New York Stock Exchange
OTC	Over-The-Counter

SEC	Securities and Exchange Commission
SME	Small and Medium-sized Enterprise
SWF	Sovereign Wealth Fund
WFE	World Federation of Exchanges
WSE	Warsaw Stock Exchange

1

Introducing the Map of the Global Stock Market

This chapter introduces the global stock market and presents the background information essential to contextualize the purpose of the book. Reflecting the multidisciplinary approach taken, it is an introduction that combines the basic economics of stock markets with their history, geography, and social scientific accounts. It starts with an outline of the roots and history of stock markets, highlighting their geographical nature, and moves on to focus on their unprecedented recent growth. As subsequent sections show, the map of stock markets around the world is highly uneven, and existing explanations of this map are insufficient. There is no end of the history of stock markets in sight, and the remaining potential for their development is high. The chapter finishes with a summary of controversies surrounding the role of stock markets in economy and society, and a roadmap for the rest of the book. Throughout the chapter up-to-date data is presented and analysed and novel measures of stock market development are introduced. Stock market development is demonstrated as a quintessential part of economic globalization. This chapter also introduces readers unfamiliar with stock markets to some basic vocabulary while explaining the structure and functions of stock markets.

The briefest history of stock markets

Stock markets are markets where stocks are sold and bought. Stocks (or shares) are issued by companies and sold to investors in order to raise capital. In contrast to debt, capital collected via issuance of shares does not ever need to be returned. Stockholders (or shareholders) are co-owners of the company, and have the right to influence corporate decision-making by exercising their votes at shareholders' meetings, the right to collect dividends (a part of company profits paid out to shareholders), and in case of the company going bankrupt, the right to obtain a share of proceeds from the sale of corporate assets left over after the repayment of debts. In addition to common stocks (ordinary shares), which give owners one vote and identical dividend rights per share, companies can issue preferred shares, with multiple votes and/or special dividend rights. When stocks are bought from the company that issues them, we refer to such transactions as the primary stock market. Shares sold and bought between investors and traders themselves constitute secondary stock markets (Mishkin 2007).

The existence of a stock market requires the existence of companies that issue stocks, known as joint-stock companies or corporations. The first joint-stock companies were created in the early seventeenth century, including the Dutch East India Company, which by 1617 had 954 shareholders (Davies 1961). This and other pioneering corporations were given charters by the state, and acted as prime agents of colonial expansion. Free incorporation, removing the need for government to authorize the purposes of a corporation, became widespread only in the nineteenth century and achieved the greatest scale in the United States, where it played a prominent part in raising capital for the rise of the United States to industrial power (Braithwaite and Drahos 2000). Indeed, the expansion of corporations transformed the whole economy, as it no longer needed to rely on family firms. In contrast to the latter, corporations could mobilize capital from thousands, and with time millions of scattered investors, and were not dependant on the life span of any particular owner. They were much less restricted by space and time.

Primary stock markets cannot survive without secondary markets, where investors trade shares and thus modify their investment portfolios. Trading can take place directly between investors, on an Over-The-Counter (OTC) market, but an overwhelming share of it became centralized in meeting places of professional stock traders, who collect orders from investors or trade on their own account. The concentration of trading in space and time, making it easier for traders to find a counterpart, judge their reputation, and exchange information, led to the creation of stock exchanges, with stocks being listed and traded according to established rules (Laulajainen 2003). Firms listing their shares on a stock exchange for the first time are referred to as going public, a process mostly combined with the issuance of new shares known as the Initial Public Offering (IPO). The first major stock exchange was established in Amsterdam in 1602 in order to trade the stocks of the Dutch East India Company. The London Stock Exchange (LSE) emerged as the premier market when French troops invaded Amsterdam in 1795, and maintained its dominance (though periodically heavily contested by the Paris Bourse) until 1914, when the New York Stock Exchange (NYSE) took over the lead in terms of size (Braithwaite and Drahos 2000).

With free incorporation taking hold in Europe and North America, in the mid-nineteenth century, the supply of new corporations was large and stock exchanges were plentiful. The United States had hundreds and large European countries tens of them (Michie 2008). Each major city had a stock exchange, where local investors traded the shares of local companies. Throughout the nineteenth century, exchanges also developed in Latin America, Africa, Asia, Australia, and Oceania, and were particularly common in British colonies. The popularization of telegraph and the invention of telephone enabled the integration of stock markets, as information relevant to stock prices could now be collected from far away and acted upon quickly. A parallel trend was the growth of corporations, operating increasingly on a national and international scale. Consequently, in the course of the twentieth century local and regional stock exchanges were decimated in all but very large economies. National stock markets were forged, with national indices and systems for the clearing and settlement of transactions (Franks et al. 2009). The period between 1900 and 1914 also witnessed a significant market for cross-border stock transactions, primarily within Europe and between Europe and North America, for example with British investments in the US railway corporations.

The main function of the stock market is to establish the value of corporate shares. A large number of transactions, that is, a high liquidity of a stock market contributes to the process of price discovery. Financial return from holding shares consists of dividends and the appreciation of share price, that is, capital gain (Solnik 1999). Thus, the estimation of a share price requires at the very least predictions about the future profitability of the firm, which in turn involves guesswork about the future condition of the entire economy. There is no upper limit on a share price, while the bottom limit is zero. This is why investments in stocks are risky, and in the long run should be more profitable than relatively safe investments, such as government bonds. Between 1900 and 2000 the US stock markets, for example, have yielded an arithmetic average of 8.7 per cent per year above inflation, with the standard deviation of 20.2 per cent, compared to US bonds with real returns of 2.1 per cent per year and standard deviation of 10 per cent (Dimson et al. 2002). As a corollary of high risk and high potential return stock markets are affected by investor sentiment and irrational behaviour, resulting in a cycle of booms and busts, with the bursting of the internet boom in 2001 being a recent example (Shiller 2005).

Although the birth and development of stock markets have been facilitated by legal inventions and the state, it was the Great Depression in the United States, triggered by the stock market crash of 1929, which provided a milestone in the regulation of stock markets. As a part of New Deal, the Securities and Exchange Act was passed in 1933, followed by the establishment of the Securities and Exchange Commission in 1934, which introduced strict entry requirements for companies willing to list their shares on stock exchanges, reporting duties for those listed, and a separation of investment from universal banking in order to insulate the latter from the vagaries of the stock market. The US model of stock market regulation spread (though with significant modifications) to many parts of the world. Many countries have emulated it, and Japan, for example, was persuaded to adopt it in late 1940s by the US military authorities (Braithwaite and Drahos 2000). Thus, while until 1930s stock exchanges operated largely as private clubs of traders, they emerged from 1940s as government controlled, semi-public institutions, granted a near-monopoly on organizing stock markets in their countries (Michie 2008).

The world of national and monopolistic stock exchanges started to crumble in late 1970s, and since then we have witnessed a gradual globalization of stock markets. The rising multinational enterprises have started listing on foreign exchanges to tap into new pools of capital and increase their visibility (Karolyi 2006). Institutional investors, including pension funds, have developed a huge demand for and means to diversify their portfolios internationally (Clark 2000). Stock exchanges themselves have been deregulated (though to various degrees in different countries), exposing them to international competition. New technology has again proven crucial, as computer networks have removed the necessity of traders meeting in one place, enabled an automatic processing of orders, and revolutionized investors' access to information. This has made virtual trading possible, and has questioned the raison d'être of stock exchanges. In response, many stock exchanges have become private publicly listed companies, engaged in international mergers and alliances, and redefined themselves as IT businesses selling listing services to issuers and information services to investors (Budd 1995; Lee 1998).

The globalization of stock markets has also involved their regulation. With companies issuing and listing shares, and investors trading on an increasingly international basis, the demand has arisen to coordinate various national rules on listing, disclosure, and illegal trading practices, as well as to integrate clearing and settlement systems to ensure quick and inexpensive cross-border payments and transfers of share ownership. The International Organization of Securities Commissions was established in 1983, and has been instrumental in promoting the application of the International Financial Reporting Standards (formerly known as International Accounting Standards) commonly applied by firms around the world, and adopted as compulsory for listed companies in the European Union in 2005 (Braithwaite and Drahos 2000). Some steps have also been undertaken, particularly within the EU, towards the coordination of listing rules as well as clearing and settlement. To be sure, it is a heavily contested process. Stock market integration lies at the core of capital market integration, and opinions on the desired extent and speed of this process differ between countries and stakeholders (Story and Walter 1997).

The development of stock markets in terms of size and significance is by no means linear – a history of continuous expansion. Stock markets first developed in the seventeenth century, but the scandalous Mississippi and South Sea Company bubbles in 1720 cast a long shadow on stock market development, resulting in stagnation, particularly in England and France, but less so, for example, in the Netherlands, allowing Amsterdam to continue as Europe's leading financial centre throughout the eighteenth century. The mid-nineteenth to early twentieth century saw stock markets flourishing, partly due to the industrial revolution and partly due to the little competition for savings from government debt, the levels of which were low in this period of relative peace in international relations. After the First World War, stock market activity was subdued in Europe (with equity crowded out by government borrowing), but it continued to boom in the United States, with an unprecedented spread of corporate ownership, exemplified by ATT owned by approx. 0.5 million people in 1930. The Great Depression halted this development decisively. In 1939, the turnover value on the NYSE was less than 10 per cent of that in 1929 and less than half of that in 1920 (Michie 2006). After the Second World War, stock market activity remained subdued. It was reinvigorated only in late 1970s with deregulation of stock exchanges, the rise of institutional investors, privatization of the corporate sector, as well as technological advances.

The development of the geographical organization of stock markets cannot be seen as a linear progression from local to global markets either. From their inception in the seventeenth century, stock exchanges were focused on trading government debt instruments and relatively few corporate stocks. Only the mid-nineteenth century saw a boom in local and regional stock exchanges focused on railway, utilities, mining, with the largest stock exchanges, like those in London and Paris, still focused on government debt and developing trading in foreign securities. To be sure the situation differed between countries, as even in late nineteenth century, German governments did not support stock market activity, which was considered as speculation (in response large banks internalized stock market transactions to avoid taxes and regulation). The regional and local stock exchanges started to disappear in early twentieth century due to technology, but also due to state intervention. Costly regulation favoured large exchanges that could afford it, and so did high levels of government debt, which does not need multiple trading venues, as in contrast to corporate equity, it is national in nature, and does not rely on local or regional knowledge base. Thus, centralization of control over stock markets, spearheaded by the Securities and Exchange Act in the United States, and spread around the world, contributed to concentration in the geographical organization of stock market industry, including stock exchanges and brokerages. The decline of regional and local stock exchanges was however slow and long. In France, exchanges were consolidated in 1967, in the United Kingdom provincial exchanges were merged with the LSE in 1973, while in few large federal states such as the United States and Germany, regional stock exchanges still exist.

Unprecedented recent growth with a qualification

Any social scientist, with the possible exception of historians, could probably be found guilty of exaggerating the significance of contemporary features and trends. Mindful of that bias, however, it still has to be argued that stock markets have never before played such an important role in the world economy, as they do at the start of the twenty-first century.

First of all, the spread of stock markets globally is unprecedented. In 1980, when the United Nations (UN) had 154 member states, fifty-nine countries had a stock exchange (Clayton et al. 2006). In July 2010, out of 192 members of the UN, 134 hosted a stock exchange and further thirteen were covered by a regional stock exchange arrangement (East Caribbean Securities Exchange and West Africa Regional Exchange). There were only twenty-one countries with a population over one million, which did not have a stock exchange, with the largest of them (over ten million) being: Ethiopia, Dem. Rep. of Congo, Burma (Myanmar), North Korea, Yemen, Madagascar, Angola, Chad, and Cuba. To be sure this spread of exchanges cannot be attributed to pure bottom-up forces of demand. It was fuelled by the collapse of communist countries, establishing or re-establishing stock exchanges; and affected by finance-led development strategies promoted by the International Monetary Fund and the World Bank. While the British Empire scattered many stock exchanges around the world in the nineteenth and early twentieth centuries, the Washington Consensus helped the proliferation of stock markets in the 1990s and 2000s (Weber et al. 2009).

The recent growth of stock markets has also been unprecedented in terms of size. In 2010, there were approx. 45,000 listed companies in the world, almost twice more than twenty years earlier (World Federation of Exchanges 2010). Since 1990, companies around the world have raised approx. $2.5 trillion through IPOs. The global stock market capitalization, the total market value of outstanding publicly traded equity at the end of 2009 was close to $50 trillion, five times that in 1990 (Figure 1.1). This represented nearly 100 per cent of the world's gross domestic product (GDP), while in 1913 (at the end of a long period of dynamic stock market development) the ratio was close to 50 per cent (Rajan and Zingales 2003*b*). This growth was most spectacular in emerging markets. Figure 1.2 shows the change in market capitalization (MC) since 2002. The top of the graph is occupied by emerging market economies,

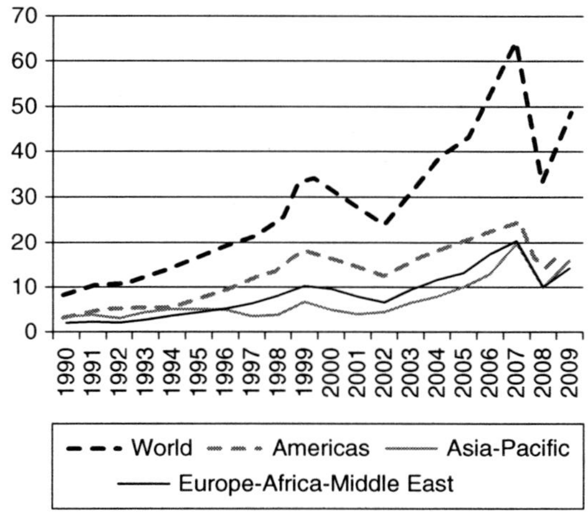

Figure 1.1. Stock market capitalization, 1990–2009 (USD trillion current prices)
Sources: Author based on data from the World Federation of Exchanges.

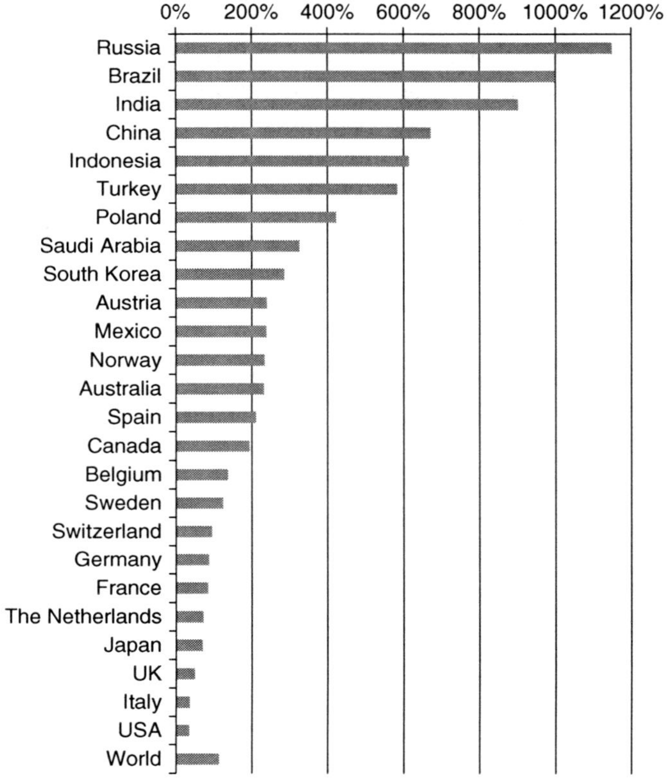

Figure 1.2. Increase in domestic stock market capitalization, 2002–9
Sources: Author based on data from the World Federation of Exchanges.

many with more than a fivefold growth, despite the downturn of 2008. The very notion of emerging markets has been commonly associated with stock markets rather than any other part of their economies or financial markets.

Stock markets have grown not only in terms of extensity (geographical spread) and intensity (size in relation to the economy), but also in terms of velocity. Since 2000, the total number of stock trades has increased eightfold (World Federation of Exchanges 2010). While in late 1980s, stock exchanges could boast of executing tens of trades per second, in 2010 some exchanges can handle a million transactions within a second. The increased velocity has been enabled by technology but also deregulation driving the trading costs down.

In the last decade the growth in secondary stock markets outpaced that in primary stock markets. In simple terms, the stock market development took the form of much larger trading activity for stocks already listed, rather than bringing new companies to the stock market. Figure 1.3 illustrates this phenomenon, presenting change in the number of listed companies between the end of 2000 and the end of 2009 for selected major economies. While the United Kingdom and particularly emerging markets steamed ahead with new listings, in the United States the number of listed companies fell by 28 per cent. In many Western European countries, primary stock markets also contracted or stagnated. The year 2000 was the peak of the Internet boom, which brought thousands of new companies around the world to the stock market. When the bubble burst, hundreds of companies ceased to exist and further hundreds left the public stock market. In some developed economies, the primary stock market still has not recovered.

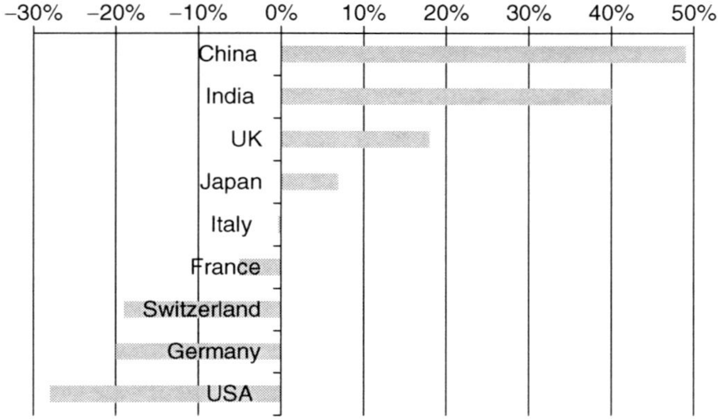

Figure 1.3. Change in the number of listed companies, 2000–9

Sources: Author based on data from the World Federation of Stock Exchanges.

Uneven development

The stock market boom of the last decades, however unprecedented, has not levelled the development of stock markets around the world. The most popular measure of stock market development is the ratio of stock market capitalization to GDP. To be sure, it is far from a perfect measure. First, it is subject to market booms and crashes. The use of short-term credit in stock trading can further inflate stock prices. The recent global financial crisis of 2007–9 serves as a warning that high ratios relating financial stocks and flows to the underlying economy cannot be used uncritically as measures of financial development and economic sophistication (Roxburgh et al. 2009). Second, MC is biased towards companies with large capitalization. A country with few but very large listed companies may appear to have a much more developed stock market than one with a large number of small listed companies. Mistakes are commonly made interpreting the ratio. Consider, for example, a report of the Scottish Enterprise (2005) evaluating the chances of Scotland becoming and international financial centre location. Drawing a profile of Milan as on of the competitors, the report states: 'Milan stock exchange accounts for 47% of national GDP' (45). An unskilled reader may even think that the stock exchange contributes 47 per cent of Italy's GDP! A semi-skilled reader may still get an impression that 47 per cent of the Italian economy is somehow represented on the stock market. Only skilled readers would know that this statement means nothing less and nothing more than the MC to GDP ratio for Italy being 0.47.

With these precautions in mind, we can move on to analysing Table 1.1 presenting the MC to GDP ratio for fifty countries as at the end of 2009. The sample includes all twenty-five largest economies in the world (according to nominal GDP), plus a selection of other countries with available data. The ratio differs greatly between countries. While the median ratio for the whole sample is 0.66, only thirteen countries have ratios within the range between 0.50 and 0.85. The highest ratio in the table, for Hong Kong, is inflated as market capitalization for Hong Kong includes Mainland Chinese companies cross-listed in Hong Kong. However, even if only Hong Kong headquartered companies were considered (which account for approximately half of the Hong Kong market capitalization), Hong Kong would still lead the list. On the other extreme, the lowest ratio is found for Argentina.

What factors account for the variation of the MC to GDP ratios? One influential body of research, known as law and finance, has highlighted the role of legal rules protecting investors, and shareholders in particular. If laws protect shareholder rights, for example, by prohibiting multiple-voting or non-voting shares, and empowering minority shareholders, stock market

Table 1.1. Stock market capitalization (MC), GDP, and legal family by country

Country	Legal family	MC 2009 (billion $)	GDP 2009 (billion $)	MC/GDP
Hong Kong	English	2,305	215	10.72
South Africa	English	799	286	2.79
Singapore	English	481	182	2.64
Malaysia	English	286	192	1.49
Australia	English	1,262	925	1.36
The United Kingdom	English	2,796	2,175	1.29
Canada	English	1,677	1,336	1.26
The United States	English	15,077	14,256	1.06
India	English	1,307	1,296	1.01
Israel	English	189	195	0.97
Thailand	English	177	264	0.67
New Zealand	English	36	125	0.28
Ireland	English	61	227	0.27
Sri Lanka	English	10	42	0.23
Luxembourg	French	105	52	2.02
Chile	French	231	164	1.41
Spain	French	1,435	1,460	0.98
Brazil	French	1,337	1,572	0.85
The Netherlands	French	628	792	0.79
France	French	1,864	2,649	0.70
Belgium	French	306	469	0.65
Colombia	French	141	231	0.61
Peru	French	72	127	0.56
Philippines	French	86	160	0.54
Egypt	French	91	188	0.49
Mexico	French	352	875	0.40
Indonesia	French	215	540	0.40
Turkey	French	234	617	0.38
Greece	French	113	330	0.34
Portugal	French	71	227	0.31
Italy	French	656	2,113	0.31
Argentina	French	46	309	0.15
Switzerland	German	1,065	500	2.13
Taiwan	German	658	379	1.74
South Korea	German	835	833	1.00
China	German	3,573	4,909	0.73
Japan	German	3,534	5,068	0.70
Russia	German	736	1,231	0.60
Germany	German	1,292	3,347	0.39
Poland	German	151	430	0.35
Austria	German	114	385	0.30
Slovenia	German	12	48	0.25
Czech Republic	German	45	190	0.24
Hungary	German	30	129	0.23
Saudi Arabia	Islamic	319	369	0.86
Iran	Islamic	59	331	0.18
Sweden	Scandinavian	403	406	0.99
Finland	Scandinavian	220	238	0.92
Norway	Scandinavian	227	382	0.59
Denmark	Scandinavian	169	310	0.55
Total		47,887	54,076	0.89

Sources: Author based on data from the World Federation of Exchange and the World Bank.

development is more likely. In their famous paper, La Porta et al. (1998) examined the relevant legal rules and their enforcement in forty-nine countries, concluding that countries with legal systems based on English common law have the strongest, French civil law countries the weakest legal protection of investors, with German and Scandinavian civil law countries in the middle. Table 1.1, next to country names, shows the origin of legal system. For several countries not covered by La Porta et al. (1998), the following decisions were made. Luxembourg was classified in the French family; Poland, Hungary, Slovenia, and the Czech Republic were considered closest to the German civil law; and so were Russia and China, although the influences on their legal systems were mixed. Finally, Saudi Arabia and Iran were labelled as having Islamic laws.

At a high level of aggregation the law and finance theory works. The median MC to GDP ratio for common-law countries is 1.16 – the highest of all legal system groups. Next come Scandinavian-law countries with median of 0.75. The median for German-law countries is 0.50, lower than for French-law countries (0.55), but admittedly the former are affected by low ratios of Central and Eastern European countries with relatively new stock markets. When we zoom in on detail, however, there are large differences within each group. Not only Hong Kong and Singapore but also South Africa and Malaysia have higher ratios than the most established stock markets of the United States and the United Kingdom, which are often considered to have the highest level of shareholder protections (Wójcik 2006). New Zealand and Ireland, with investor protection very similar to that in the United Kingdom, have some of the lowest ratios in the table. Large contrasts can also be found within the French and the German legal system families. Even within a compact Scandinavian group, there is a marked difference between high ratios for Sweden and Finland, and low for Denmark and Norway.

While stock markets are often presented in economics textbooks as a higher form of finance in relation to banks, and their development as a sign of sophistication of a national financial system (Mishkin 2007), there is no simple relationship between stock market development and general economic development, as measured, for example, by GDP per capita. Out of ten countries with the highest MC to GDP ratios in the table, six are emerging markets (Hong Kong, South Africa, Singapore, Malaysia, Chile, Taiwan). In contrast, the long-established wealthy economies of Germany, Italy, and the aforementioned Ireland and New Zealand, have ratios in the bottom fifteen of the list. Remarkably, the largest emerging market economies of Brazil, China, and India are already in the top half of the list, and so is Saudi Arabia. In other words, just as we stressed that the history of stock markets cannot be interpreted as a story of unstoppable gradual expansion and globalization, neither can stock market development be seen as a simple corollary of economic development.

We have to be skeptical of the treatment of stock markets in law and finance and economics, but we also need to be suspicious of the conceptualization of stock market development in political economy and other social sciences. According to varieties of capitalism – a school of thought influential in social sciences – stock markets are prominent in liberal market economies (LME) but play a lesser part in coordinated market economies (CME). In the latter type, a strong stock market would not be compatible with the significant role of stakeholders other than shareholders (workers, local communities, government) and considerable redistribution of wealth (Hall and Soskice 2001). A related strand of literature actually uses the term 'stock market capitalism', and contrasts it with welfare capitalism. The MC to GDP ratios are consistent with these approaches as far as the archetypes of LME and stock market capitalism (the United States and the United Kingdom), and CME and welfare capitalism (Germany, Japan) are concerned. However, there are important examples undermining these simple distinctions. Sweden and Singapore have arguably much more coordinated and welfare-oriented economies than Ireland or New Zealand, but they have much more developed stock markets. The percentage of households investing in stocks or mutual funds in Sweden was reported as higher than in the United States (Guiso et al. 2003).

A simple but important lesson here is that there is no single driver or theory that would explain the uneven development of stock markets across countries. Additional factors that should be thrown into the mix of explanations include the role of big companies. Where those are missing and an economy is dominated by small firms, stock market capitalization is likely to be small, as small firms can rely to a larger extent on bank financing, without resort to stock markets. This may explain some of the differences between low MC to GDP ratios in Ireland, New Zealand, and Denmark in relation to Finland (with Nokia accounting for the bulk of market capitalization). The relative significance of debt financing also plays a part. Denmark has a large bond market, which absorbs the funds of investors, possibly at the expense of equity market. In Chile, which followed the prescriptions of the Washington Consensus more closely than any other Latin American country, massive privatization programmes and shift to funded pensions were decisive in the development of stock market. Last but not least, there is a strong coincidence between the role of a country in international finance and its level of stock market development. Hong Kong, Singapore, Luxembourg, and Switzerland claim four of the top five spots on the list.

Underused potential

The recent boom in stock market development may give an impression that many economies are so penetrated by stock markets that potential for further development is limited. The MC to GDP ratios close to or exceeding 1 in many countries may reinforce that impression. Such judgement however is wrong. To prove that this section focuses on primary stock markets and proposes novel and simple to interpret measures of stock market development, which complement the MC to GDP ratios.

To assess the level of stock market development a simple question is asked: What percentage of companies that could possibly be traded publicly is already present on the stock market? Table 1.2 answers the question, presenting the number of publicly traded companies as a percentage of all large, and all very large companies registered and headquartered in a given country. The thresholds of €50 million and €200 million in annual turnover are used to classify a company as large or very large, respectively. The threshold of €50 million is used officially in the European Union to distinguish large from small and medium sized companies. The thresholds were adjusted to the price level

Table 1.2. Stock market participation of companies

Country	Number of publicly traded companies	Number of large publicly traded companies / number of large companies	Number of very large publicly traded companies / number of very large companies
Austria	109	0.07	0.14
Belgium	159	0.04	0.09
Czech Republic	37	0.02	0.05
Denmark	178	0.07	0.12
Finland	134	0.10	0.16
France	946	0.06	0.11
Germany	1014	0.05	0.08
Greece	336	0.27	0.45
Hungary	37	0.04	0.09
Ireland	114	0.05	0.11
Italy	292	0.03	0.09
Japan	3858	0.25	0.47
Luxembourg	49	0.10	0.18
Norway	277	0.11	0.16
Poland	241	0.07	0.13
Portugal	73	0.05	0.14
Spain	198	0.03	0.09
Sweden	395	0.09	0.15
Switzerland	274	0.15	0.23
The Netherlands	224	0.04	0.09
The United Kingdom	2542	0.07	0.12
The United States	8861	0.11	0.22
Average	n/a	0.09	0.16

Sources: Author based on data from ORBIS provided by Bureau van Dijk Electronic Publishing.

in a given country. They are used for two reasons. First, it is not possible to consider all companies existing in an economy due to the difficulty of obtaining internationally comparable data. Second, such an approach would fail to recognize that companies participating in stock markets are relatively large, mainly as a result of fixed costs of stock market participation such as reporting costs or listing fees (Pagano et al. 1998).

Publicly traded companies are defined broadly as all those admitted to be traded on regulated markets (for EU countries) and those that are publicly listed or at least quoted and traded on public markets. This definition is inclusive, covering small company, alternative, and technology-focused segments of stock markets. To be sure, the requirements for companies to be publicly traded vary across countries and lenient rules can result in a large number of publicly traded companies, not to be mistaken for a high level of stock market development. Within the EU, the rules on becoming a publicly traded companies are now harmonized, but the variation in the total stock of such companies across countries is still affected strongly by the old diversity of rules.

Table 1.2 documents a very low level of corporate participation in stock markets. On average, only every eleventh large company is publicly traded. The percentage varies from 27 and 25 per cent for Greece and Japan, respectively, to 2 per cent for the Czech Republic. Even in the United Kingdom only every fourteenth company is present on the stock market. Stock market participation grows with company size but only slowly. On average only every sixth very large company is publicly traded. In short, companies present on the stock market represent an absolute minority of the total population of companies, even in countries with the most developed stock markets. This clearly shows that the corporate sector is far from being saturated with publicly traded companies, but it also raises issues of how unrepresentative the stock market can be of the underlying economy (Wójcik 2007). We should keep that in mind whenever we see a stock market index presented as a barometer of the whole corporate sector and economy.

Stock market controversies

While explaining the level of stock market development is complicated, explaining its impact on the economy and society is even more difficult and controversial. The size and structure of stock markets has significant implications for the whole economy and society. There are strong disagreements on the virtues and vices of stock markets between mainstream/orthodox economics and more socially oriented research in sociology, political science, geography, and heterodox economics.

One characteristic of stock markets, commonly acclaimed by mainstream economists, is their impersonal nature in comparison with bank lending, as an alternative way of channelling capital from savers to firms. Bankers can act in their own interest, at the expense of depositors' interest, for example, colluding with managers of borrowing firms. In other situations, banks can exert too much power over borrowers, if the latter do not have any alternative source of financing (Wenger and Kaserer 1998). Stock markets bypass the intermediary, channelling funds to firms directly from the public. In addition, stock markets are seen as enhancing competition between companies. Shares of companies that underperform can be acquired by competitors more easily if they are traded on a stock market. In general, acting impersonally, stock markets are believed to be better than banks at applying the 'axe' of creative destruction. Banks, with established long-term relationships with borrowers, are less likely to let them go bankrupt, even if bankruptcy is justified (Rajan and Zingales 2003*a*). Finally, stock markets provide a forum where multiple opinions (expert and non-expert) on firms and their decisions clash with each other, while in bank lending such evaluations are made by few experts within one organization. As such, it is argued, stock markets improve the allocation of capital and at the very least complement banks.

Another important way in which stock markets may outperform or at least complement banks concerns innovation. It is claimed that banks have an inherent bias towards prudence, low-risk investments, and borrowers that offer tangible collateral to secure their loans (Morck and Nakamura 1999). Young and innovative firms, with potentially highly profitable but very risky projects, are therefore likely to struggle to obtain bank financing. Stock market investors would be more willing to fund such firms, since shares allow the provider of funds to participate in the success of the firm without an upper limit on their return (Wójcik 2008). Thus, bank-centred financial systems may be more conducive to the funding of mature, less risky firms, while more market-based systems better support the growth of newer, riskier sectors (Levine 2005). Strong stock markets may therefore enhance the innovativeness and competitiveness of an economy. The relatively high growth of the US economy in the 1990s and early 2000s, and high levels of technological innovation in the United States have often been associated with large and liquid stock markets, fed with hundreds of IPOs of high-technology companies.

Many countries have tried to replicate the US model to capitalize on synergies between stock markets, venture capital, and high technology sectors. In Europe, a set of new stock markets (with the German Neuer Markt and French Nouveau Marché in the lead) was created in the late 1990s, modelled after the US NASDAQ, during the US-led boom of Internet stocks. Although these markets did not survive the end of the boom in the early 2000s, they helped raise tens of billions of Euro for new ventures and contributed to the development of venture capital industry in Europe. Thousands of new companies and millions of new investors entered the stock market for the first time in a span of just a few years. Before the mid-1990s, small and medium-sized firms in Europe were shut out of stock markets and dependent on banks (Posner 2005).

On the other side of the corporate spectrum stock markets facilitate the existence of very large companies, which may find it difficult to satisfy their capital needs with bank loans. Stock markets can mobilize capital for large capital projects. Arguably the development of infrastructure (including water, gas, canals, and railways) in the nineteenth and early twentieth centuries in the United Kingdom and particularly in the United States would have been difficult without stock markets. In the process, stock markets transform short-term investments, made by people who want to trade stocks for capital gains only, into long-term corporate projects, by the virtue of combining the primary with an active secondary market. In addition, borrowed money can be used for trading in secondary stock markets. Thus, the stock markets bridge the divide between short- and long-term investments, as well as between money, capital, and credit markets. This allows flows of money between different parts of financial markets and the integration of these markets (Michie 2006).

In contrast to orthodox economics, behavioural economics stresses the role of irrational behaviour in stock markets. Prices can rise or fall, even for years, without any changes in underlying fundamentals (e.g. in terms of corporate profitability) that would justify such price movements (Akerlof and Shiller 2009). In other words, bubbles and crashes are common in stock market history, and their effects on the distribution of wealth can be tremendous. Those who bought shares towards the end of a bubble, presumably the most vulnerable, lower income investors, lose most (Kindleberger and Aliber 2005; Shiller 2005). If considerable over- and underpricing are common on stock markets, and bursting bubbles lead to perverse distributional outcomes, this seriously undermines claims about the efficiency of stock markets as a mechanism allocating capital to firms, and a mechanism providing reliable investment returns on savings, including savings for retirement (Engelen 2003). On the other hand, we may wonder, for example, whether some valuable Internet-related innovations would have occurred without the Internet boom of late 1990s, however irrationally exuberant it was.

In addition to irrationality, stock markets may be subject to manipulation, with the main suspects including investment banks and corporate managers. Investment banks and investment banking departments of universal banks advise firms on their stock market entry (IPOs) and other capital market activities, such as mergers and acquisitions, which gives them access to corporate information, before other investors have it. On the other side of their business, their investment advisors and analysts influence investors' opinions and decisions. This gives investment banks and bankers a position of power in stock markets, which contributes to their very high profitability and legendary pay packages, and which they could abuse, for example, by using inside information when trading on their own account (Bodnaruk et al. 2007; Crotty 2008).

Stock markets enable the creation of a class of salaried managers, thus professionalizing corporate management and transforming labour markets. This, however, implies the preponderance of corporations with a multitude of small owners, none of which on their own can counterbalance the power of corporate managers (Clark and Wójcik 2007). Since 1990s, in order to align the interests of managers with those of shareholders, it has been popular to award managers with stock options, which promise them big payouts if the stock price of the company goes up (Wójcik 2009). Arguably, however, this may fixate managers' interest on short-term stock market performance, and even enhance incentives to manipulate accounting figures (Bebchuk and Fried 2004; Froud et al. 2006). Corporate scandals at Enron, WorldCom, or Ahold, where managers, investment bankers, and other intermediaries colluded with each other, as well as the recent failure of corporate governance in banks exposed in the global financial crisis of 2008–9, exemplify in an extreme fashion that stock market relations are not as impersonal as orthodox economists paint them (Clark et al. 2006).

Even if we assume that stock markets genuinely discipline corporate managers to maximize the value of shares, the 'shareholder value' orientation is in itself problematic, as it can undermine the interests of other corporate stakeholders, such as labour and local communities (Lazonick and O'Sullivan 2000; Dore 2008). Takeovers, facilitated by stock markets, can further erode the power of labour and local communities, as they result in abrupt closures and layoffs that may be socially harmful, while benefiting nobody but corporate raiders (Shleifer and Summers 1988). Indeed, financial economics has no conclusive evidence that hostile takeovers improve the performance of target firms (Becht et al. 2003). Thus, as the literature on financialization stresses, stock markets may be seen as turning firms into commodities, things made for sale on the market, stripped of complex and locally embedded social relations that they represent (Aglietta and Reberioux 2005).

On the investor side, stock markets allow diversification of investments. By investing in the shares of local private health care companies or local water suppliers, individuals can insure themselves to some extent against the rising prices of these services. At an international scale, benefits of diversification are even larger. Investors from Norway, for example, can insure their future welfare by investing in the stock markets of foreign economies that benefit if the prices of oil and gas fall (Clark 2005). Cross-border equity investment arguably lowers the incentives of the public to support, and of the governments to introduce, policies that adversely affect the corporate sector of foreign countries (Doremus et al. 1998). On the other hand, the growing exposure of households to stock market investments, either directly or via pension funds, may be seen as contributing to the rise of casino capitalism, where welfare provision is privatized, with individuals focusing on their own risky bets, and neglecting the need for social cooperation (Strange 1997; Dore 2000; Martin 2002; Langley 2008).

What is the verdict of empirical research on the relative virtues and vices of stock markets? One recent review states that there is no conclusive evidence from cross-country studies that stock market-based or bank-based financial systems are better at fostering growth (Levine 2005). There is not one optimal structure for providing financial functions to the economy (Merton and Bodie 2004; Peck and Theodore 2007).

Rethinking stock markets

This chapter stresses the fundamentally geographical nature of stock markets. The very act of creating a joint-stock company, a prerequisite for stock market development, is about freeing an enterprise from the constraints of time and space, facilitating its existence beyond the lifespan and immediate environment (family and friends) of the founders. The essence of primary stock markets – selling corporate shares to the public – is spreading the ownership of a company, reaching new investors. While many investors can be found within a city or a region, spreading ownership ultimately necessitates reaching investors in more and more places. Finally, the secondary stock market is based on interactions of investors and traders from different places, with flows of information and transactions across space, which necessitate physical (technology, infrastructure) and institutional (rules, language) connections between places.

The development of stock markets is a quintessential part of globalization. As globalization, stock market development unfolds unevenly in both time and space. It is not a linear, gradual, and unstoppable force operating throughout history, nor does it take the same shape everywhere. And just as globalization, stock market development can be analysed across four dimensions: extensity, intensity, velocity, and impact propensity (Held et al. 1999). Extensity is evident in the spread of stock markets and stock exchanges around the world. Intensity is reflected in the magnitude of stock market activity (market capitalization or trading values and volumes) in relation to the whole financial system and economy, and the participation of companies and investors in stock markets. Velocity concerns the frequency and speed of transactions conducted on stock markets. Impact propensity involves the influence of stock markets on economic growth, economic stability, governance of companies, and the whole economy. On all four counts, the last twenty years have seen a spectacular wave of stock market development. It has been unprecedented historically, uneven and controversial, but by no means exhaustive – stock market development has not run its course yet.

This chapter is just an introduction to the map of the globalizing stock market. For all research on stock markets accumulated in financial economics, business studies and in the industry, our knowledge of this map is still very limited. Many important questions beg for systematic answers. What is the spread and intensity of stock market activity within countries? To what extent does stock market activity remain local and regional as opposed to national or international? What economic interactions does the development of the global stock market forge between cities and regions? How do stock markets affect regional, local, and urban development? How do they affect competition between financial centres? What is the impact of financial crises on the spatial organization of stock markets?

The remainder of the book breaks away from the tradition of treating nation-states as the exclusive spatial unit of analysis in research on stock markets, as homogeneous containers of stock market activity. After all, cities, not states, were some of the first issuers of securities, as they had revenues from business, but unlike states they were not above the law, and could be pressurized into paying back (Michie 2006). Mainstream research on stock markets, obsessed with prices and returns, effectively imagines the stock market as a set of transactions among anonymous actors, an epitome of free markets and their invisible hand at work (as opposed to studies on banking, where agency is taken more seriously). The focus of this book is on actors and relations between them, both in primary and secondary markets. Actors come from specific places, and interactions among actors forge connections among places. This logic is reflected in the structure of the book, with Chapters 2 and 3 focusing on issuers, Chapters 4 and 5 on investors, and Chapters 6 and 7 on intermediaries. Chapter 8 consolidates the findings proposing a theory of stock market centres and their networks, further refining the understanding of stock market development as a crucial part of globalization.

2

Biased Listings: Proximity in Domestic Primary Markets

Although Initial Public Offerings (IPOs) are one of the most publicized events on financial markets, and one of the most researched areas in finance and economics, little research has been conducted within these disciplines on the geography of IPOs within countries, as if it was assumed that geography of regions and urban centres did not matter for public equity markets. Such an assumption stands in stark opposition to the work of economic geographers, for whom diversity, heterogeneity, and differentiation within domestic financial markets are as important as those between markets. Their research has established that an important part of information used in financial markets is not easily transferable across space, resulting in the significance of local financial relations and spatial concentration of financial firms (Corbridge, Thrift, and Martin 1994; Martin 1999). The latter is further enhanced by localization and agglomeration economies, whereby financial and related firms concentrate spatially in order to benefit from common infrastructure and labour markets. Beyond the role of information and economic incentives, geographers have documented the role of political, social, and cultural factors in the formation of financial centres (Leyshon and Thrift 1997), as well as systematic differences within domestic economies in terms of corporate ownership and governance (Clark and Wójcik 2007). Thus, for economic geographers, mobility of capital within countries has always been restricted, and access to capital within countries has always been uneven, with implications for the continued significance of local and regional equity markets (Klagge and Martin 2005).

Recent empirical research in financial economics, however, starts to recognize that location within countries matters in public equity markets. The growing literature on 'local bias' documents that investors' equity portfolios are skewed towards local firms and that this may be accompanied by the ability to obtain superior returns driven by access to information available to local but not to remote investors. Loughran and Schultz, for example, demonstrate that in the US rural firms trade less, are covered by fewer analysts, and are owned by fewer institutions than urban firms (2005). A more recent inquiry builds on the information-based explanation of the 'local bias', claiming that companies located in urban areas have more potential shareholders than their rural counterparts, and as a result, have better access to public equity markets (Loughran 2008). Consistent with this hypothesis, they show that US rural firms wait longer to go public, are less likely to conduct seasoned equity offerings, use lower quality underwriters, and have more debt in their capital structure. This is an important finding, which is expanded in this chapter to show that access to local information is one of many aspects of the uneven geography of primary equity markets.

This chapter develops the geography of primary public equity markets both theoretically and empirically. Conceptually, it combines insights from financial economics and economic geography, and enhances them with a highly relevant interdisciplinary debate on corporate governance. Just as the development of geographical economics by Paul Krugman and others have rested on adding the ideas of imperfect competition, increasing returns to scale, and agglomeration economies to the mainstream trade theory, so does recent research in financial economics rest on incorporating ideas about geography of information. Here, I use the ideas of increasing returns to scale and agglomeration economies to explain the mechanisms of the primary public equity markets, but I also want to go beyond what we could call geographical finance, by considering genuinely social and institutional factors. This theoretical contribution is enhanced with comprehensive empirical coverage of public equity markets in thirty European countries as well as the United States and Japan, which is important given that existing research on IPOs is US-centric (Jenkinson and Ljungqvist 2001).

I argue that there are strong theoretical reasons and empirical evidence that provincial firms are less likely be public than firms from financial centres. This phenomenon, that I call the financial centre bias, is inconsistent with a view of efficient primary equity markets where information is ubiquitous. It should be added to the phenomena of underpricing and long-term underperformance, as an anomaly worthy of further consideration by finance practitioners, researchers, and policymakers. My empirical analysis shows that financial centre bias holds in an absolute majority of European countries, the United States, and Japan. I explain how this phenomenon is likely to be underpinned by the following: tacit knowledge and face-to-face contact, access to labour markets, corporate governance incentives, and institutional factors. In addition, the chapter presents an exploratory analysis on why the degree of financial centre bias differs between countries, with results pointing to the significance of public policy and corporate governance.

The next section develops hypotheses on why provincial firms are less likely to go public. The following sections introduce data and empirical methodology, and discuss empirical results. The last section concludes with implications and speculations on the future geography of IPOs.

Why are provincial firms less likely to go public?

There is extensive theoretical and empirical literature on why companies go public (for reviews, see Röell 1996; Ritter and Welch 2002; Bancel and Mittoo 2008), and why propensity of companies to go public differs between countries (Ritter 2003), as well as industries (Brau and Fawcett 2006). However, to my knowledge there is no systematic literature on why propensity to go public could depend on corporate location within a country. In this section, I propose four groups of factors, which can make provincial firms less likely to go and to be public. To be sure, these factors are bound to differ between regions, cities, and communities. Nevertheless, I argue that the main distinction that affects the participation of firms in public stock markets is between provincial areas and financial centres. The latter are defined as cities that are concentrations of financial and other advanced business services. The term is relative as there could be regional, national, and international financial centres. This analysis does not preclude a relative definition of financial centres, but it focuses on the national scale.

Tacit knowledge and face-to-face contact

IPO is a multi-stage process of intensive exchange of information. First the company going public produces a prospectus. To this end, it appoints an investment bank as the lead manager, which performs the due diligence investigations to produce information required to satisfy the appropriate regulatory authorities. The leading bank can also create a syndicate with other banks that will underwrite and/or market the issue to investors. Once the prospectus is ready, marketing of the issue to investors takes place. Senior managers of the issuer go on road-shows, giving presentations in places with large concentrations of investors, while investment bankers in the syndicate bring the issue to the attention of their client investors. The marketing stage generates information that is crucial for setting the price of the issue. The final phase of an IPO involves pricing and allocation of shares through one of three methods: fixed price, book building, and auction. In the fixed price method, the share price is determined prior to collecting bids from investors. If the issue is undersubscribed, the remaining shares are paid for by the underwriting banks. If it is oversubscribed, shares are allocated according to predetermined rules. The book-building method starts with the investment bank inviting selected investors to participate and submit their indications of demand. Once the bank knows the demand curve for the issue, it determines the issue price and the allocation of shares to investors. While the final allocation may reflect the preferences of the issuer, the investment bank retains considerable discretion. IPO auctions, in contrast, involve pre-determined rules of pricing and allocation, which can be executed by a computer. Finally, after shares are allocated, the role of the investment banks often continues as they stabilize the share price, support liquidity for the shares, and provide analyst coverage of the company (Jenkinson and Ljungqvist 2001).

From the description of the IPO process it is apparent that the central relationships in an IPO are those among issuers, investment banks, and investors. What is more, IPOs involve tacit knowledge, defined broadly as knowledge that cannot be created successfully through exchange of information at a distance, but necessitates frequent face-to-face contact (Gertler 2003; Bathelt et al. 2004; Storper and Venables 2004). The investment bank has to know the prospects of the issuer and the likely investor demand. Beyond financial statements and plans, as available in a codified form of spreadsheets and reports, the bank needs to know the integrity and reputation of the issuer's executives. In turn, the issuer needs to know the reputation of the bank, and has to trust that the bank will set the right issue price, neither too low (reducing the issuer's revenue from IPO) nor too high (ending in undersubscription).

What helps an issuer in their relationship with investment banks is the issuer's own knowledge about likely investor demand. Potential investors are unlikely to publicize their intentions with regard to an IPO, as this would undercut their chances of outperforming other investors, for example, by buying new shares at a low price. Thus, issuers have to judge the potential demand on the basis of personal confidential contacts and even rumours. Investors on the other hand, need information about issuers to reduce their investment risk. Proximity to the investment bank and issuer may also help an investor obtain additional information and/or favourable treatment in the process of price-setting and allocation. In short, proximity helps information flows in an IPO, and is indispensible for establishing mutual trust between the issuer and the investment bank, central to the whole IPO process (Ellis et al. 1999; Corwin and Schultz 2005). What highlights the role of tacit knowledge and face-to-face contact further is unstable information environment of an IPO, as investor sentiment and decisions on competing IPOs can change rapidly.

Figure 2.1 depicts the key information flows in an IPO, indicating that proximity is significant also within different groups of actors. Proximity among investment banks helps information flows needed to build and run a syndicate. Spatial concentration of investors helps them observe each

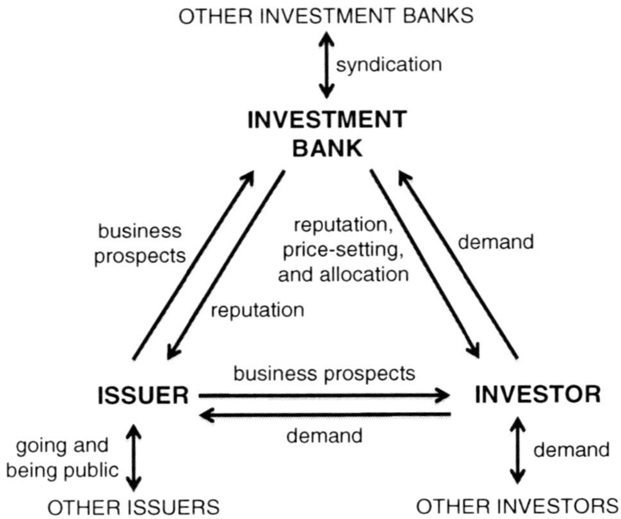

Figure 2.1. Key information flows in an IPO
Source: Author.

other's interest in the issue. Finally, proximity of other companies that are already public or are going public helps the inexperienced issuer to assess the costs and benefits of an IPO, as well as to avoid mistakes and piggyback successful practices of their peers. What Figure 2.1, for the sake of simplicity, does not show are other intermediaries involved in an IPO. It is typical of companies going public to appoint new lawyers and new auditors, usually ones that are more recognizable to public investors (Burton et al. 2004). Given the role of tacit knowledge, proximity of an issuer to investment banks, investors, other issuers, and other specialized service providers makes the IPO process less costly. As Burton et al. (2006: 689–90) summarize their empirical survey of IPOs in the United Kingdom 'the time top management had to spend with advisers including bankers, brokers, lawyers, and accountants was significant, and often resulted in some focus being taken off the business, so that the performance of company declined in short term'. If interactions with IPO advisors are so costly, savings afforded by proximity can be important.

There is another important aspect of tacit knowledge involved in the IPO process. According to the literature on 'local bias' investors proximate to the headquarters of the issuer form a crucial set of informed investors and a pool liquidity for the issuer's shares. If an area has few potential investors and little capital that could be invested in equity, then firms from this area are likely to find it difficult to access public equity markets. This is exactly the reasoning behind the findings that rural firms in the United States are less likely to go public, and when they are public, suffer from lower liquidity of their shares than urban firms (Loughran and Schultz 2005; Loughran 2008). The role of liquidity is also highlighted by Subrahmanyan and Titman (1999) who argue that 'the net benefit from going public depends on the size of public markets – that is, the number of firms already trading publicly. The benefit from going public is greater in a large, liquid public market'. Consequently, they underscore path dependence in the development of public stock markets, with 'bad equilibria', in which many firms remain private, and 'good equilibria' in which most firms are publicly traded. While Subrahmanyan and Titman's theory is concerned with national stock markets, it is plausible that the positive externalities of many firms being or going public are not necessarily country-wide, they may be regional and local. Simplifying, within a country, a financial centre may be in the state of 'good equilibrium', with provinces in general (or individual regions) in the state of 'bad equilibrium'.

Thus, tacit knowledge is important for firms not only when they go public but also afterwards, when they are public. A public company needs a continued relationship with investment banks (e.g. to conduct secondary public offerings or interact with stock analysts), investors, auditors, and lawyers (to prepare reports required from public companies), and other specialized service providers. Put differently, tacit knowledge required for going and being public implies benefits from the co-location of relevant actors. Consequently, the proportion of potential issuers that are public should be higher in financial centres than in provincial areas.

Access to specialized labour markets

Access to specialized labour markets is another element of localization and agglomeration economies, which is important for firms going and being public. First, being close to investment banks, major investors, and specialized service providers, implies staying close to a large pool of specialized highly skilled labour that these institutions require. There is however a direct impact as well, since a firm going public needs to employ new specialists, including: executives (particularly financial executives), non-executive directors, investor relations experts, and accountants skilled in financial reporting required from public companies (Burton et al. 2004, 2006). Such specialists are most likely to be found in financial centres.

Principal–agent problem and private benefits of control

We now move to hypotheses related to corporate governance, which narrowly defined refers to relationships between corporate managers and shareholders, and broadly defined – relationships among all stakeholders of a company (Wójcik 2009). The principal–agent problem is the central issue of corporate governance and occurs with the separation of ownership and control, that is, when owners (principals) are different people than managers (agents). The problem is how to make managers act in the interest of owners.

In a typical private firm, owners are identical with managers (e.g. a member of the family who owns the firm is the manager), are closely related to them (a trusted friend of the owners) or at least there are dominant owners in the firm who control the managers. As a result the interests of managers are aligned tightly with the interests of owners. IPO by nature involves the introduction of public (minority/small) investors into the ownership structure. As a result the interests of managers and owners diverge, and the former have incentives to extract private benefits of control (also called perquisite consumption) of pecuniary (e.g. diversion of corporate resources to other companies owned by managers or their families) and non-pecuniary (e.g. financing glamorous projects) character (Dyck and Zingales 2004). To be more precise, agency problems that arise with an IPO may take three forms. Minority shareholders can be exploited by (*a*) managers, (*b*) dominant owners, and (*c*) managers and dominant owners. Exploitation by managers is a typical problem in Anglo-American corporate governance; by dominant owners in Japan and Continental Europe (Shleifer and Vishny 1997; La Porta et al. 1998). One way or another, corporate governance theory posits that managers' (and/or dominant owners') incentives to maximize private benefits rather than firm value increase in the fraction of equity capital held by outside/small shareholders (Jenkinson and Ljungqvist 2001).

The issue here is whether the agency problem could differ between firms from financial centres and provinces. Recent research in corporate governance offers some clues. First, Landier et al. (2009) show that in the United States, multi-branch firms that downsize their activities tend to close branches and lay off employees in remote locations before they downsize activities close to the headquarters. This local employee protection afforded by managers is significant only when the firm is headquartered in a less populated county. Interpretation offered is that close social interactions, more typical of smaller communities, increase managerial concern for employees and status in the community. Holmén and Högfeldt (2004), in turn, in a paper on Swedish corporate governance suggest that a relation-based environment like Scandinavia, where informal rules and social standing are important checks and balances, limits the dominant owners' incentives to myopically extract pecuniary benefits. Put differently, they claim that in Sweden social norms and informal institutions can protect minority owners from majority owners and managers.

Thus, Landier, Nair, and Wulf seem to suggest that incentives to extract private non-pecuniary benefits of control are higher in the provinces (with more closely knit, less anonymous communities), while Holmén and Högfeldt claim that incentives to extract private pecuniary benefits may be higher in large urban centres. It stands to reason that on balance provincial firms face higher agency costs when they go public. An IPO, conducted outside of the province, in the financial centre, introduces investors that are not only small but also relatively distant. First, these investors (in contrast to local investors) will not participate in non-pecuniary benefits that managers (and dominant owners) may extract. Second, these investors have limited means to oversee whether managers in provincial companies are not colluding with local political and business elites to extract pecuniary benefits. If this speculation is correct, and the scope for and incentives for private benefits are larger in provincial companies, then public investors (particularly distant ones) will be less willing to buy shares in these companies. Lower demand for their shares would consequently lead to lower participation of provincial companies in public equity markets.

Managerial entrenchment

Being public implies increased pressure on senior management due to closer public scrutiny (Röell 1996). As public companies are more transparent than private firms, performance of managers in public companies is more readily comparable. In addition, public companies may be subject to a market for corporate control, facing the threat of a hostile takeover. In general, managerial entrenchment in a public company is smaller than in a private firm. The reduction in entrenchment as a result of going public, however, could have different ramifications for managers in provincial firms than for those in financial centres. If the manager of a provincial firm going or being public is unsuccessful, she/he faces the threat of losing a job and possibly reputation in a small labour market and generally smaller social environment. To get a new job and regain reputation the manager may need to relocate. Thus, the potential personal cost of going public may be greater for provincial managers than for those from financial centres. Arguably, the potential reward is greater as well, as it is easier for a provincial manager to become a local business celebrity solely on the basis of a successful IPO. While the expected value of net benefits from going public may be similar in the end, psychology and behavioural economics suggest that when faced with two options with same expected value, people tend to chose one with lower downside risk (Kahneman and Tversky 1979). Thus, even if financial centre-based and provincial managers have the same level of risk aversion, the latter may be less willing to take their companies public.

Institutional factors

Behaviour of firms in particular places is shaped to a large extent by the underlying institutional architecture of these places, which in turn is shaped by their culture and history. The international political economy literature stresses the differences between institutional foundations and resultant corporate behaviour between nation-states (Crouch and Streeck 1997). Varieties of capitalism perspective in particular places developed capitalist countries on a spectrum from liberal to coordinated market economies, with the former relying to a much greater extent on stock markets (Hall and Soskice 2001). The role of stock markets is so central to this literature that some have even suggested a distinction between stock market capitalism and welfare capitalism (Dore 2000). Economic geographers have stressed that institutional architecture can also vary systematically between regions within countries (Martin 2000). Wójcik (2002*b*), for example, shows significant differences in corporate governance regimes between German regions.

One implication of the institutionalist literatures is that propensity of firms to enter stock markets is likely to vary systematically between countries and regions in ways that complement other institutions in these places. This does not however rule out the possibility of systematic differences in terms of stock market participation between financial centres and provinces. Stock markets, exposing listed firms to short-term oriented valuation by investors and to takeovers, thus inducing a changing demand for labour, can complement the larger, deeper, and more fluid labour markets existing in financial centres. Provincial firms, in contrast, with smaller and less fluid labour markets may rely more on long-term employment relations, which are less compatible with stock markets. Smaller labour markets and sectoral specialization of provincial local economies may be coupled with stronger incentives to inter-firm product and labour market cooperation, leading to cross-shareholdings which can seal and stabilize links between firms. Cross-shareholdings, in turn, are not compatible with stock markets which flourish on dispersed ownership and arm's length relationships between firms. In other words, the tentative proposition here is that while institutional differences between countries and regions remain paramount, financial centres may tend to exhibit more features of a liberal and fewer features of a coordinated market economy than provincial regions in the same countries.

Methodology and data

In order to test whether provincial companies are less likely to participate in public stock markets than companies from financial centres, we need to define participation in the public stock market, as well as identify the population of companies that could potentially participate in these markets. The operational definition of a financial centre is also required, but this will be discussed at the start of the next section.

Companies participating in the stock markets are defined as all companies that are publicly listed or at least publicly quoted and traded. A detailed list of each country's market segments covered in the chapter is presented in Appendix 1. All alternative, smaller company, and technology-focused segments of stock markets are covered, and this generous coverage is consistent with the chapter's objective to evaluate the geographical bias of the public stock market in its entirety. Companies are considered stock market traded, if they are traded on any stock market in the world, not necessarily their home country market.

What broader population of companies in the underlying economy should we compare the set of stock market issuers to? It is not possible to consider all enterprises existing in an economy due to the difficulty of obtaining internationally comparable data. Such an approach would also fail to recognize that companies participating in stock markets are relatively large, mainly as a result of fixed costs of stock market participation such as reporting costs as well as initial and ongoing listing fees (Pagano et al. 1998). For this reason, we will compare the set of stock market companies to all companies with turnover in excess of €50m, which is the threshold used officially in the European Union to distinguish between medium and large companies. In addition, very large companies are defined as those with turnover in excess of €200m.

The following measures of financial centre (FC) bias are proposed:

$$\text{FC Bias Index} = \frac{N_{\text{Listed\_FC}}}{N_{\text{Large\_FC}}} \div \frac{N_{\text{Listed\_Provinces}}}{N_{\text{Large\_Provinces}}}$$

$$\%\text{Bias for large firms} = \left[\left(\frac{N_{\text{large\_Listed\_FC}}}{N_{\text{Large\_FC}}}\right) \div \left(\frac{N_{\text{large\_Listed\_Provinces}}}{N_{\text{Large\_Provinces}}}\right) - 1\right] \times 100$$

$$\%\text{Bias for very large firms} = \left[\left(\frac{N_{\text{VLarge\_Listed\_FC}}}{N_{\text{VLarge\_FC}}}\right) \div \left(\frac{N_{\text{VLarge\_Listed\_Provinces}}}{N_{\text{VLarge\_Provinces}}}\right) - 1\right] \times 100$$

The FC Bias Index captures all listed companies, including those with turnover below €50m, and relates them to the number of large companies in the underlying economy. The other two measures exclude listed companies with turnover below €50m, but are more straightforward to interpret. The first shows by what percentage large companies headquartered in the financial centre are more likely to be publicly traded than large companies not headquartered in the financial centre. The second shows by what percentage very large companies headquartered in the financial centre are more likely to be publicly traded than very large companies not headquartered in the financial centre.

To be sure, what counts as a publicly traded company in one country, would not necessarily be recorded as such in another country. Listing rules differ between countries and between stock exchanges. Lenient listing rules can result in high and strict rules in low numbers of recorded issuers. This is however not a major problem for this analysis, which does not focus on the percentages of companies that are publicly traded, but rather on the ratios of such percentages between financial centres and provincial areas. In other words, the objective is to evaluate the geographical bias of the public stock market, irrespective of the definition of the public stock market in a given country.

Data

Data were obtained from the ORBIS database, provided by Bureau Van Dijk Electronic Publishing (BDEP). They were harvested by the author in October 2006, but the database was last updated by the BDEP at the end of September 2006. The data were obtained for all twenty-seven European Union member states (including Bulgaria and Romania), Iceland, Norway, Switzerland, as well as Japan, and the United States, giving a total of thirty-two countries. Data on the numbers of publicly traded companies are valid for the end of September 2006. The data were compared with those available from such sources as the World Federation of Exchanges, the Federation of European Stock Exchanges, and websites of individual stock exchanges. No major discrepancies were detected.

Data on the number of companies operating in the underlying economies were collected by filtering companies with turnover in excess of €50m and €200m, respectively, out of all companies included in ORBIS. Turnover figures were based on consolidated financial statements, if available (unconsolidated otherwise), for the last financial year, for which they were available (mostly 2005). The thresholds of €50m and €200m were adjusted to the country price level, using Eurostat-OECD comparative price levels for 2005, based on the price of a representative basket of consumer goods and services (for details see OECD 2006). The comparative price level for the thirty OECD countries combined is set at 1; indices for individual sample countries in 2005 ranged from 0.40 for Bulgaria to 1.46 for Iceland. The adjusted turnover thresholds were calculated by multiplying €50m and €200m, respectively, by a country's comparative price level, and for non-Eurozone countries were translated into domestic currency using the respective Euro exchange rates as at the end of September 2006.

An important issue is whether the ORBIS database captures reliable numbers of all large companies operating in the sample countries. Unfortunately, it is not possible to compare the ORBIS data with those from the Eurostat's New Cronos database, since the latter defines large companies on the basis of the number of employees, not turnover, and the data are often out-of-date and available only for few countries. The use of multiple sources of corporate data by the BVDEP, resulting in impressively high numbers of companies included in ORBIS serves as an important source of assurance. While the numbers of publicly traded companies for European sample countries, Japan, and the United States were 8646, 3858, and 8861, respectively; and the numbers of large companies were 59,300, 12,338, and 35,407; the numbers of all companies covered by ORBIS were over ten million, over one million, and nearly two million, respectively. Thus, large companies represent less than 1 per cent of all companies in the ORBIS database. Given that the likelihood of the BVDEP having data on a company grows with the size of the company, the coverage of large companies used here should be reliable.

Empirical evidence on the financial centre bias

Let us move to the results on the extent to which stock markets are biased towards companies from financial centres. For six European countries without an obvious single financial centre, the ratios were calculated for two or more major financial centres combined: Berlin, Düsseldorf, Frankfurt am Main, and Munich in Germany; Milan, Rome, and Turin in Italy; Amsterdam and Rotterdam in the Netherlands; Lisbon and Porto in Portugal; Barcelona and Madrid in Spain; Basel, Geneva, and Zürich in Switzerland. For the United States, two alternative specifications were used: one with the Metropolitan Statistical Area (MSA) of New York as the sole centre, the other combining data for the MSAs of New York, Chicago, Los Angeles, San Francisco, and Boston. Chicago hosts the US largest derivatives trading industry, while Los Angeles, San Francisco, and Boston are the largest asset management centres after New York. As companies are assigned to places where they are headquartered, it is important to carefully delimit the spatial scope of financial centres. The general objective was to treat financial centres as agglomerations, including adjacent urban areas, even if from an administrative point of view they constitute separate cities or townships. Considering the idiosyncratic character of spatial and administrative structures of large cities, details of the financial centres covered, including their spatial scope, are presented in Appendix 2.

Table 2.1. Financial centre bias

Country – financial centre(-s)	FC Bias Index	% Bias for large firms	% Bias for very large firms
Austria – Vienna	3.22	86	79
Belgium – Brussels	2.37	124	133
Bulgaria – Sofia	0.10	−89	−50
Cyprus – Nicosia	2.35	−12	33
Czech Republic – Prague	1.04	15	33
Denmark – Copenhagen	1.88	59	57
Estonia – Tallin	1.62	85	n/a
Finland – Helsinki	1.15	0	22
France – Paris	1.70	86	60
Germany – four centres	2.19	68	27
Greece – Athens	1.19	−16	−39
Hungary – Budapest	0.60	−73	−86
Iceland – Reykjavik	0.68	n/a	n/a
Ireland – Dublin	1.59	−12	−17
Italy – three centres	1.74	54	13
Latvia – Riga	0.29	−71	−71
Lithuania – Vilnius	0.33	−46	−60
Luxembourg – Luxembourg	5.55	232	90
Malta – Valletta	1.78	100	n/a
Netherlands – two centres	2.03	67	7
Norway – Oslo	1.21	11	45
Poland – Warsaw	1.00	14	25
Portugal – two centres	1.76	160	151
Romania – Bucharest	0.42	−46	−87
Slovakia – Bratislava	0.60	−49	−75
Slovenia – Ljubljana	0.77	1	10
Spain – two centres	2.36	49	64
Sweden – Stockholm	1.43	23	30
Switzerland – three centres	0.71	7	−6
The United Kingdom – London	1.82	26	11
EU 15 – all centres	1.76	42	32
EU Transition 10 – all centres	0.66	−20	−19
Europe – all centres	1.50	34	26
Japan – Tokyo	1.67	63	17
The United States – New York MSA	1.22	15	−4
The United States – five centres	1.42	27	9

Notes: The 'FC Bias Index' is calculated by dividing the ratio of the number of publicly traded companies to the number of companies with turnover in excess of €50m in the financial centre of the country, by the equivalent ratio for the rest of the country. % Bias for large companies shows by what percentage companies with turnover in excess of €50m headquartered in the financial centre are more likely to be publicly traded than companies not headquartered in the financial centre. % Bias for very large companies does the same for companies with turnover in excess of €200m. Figures for EU 15, EU Transition 10, and Europe were arrived at by adding the respective numbers of companies, and calculating indices and percentages on the basis of the resulting totals, not by averaging figures for individual countries. Details of the financial centres covered are presented in Appendix 2. MSA – Metropolitan Statistical Area.

In Estonia and Malta, there are no very large companies headquartered in the provinces, so the figure for % bias for very large companies is not available. In Iceland, there are neither large nor very large companies headquartered in the provinces, so the figure for % bias for large and very large companies is not available.

Sources: Author based on data from BDEP and OECD.

As Table 2.1 shows, the FC Bias Index is greater than one in twenty-two out of thirty-two countries. This means that for a majority of countries as well as for EU 15 and Europe as a whole, the ratio of issuers to potential issuers is larger in the financial centres than in the rest of the country. This is confirmed when we analyse the percentage bias for large companies. In twenty-one countries, a large company is more likely to be listed if it is headquartered in the financial centre. In EU 15, a large company is 42 per cent more likely to be listed if it comes from the financial centre. This is more than in the United States but less than in Japan. The FC bias prevails in each of the five largest economies of the EU – France, Germany, Italy, Spain, and the United Kingdom.

If we extend analysis to very large companies, the FC bias holds for nineteen countries out of twenty-nine for which data are available. In EU 15, a very large company is 32 per cent more likely to be listed if it comes from the financial centre, in Japan 17 per cent more likely to be listed. In the United States, a very large company from New York City is actually 4 per cent less likely to be listed than a very large company from the rest of the country. The relationship between results for large companies and those for very large companies is significant. The FC bias is stronger for large companies than it is for very large companies. This is the case for nineteen countries, including the United States and Japan, as well as the EU15 as a whole. Therefore it seems that the factors described as inhibiting provincial companies' participation in public stock markets have a stronger impact on relatively small companies. Very large companies may find it easier to participate in the networks of information exchange with intermediaries and investors in financial centres; easier to access specialized labour markets; and it may be a more pressing need for them to obtain external equity capital in spite of potential entrenchment and private benefits of control.

The results for the United States demonstrate the sensitivity of the FC bias to the definition of a financial centre. It is not surprising that the FC bias figures are all lower if New York is considered the single financial centre than in the case where five largest centres are combined. In other words, the primary equity markets in the United States are biased towards companies from New York and against the rest of the country, but a much stronger bias exists against companies from outside the top five financial centres. In fact, a closer inspection of the data reveals that the high-tech focused centres of San Francisco and Boston have higher percentages of firms participating in stock markets than New York itself.

There is one methodological issue, which further reinforces the findings on the existence of the FC bias. Recall that potential issuers in each country are identified as companies exceeding €50m in turnover. The threshold of €50m is adjusted to the country price level, but the difference in the level of prices between financial centres and the rest of the country is not accounted for. If higher prices in financial centres were accounted for, relatively more companies would be counted as large in the provinces, resulting in higher values of the FC Bias Index and higher percentage bias for large and very large companies.

Is financial centre bias driven by sectoral bias?

Does the geographical bias exist because financial centres are concentrations of highly represented sectors, such as financial services or high-technology firms? Answering the question requires data on sector affiliation as well as location for each company. Such data are available only for the United Kingdom. With London as the hub of global finance, and of the British venture capital industry, the United Kingdom is a very useful case. Given that the FC bias in the United Kingdom is lower than the European average, it may be particularly sensitive to sectoral bias.

In order to test the relationship between geographical and sectoral stock market representativeness for the United Kingdom the FC Bias Index was calculated separately for each of the fifty-six NACE sectors (by Eurostat, as amended in 2001, also known as Rev.1.1 NACE codes), for which there are any publicly traded UK firms. A company is considered as located in London, if it is headquartered in Greater London. Results show that the FC Bias Index is higher than 1 for thirty-eight, that is, approx. 68 per cent of sectors. Thus, in an absolute majority of sectors, companies from London are more likely to be publicly traded than provincial firms. For financial intermediation the FC Bias Index is 1.01. While London hosts approx. two-thirds of the UK publicly traded financial intermediation firms, it also hosts approx. two-thirds of all large financial intermediation firms that exist in the United Kingdom. Within high-technology manufacturing, the FC Bias Index is above one for manufacturing of radio, television, and communication equipment (1.37), as well as medical, precision, and optical instruments (1.19), but below one for office machinery and computers (0.59). Within high-technology knowledge intensive services, the index is above one for post and telecommunications (1.39), but below one for computer activities (0.97), and research and development (0.77). Considering large sectors, with large absolute numbers of firms, the highest levels of London advantage are found in the manufacturing of chemicals and the manufacturing of machinery and equipment, with the FC Bias Index values of 2.38 and 3.13, respectively.

To summarize, in the United Kingdom the FC bias prevails in an absolute majority of sectors. Its existence is not determined by sectors concentrated in London having an advantage over sectors concentrated in the provinces in terms of their stock market participation.

Why financial centre bias differs between countries?

The empirical evidence shows that the degree of FC bias differs greatly between countries. This section presents exploratory analysis of the potential reasons behind these differences.

If FC bias is affected by proximity of potential issuers to investment banks and other specialized intermediaries, then the bias could be greater in countries where the average distance between potential issuers and the financial centre (or centres) is greater. Simplifying, we might expect a larger FC bias in larger countries. Table 2.1, however, shows little evidence for such a relationship. There are small countries such as Luxembourg or Belgium with strong FC bias, and large countries such as Sweden or Finland with weak bias. This suggests that the financial centre bias may have more to do with social and cultural proximity of issuers to financial centres and specialized intermediaries than with physical distance.

Another factor that could explain the FC bias is the existence of financial centres alternative to those included in the calculation. If such surrogates were available, we would expect a weaker bias. This is a difficult hypothesis to test in quantitative terms; nevertheless a closer look at Table 2.1 lends some support to it. First, as already discussed, the FC bias is lower for US – New York than for the United States – five centres. Second, other countries where more than one centre is considered tend to have relatively high FC bias.

The level of FC bias could also be related to the general level of stock market development. Companies from the financial centre may be the first ones to get listed, but as stock market develops it could penetrate other parts of the country. We test this hypothesis with two measures of stock market development: the ratio of market capitalization of domestic companies to GDP (MC/GDP); and the percentage of large companies that are publicly traded (PL/AL). Table 2.2 presents results, separately for the samples of all thirty-two countries, twenty-two non-transition, and ten transition countries, which

Table 2.2. Financial centre bias vs. country size, stock market development, and corporate governance

Index	Countries included	Area	PL/AL	MC/GDP	PWH/P
FC Bias Index	All	−0.098	−0.305*	0.447***	0.211
	Non-transition	−0.351	−0.484**	−0.356	−0.448**
	Transition	−0.244	−0.476	0.649**	0.103
% Bias for large firms	All	−0.059	−0.304*	0.489***	0.214
	Non-transition	−0.205	−0.422*	−0.063	−0.346
	Transition	−0.241	−0.262	0.561*	0.006
% Bias for very large firms	All	0.043	−0.239	0.382**	0.213
	Non-transition	−0.123	−0.288	−0.299	−0.432*
	Transition	−0.025	−0.050	0.427	0.467

Notes: The table reports Spearman's rank correlation coefficients between the measures of the financial centre bias and: the total area of a country (Area); the percentage of publicly traded firms among all firms with turnover in excess of €50m (PL/AL); the ratio of domestic market capitalization to GDP (MC/GDP); and the percentage of publicly traded companies that are widely held, that is, have no shareholders owning more than 25 per cent of shares directly or indirectly (PWH/P). Coefficients are significant at 10 per cent (*), 5 per cent (**), or 1 per cent (***).

Sources: Author, based on data from BDEP, OECD, World Bank, and the World Federation of Exchanges.

lend some support for the hypothesis. There is indeed a negative correlation between FC bias and the percentage of large companies that are publicly traded, particularly in non-transition countries. Thus, diffusion of stock market engagement from the financial centre to the rest of the country may indeed take place.

The third hypothesis, on the relationship between the FC bias and corporate governance, stems from my previous research on Germany demonstrating that the institutional concentration of ownership in companies is higher in regions that are relatively closed to investors from outside the region (Wójcik 2003). For example, in Hesse and Hamburg in contrast to Baden Württemberg, fewer public companies have dominant owners and there are more investors from outside the region (Wójcik 2002*b*). Thus, concentrated ownership tends to coincide with local ownership. This suggests a potential relationship between corporate governance and geographical bias in primary equity markets. Countries with higher institutional concentration of corporate ownership may rely on more locally/regionally based financial interactions and have financial centres that are more 'closed' to provincial firms than countries with relatively open ownership structures. In other words, institutional closeness/openness of a corporate governance regime may coincide with its geographical closeness/openness. To test the relationship between corporate governance and the FC bias, we use data on the percentage of publicly traded companies that are widely held (PWH/P), that is, with no shareholders owning more than 25 per cent of shares directly or indirectly. For non-transition countries, there is indeed a negative and significant correlation between FC bias and the percentage of widely held companies. To be sure, the relationship between corporate governance and the FC bias is likely to be a two-way relationship. Since IPOs dilute corporate ownership, the FC bias would reinforce the difference between relatively high ownership concentration in the provinces and low concentration in the financial centre.

The power of explaining the FC bias with the level of stock market development and corporate governance is limited due to the most striking feature of the results in Table 2.1. Namely, in transition countries the FC bias is non-existent or very weak, although these countries have underdeveloped stock markets, particularly in terms of MC/GDP, and closed ownership structures in comparison with Western Europe or the United States. In my view, this apparent anomaly can be explained with the role of privatization as a major route of firms entering public stock markets in transition countries, as well as public policy aimed at geographically inclusive markets. First, in transition countries the share of companies that entered public equity market via privatization of formerly state-owned enterprises is higher than in 'mature' market economies (Perotti and Oijen 2001). As a result the geography of IPOs and public equity markets in transition countries has been shaped significantly by the state's priorities of privatization and raising revenue from it, which have subdued the barriers and disincentives faced by provincial firms and related to tacit knowledge, access to specialized labour markets, and corporate governance. In addition, stock exchanges in these countries were developed and at least until recently owned by the governments as not-for-profit organizations, and tools of capital market development policy, with one of its objectives being to reach potential issuers in different parts of the country. The impact of public policy on stock exchange strategy will be further elaborated in Chapter 6.

To summarize, it is not surprising that stock market development, corporate governance, or the role of privatizations, all of them elements of nation-state institutional structures, seem to explain the difference in the level of FC bias between countries. After all, we have hypothesized before that the very existence of the bias may be driven by differences in institutions. The list of institutional factors that could explain the cross-country variation of the FC bias could be extended to include the level of competition among intermediaries (mainly investment banks) that assist firms going public, rules of stock exchange listing prevailing in a country, or tax systems encouraging or discouraging firms from going public. Due to the difficulty of collecting and quantifying data on such factors, as well as exploratory character of the analysis in this section, these issues are left to future research.

Towards disintermediated IPOs?

Research on IPOs has been focused on two anomalies: underpricing and long-term underperformance. There is, however, another anomaly that has escaped the attention of financial economists – the FC bias, the fact that firms from financial centres are more likely to go public than their provincial counterparts. This chapter assembles theoretical reasons for and empirical evidence on the FC bias. The primary reasons of the bias are likely to be the benefits of issuers' proximity to IPO intermediaries and specialized labour markets. Second, there are corporate governance incentives that could lower both the supply and the demand for provincial IPOs. In addition, institutional differences between financial centres and provinces may also make provincial firms' IPOs less likely. Empirical analysis covering thirty-two countries, including the whole European Union, as well as the United States and Japan, shows that even according to conservative measures, the FC bias is common, and is particularly strong in countries with underdeveloped stock markets and closed corporate governance regimes. However, the FC bias is still present in countries with the most developed stock markets and most open corporate governance, such as the United Kingdom and the United States. In fact, in almost all countries where there is no FC bias, this is most likely due to state intervention, in particular the role of privatizations in taking companies public, and capital market development policy.

In the age of Internet, it may sound strange to talk about provincial firms or the role of proximity to financial centres. After all, we have seen successful Internet IPOs, such as Google's, whereby collection of buy orders, pricing, and allocation of shares were executed through computer networks. Does not it imply the arrival of disintermediated IPOs that would make the FC bias history? Most probably not. First, Internet auctions have certain disadvantages, which may explain why they are the least popular, while heavily intermediated book-building remains the most popular IPO method. In book-building, discretion afforded to bankers and issuers makes it easier to reward investors undertaking costly information seeking and research and thus contributing to price discovery, while fully disintermediated auctions face problems of free-riding, with investors waiting for others to undertake such activities (Jenskinson and Ljungqvist 2001). A likely development in the future are hybrid IPO methods, with auctions encouraging the broad participation of retail investors, but at the same time retaining a significant degree of intervention and discretion on the side of investment banks and issuers. Finally, even if IPOs were to be fully disintermediated, the FC bias could still remain due to the geography of corporate governance, labour markets, and institutional factors.

This chapter opens new research avenues in financial economics and economic geography. Financial economists should be reminded that in addition to the geography of national and international financial systems, there is also an important geography at the sub-national scale of analysis. If we simplify this geography to the distinction between financial centres and provinces, we may expect more arm's length relationships and stock market based financing in financial centres, with more relationship-based finance and higher reliability on bank credit in the provinces. Of course, for geographers this distinction should not suffice. Provincial regions, cities, and communities differ in respect of their financial systems. Hence the need for more research on how public stock market participation of firms, but also investors, differs within countries.

There is another issue that merits our attention. Could the FC bias, so prevalent in the domestic context, apply to situations where firms list their shares on foreign stock markets? This triggers further questions. When the headquarter location of the issuer and the location of the host stock market are in different countries, how do we judge which places in the home market are closer to the host market? And what institutions help issuers to bridge the distance between the home and the host market? We turn to these questions in Chapter 3.

3

The Footprint of Foreign Listing: Issuers from Emerging Markets

Foreign listing, referred to as the listing and trading of corporate shares on stock markets outside of the home country of the issuer, has a long history. In late nineteenth and early twentieth centuries, there were hundreds of foreign stocks traded in London and Paris (Cassis 2006). Like most types of international financial flows, foreign listing was curtailed between 1914 and the 1980s. Out of 3683 foreign listings at the end of 2006, approximately 85 per cent took place after 1980, and 65 per cent after 1990 (Sarkissian and Schill 2008). Between 2005 and 2007 alone, above $130bn of new capital was raised globally through depositary receipts, the dominant mode of foreign listing (BNYM 2008).

Foreign listing is cyclical. It is popular when stock prices grow, but can come to a standstill when they fall, as has been the case between the middle of 2008 and the end of 2009. Interestingly, historical waves of foreign listing are much more similar in terms of destinations (host stock markets) than in terms of origins (countries where foreign listing issuers are headquartered). The United States and the United Kingdom have been the top host markets since the 1960s, and their share in the total number of foreign listings in 2006 was approximately 60 per cent. Luxembourg claimed the third place, although far behind the top two destinations (Sarkissian and Schill 2008). The geography of foreign listings in terms of their origins, however, has witnessed a major shift. While until late 1990s, issuers entering foreign stock markets would come mostly from Europe, North America, and Australia, the 2000s saw a boom in foreign listings from emerging markets, with their rapidly developing corporate sectors demanding external capital and international securities market expertise. The four largest emerging market economies of Brazil, Russia, India, and China in 2007 accounted for 73 per cent of new depositary receipts listed on foreign stock exchanges, 63 per cent of capital raised, and 48 per cent of trading value (BNYM 2007). At the end of 2008, the share of the four countries in the total number of outstanding foreign listings reached approx. 20 per cent.

While the global pursuit of stock issuers from emerging markets has been well covered by media and consultancy reports (e.g. Research Republic 2008), it has received little attention in social sciences beyond financial economics. The latter, however, has thus far focused on studying foreign listings as relationships between home and host countries, with little interest in whether and where foreign listing activity is concentrated within home and host countries. While Fernandes and Giannetti (2009: 1) note that 'countries whose exchanges manage to attract more foreign listings are likely to be the winners of the competitive struggle to become (or remain) major financial centres of the global economy' there is no research applying a sub-national scale of analysis to foreign listing. It is also striking that its political nature has hardly been studied.

This chapter presents an exploratory analysis of a comprehensive dataset on companies from Brazil, Russia, India, and China (BRIC) listing their shares on stock markets in the United States, the United Kingdom, and Luxembourg at the end of 2008. These four home and three host countries represent the most dynamic part of the market for foreign listings. We will identify similarities and differences in the cross-listing patterns between and within the BRIC countries at four levels:

- intensity of cross-listing by country of origin of cross-listing firms
- sub-national geography of cross-listed firms
- intermediaries involved in the cross-listing process
- destinations of cross-listing

The next section presents diverse literatures in geography and economics that are most relevant to the study of cross-listing. This is followed by a description of data used in the chapter. The core sections document and account for the different aspects of the geography of foreign listing, from the national and sub-national origins of foreign listed firms, through the role of intermediaries, to cross-listing destinations in terms of countries and stock markets. The last section concludes, and draws implications for further research.

Economics, financial geographies, and foreign listing

Our analysis of cross-listing from the BRIC countries focuses on: the national origins of cross-listing firms, their sub-national origins, intermediaries involved in the process, and cross-listing destinations. This section justifies our emphasis on these issues by reviewing relevant literature on factors affecting cross-listing. The goal is not to formulate hypotheses, but to identify the shortcomings and gaps in the existing research, and to highlight the significance of the cross-listing phenomenon to the field of financial geographies.

What makes a company list its shares abroad? In an integrated frictionless global capital market, investors would have no regard for the country of origin of stocks or the location of their trading venue. Issuers' choice of where to list their shares would have no effect on their pool of investors. In reality, trading shares listed on foreign stock exchanges is still more costly than dealing with stocks listed domestically, not least because of the complexities of cross-border clearing and settlement. Information relevant to share price of foreign issuers is often available only in a foreign language, and even if translated, making sense of it requires understanding foreign laws and customs. In addition, institutional investors in many jurisdictions still face restrictions on the share of their portfolio that can be invested in shares traded on foreign exchanges. In these conditions, listing shares abroad makes shares more accessible to investors in the host market, and overcomes international stock market segmentation (Karolyi 2006).

Foreign listing can also give rise to a change in corporate governance (Stulz 1999). A firm listing abroad enters the legal and regulatory environment of the host market, and firm's insiders (managers and/or large, controlling shareholders) can 'bond' themselves to a legal system with more effective protection of minority shareholders. A host market may also require a more stringent disclosure of information relevant to investors. Beyond laws and regulations, foreign listing may expose a firm to a market for corporate control, whereby it can be taken over if management underperforms. Finally, foreign listed firms may become subject to the scrutiny by intermediaries such as analysts and investment banks that have more expertise than institutions present in the firm's home market. All these factors should make a company friendlier to minority shareholders, and increase its share price (Doidge et al. 2004).

Demand for 'bonding' and the need to overcome international stock market segmentation seem consistent with the recent boom in cross-listings from emerging markets. Firms from such markets should have more incentives to seek foreign listings than those from more developed capital markets. Listing on foreign markets presents firms from emerging markets with multiple opportunities: lower transaction costs for investors, more informative financial reporting, more accurate analyst forecasts, and ultimately better access to capital (Edison and Warnock 2008). By extension, differences in the intensity of cross-listing between countries would be driven by their companies' demand for external capital and/or 'bonding' services, as well as barriers faced by foreign investors in accessing their domestic stock markets.

Political and regulatory barriers may hinder the ability of firms to cross-list, acting as tariffs on importing foreign financial services in order to protect the domestic financial sector. This might be justified in the light of mixed research on the impact of cross-listing on domestic stock markets, particularly in emerging economies. On the one hand, foreign listing may put pressure on domestic intermediaries to compete with foreign markets, and on domestic regulatory authorities to make capital market more shareholder-friendly (Karolyi 2004). On the other hand, foreign listing may erode trading and issuance on the domestic market so much, that incentives for local intermediaries to innovate are reduced (Moel et al. 2001). Domestic market can suffer as some trading moves abroad, the liquidity of the domestic market falls and the costs of trading (some of which, e.g. that of clearing and settlement infrastructure, are fixed) per trade increase. To be sure, the willingness and ability of emerging economy governments to erect barriers to cross-listing can be affected by their commitment to economic and financial liberalization, including the forum of the World Trade Organization (WTO) (Germain 1997; Sarre 2007). Mature economies, with the United States in the lead, may expect from emerging economies a commitment to unhindered imports of financial services in exchange for freer exports of goods.

Moving to the sub-national origins of cross-listed firms, literature in economics shows that cross-listing firms are typically large, and come from high-growth, capital, and export-intensive sectors (Pagano et al. 2002). There is however no research on the consequences of such differential propensity to cross-list at the regional and urban level. We could, for example, expect regions and cities with clusters of high-technology firms to be prominent in cross-listing, thus bypassing their national capital markets and institutions (Clark and Wójcik 2007). Chapter 2 demonstrates that even if we control for corporate size and sector, corporate participation in stock markets is uneven in space. In particular, firms from financial centres are more likely to list on the stock market than provincial firms, due to a combination of factors, including the benefits of proximity to intermediaries, specialized labour markets, corporate governance incentives, and institutional factors. Geographical biases could also apply to cross-listing.

Considering factors affecting the destinations of foreign listing, according to the theories of international market segmentation and 'bonding', the most popular destinations of foreign listing should be markets that offer best access to capital and shareholder-friendly corporate governance regimes. Sarkissian and Schill (2004) go further demonstrating that proximity between the host and home market (distance, foreign trade links between the host and home country, language and colonial links, as well as similarity in terms of industrial structure) play a crucial part in choosing the foreign listing venue. In other words, while foreign listing is about entering new capital markets, firms tend to be attracted to markets that are already familiar with them, or those that are more likely to become familiar. Recent research has also investigated the unequal distribution of foreign listings over time. In the 1990s, for example, the Internet boom attracted hundreds of foreign firms to list in the United States (Pagano et al. 2002).

While acknowledging the role of geography in the matching of home and host markets, existing research neglects the sub-national scale, despite the fact that cross-listing in most cases involves a listing on a stock exchange, and intermediation of firms located in a leading financial centre. Comprehensive research on cross-listing has to consider financial centres as destinations of cross-listings, as well as the agency of intermediaries involved in the process, in keeping with the broad literature on financial geographies (Leyshon and Thrift 1997; Martin 1999). There is silence in research on the agency of intermediaries acting on the foreign listing market. There is some interest in stock exchanges competing for foreign listings, but who are the institutions that assist on issuer's way to foreign markets?

To summarize, the engagement of financial geographies with the cross-listing phenomenon offers major opportunities. A geographical perspective helps to compare patterns of cross-listing between and within countries, instead of treating them as homogenous national markets. Comparative analysis of cross-listing from the BRIC countries in particular counteracts the trend to treat them as similar by nature, and to put them simply in the basket of emerging economies (Sidaway and Bryson 2002). Second, a geographical approach helps analyse cross-listing as a factor affecting the development of financial centres as well as regions. Finally, cross-listing may be seen as an important process within financial globalization and financialization, through which companies, cities, and regions in emerging economies are increasingly exposed to the standards and practices of host financial markets and centres (Froud et al. 2006).

Data

Foreign listing refers to the listing of corporate shares on a stock market outside of the home country of the issuer (the country where the issuing company is headquartered). While a foreign-listed firm does not necessarily need to be cross-listed (i.e. listed on more than one market), there are very few such firms in practice, and so we use the terms foreign listing and cross-listing interchangeably. The dominant vehicle of foreign listing are Depositary Receipts (DRs), which represent equity (ownership rights) in a foreign company, but are denominated in the currency of the host market, and can be bought and sold just like domestic stocks, following the same clearing and settlement procedures. Their objective is to make investment in foreign shares as easy and convenient as in domestic shares. DRs can be exchanged at any time for the actual foreign shares, which ensures the link between the price in the domestic and foreign market. The best known types of DRs are the American Depositary Receipts (ADRs) traded over-the-counter or on the US exchanges, and Global Depositary Receipts (GDRs), which combine an ADR with a DR in Europe. As an alternative to DRs, some stock exchanges allow foreign issuers to list directly (JP Morgan 2009).

The objective of our data collection was to cover all foreign stock issuers from Brazil, Russia, India, and China present on the stock markets of the United States, the United Kingdom, and Luxembourg. Few companies from the BRIC countries have foreign listings outside of the three host markets. While Hong Kong is a major listing location for Mainland Chinese firms, data on these foreign listings is less readily available than that for the US, the UK, and Luxembourg markets. As a result, with regard to China, we focus exclusively on Mainland Chinese firms, and leave their cross-listing in Hong Kong beyond the scope of the chapter.

Data on listings in the United States and Luxembourg was derived from a database on DRs from the Bank of New York Mellon (BNYM). To the best of our knowledge, there are no issuers from the BRIC countries that list in the United States or Luxembourg without using DRs. Data on listings in the United Kingdom comes directly from the London Stock Exchange (LSE). Data on the segment of the LSE called the Alternative Investment Market (LSE AIM) specifies the country of incorporation of the foreign issuers, and the main country of operation. Included in the sample are 116 companies that have main operation in one of the BRIC countries, but are incorporated in the United Kingdom or tax havens like the Cayman Islands. This gives a total of 446 foreign listings. For each we have: name of the company, host stock exchange, date of foreign listing, location of corporate headquarters (country and city), sector, and value of sales (turnover) for the last year for which data is available (2007 in most cases), obtained from database Orbis and provided by Bureau van Dijk (BvD). Data on the city in which corporate headquarters are located is not available for the subset of 116 companies. Fewer than ten companies have a foreign listing in more than one of the three selected markets. The data can be considered as valid for the end of 2008.

To study intermediaries, we use a dataset from Citibank documenting all capital raising events between the start of 1990 and end of May 2009, which were conducted with the use of DRs. Not all foreign listings covered in the previous dataset had any capital raising events, since DRs can be issued on the basis of shares already in circulation in the issuer's home market. In contrast, some issuers could have more than one capital-raising event. The virtue of the Citibank database is that for each event it gives the name of the institution sponsoring the issuer (administering the DRs), and the investment bank acting as the lead manager for capital raising. We would not be able to find data on intermediaries for all listings in the core dataset. In total, DR issuers from the BRIC countries have 359 capital raising events, out of which at least 311 were conducted on the US, the UK, or Luxembourg stock market. For fifty-four issues, data on the host market is unavailable, and five were conducted on other markets.

National origins of foreign listed companies

To compare the intensity of foreign listing between the BRIC countries, Table 3.1 presents basic data at the national level as at the end of 2008, while Figure 3.1 shows the cumulative number of foreign listed firms over time, revealing a pattern of consistent growth. No significant effect of the Asian crisis of 1997–8 can be detected. Actually, it was 1999, not the years of the crisis that recorded the smallest absolute increase in the number of cross-listings since 1995. Years 2000–2 recorded dynamic growth of cross-listing in all four countries, with a slow-down in 2003. The activity was thus remarkably resilient in the conditions

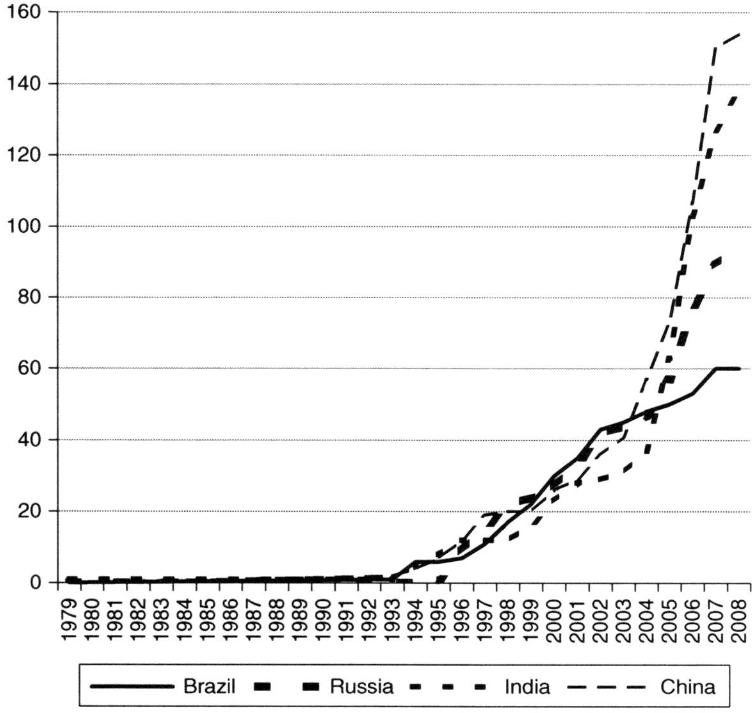

Figure 3.1. Cumulative number of foreign-listed firms from the BRIC countries
Sources: Author, based on data from BNY Mellon and LSE.

Table 3.1. The number of foreign listings from the BRIC countries

	Brazil	Russia	India	China	Total
Number of foreign-listed firms	60	94	138	154	446
Median turnover of foreign-listed firms (million €)	1712	527	92	99	178
Median turnover of domestically listed firms (million €)	123	37	4	113	19
Number of foreign-listed firms as percentage of:					
Number of domestically listed firms	10	10	10	8	9
Number of firms with turnover €50m	20	16	15	12	14
Number of firms with turnover €200m	30	34	41	26	32
Number of firms with turnover €1b	80	138	194	105	124

Sources: Author, based on data from BNY Mellon, LSE, and BvD.

of depressed stock markets in the United States and Western Europe, which lasted from the end of the Internet boom in 2000 until 2003.

The BRIC countries arrived at the end of 2003 with quite similar numbers of foreign-listed firms, but in the following two years considerable divergence has started. While cross-listings from Brazil continued to grow incrementally at the old pace, their growth accelerated in China (from 2004), as well as in India and Russia (from 2005). Between 2004 and 2007 the number of cross-listed firms doubled in Russia, tripled in China, and quadrupled in India. In 2006 alone, nearly a hundred companies from the BRIC countries listed abroad. The financial crisis in 2008 slowed down, but did not stop the activity.

Table 3.1 relates the number of foreign listed firms to the number of all domestically listed firms and the number of large firms. All four countries seem far from saturated with foreign listed firms. In each the number of firms with more than €200m in turnover is at least four times larger than the number of foreign listed firms, and the number of domestically listed firms at least seven times larger. To put it simply, there are thousands of large companies in these markets that are not listed abroad. By these measures, Mainland China seems least penetrated by foreign listings.

Table 3.1 shows a significant difference between the size of foreign and domestically listed firms. Issuers that have foreign listings are typically larger, but the difference depends on the market. In Russia and Brazil, a foreign listed firm is typically fourteen, and in India twenty-three times bigger than a domestically listed firm. In China, however, foreign listed firms are similar in size to domestically listed firms. Company size is definitely a factor affecting the propensity of companies to list abroad. Large companies are more likely to need foreign capital, and are more capable to absorb the costs of foreign listing. This is however not a universal pattern across all countries. There are also marked differences in the absolute size of foreign listed firms. While a typical foreign listed firm from India or China has just below €100m in turnover, in Russia the average is above €500m, and in Brazil €1.7bn. As we will show in the following sections, this is related to the sector structure of foreign listed firm and the features of foreign markets on which they list.

To be sure, the significance of foreign listings in the BRIC countries and their potential to generate future foreign listings cannot be explained solely with basic economic variables such as company size. In China, the government decides on whether to foreign list state-owned enterprises undergoing privatization. The China Securities Regulatory Commission (CSRC), which directly controls the stock exchanges in Shanghai and Shenzhen, draws up a list of candidate companies, which is subject to approval by the State Council (Hung et al. 2008). With regard to private firms, while the CSRC claims that it promotes foreign listing, in the mid-2000s the formalities faced by these companies have become more cumbersome (Ling 2005). The Chinese authorities appear particularly displeased with firms that use tax havens, such as Cayman Islands and Bermuda, for incorporation and later list their shares abroad as non-Chinese companies. In addition, while demand for domestic stocks in China is high due to high savings rate, popularity of stock market investing among individuals, and severe restrictions on investment in foreign stocks, foreign listing might be seen as limiting the supply, and increasing the likelihood of stock price bubbles. Options being considered include the repatriation of foreign listed firms via multiple listings (on both domestic and foreign exchanges), as well as opening the Chinese stock market to foreign issuers.

In 2005, in Russia, the financial regulator (at present the Federal Financial Markets Service) expressed their discontent with Russian companies setting up holding companies abroad (mainly in Cyprus) and then listing abroad as non-Russian incorporated companies. Amendments to securities laws drafted and aimed at closing this 'loophole' were never introduced, however, as they were seen as against international practices. Instead, Russian authorities make plans to facilitate multiple listings.

Brazil and India seem to have taken a more liberal approach to foreign listings, which may be explained by the shortage of domestic capital available for the corporate sector, most severe in the case of India. In Brazil, a large part of the privatization programme of the 1990s, has been conducted with share issues on the US markets. Recent reforms of financial reporting and corporate governance, however, are said to have contributed to an increase in both domestic and foreign investment in equity to the extent to which foreign listing may be needed less than before (Karmel 2006). The national Brazilian stock exchange BOVESPA itself is listed domestically following a successful initial public offering in 2007. In 2009, Brazil, as the only BRIC country, was classified by the FTSE Global Equity Index Series as an advanced emerging, not secondary emerging market. No major signs of opposition to foreign listings can be found for India either, where foreign listings seem to be celebrated as business success stories.

A relatively liberal approach to foreign listing in Brazil and India coincides with the fact that both countries joined the WTO in 1995, four years before the Financial Services Agreement, WTO's framework for liberalizing trade in financial services, came into effect. China joined only in 2001, and Russia as of 2009 was still negotiating accession. Their commitment to WTO makes foreign listing unlikely to be banned. Regulators' intentions of making foreign listing more difficult in these countries, which surfaced in the mid-2000s, might have actually backfired. Companies could speed up their foreign listing in anticipation of such move becoming more difficult and expensive in the future.

We should resist the temptation of labelling concerns about the impact of firms' migrations to foreign stock markets on domestic markets as expressions of protectionism and economic nationalism. There is no conclusive research on the net benefits of foreign listings for domestic stock markets. While benefits for foreign listing firms may be clear, there can be significant costs to domestic firms that do not list abroad, and the domestic stock market as a whole. Thus, it is important to know who the foreign listing companies are in relation to the rest of the domestic stock market, which is the focus of the next section.

Sub-national origins of foreign listed companies

This section explores the diversity of cross-listing firms by sector and location of corporate headquarters. Table 3.2 presents the structure of foreign listings by sector, using the FTSE Dow Jones Industry Classification Benchmark. This is compared to the structure of domestically listed firms to gauge the propensity of firms in different sectors and countries to cross-list. In addition, the table shows the median firm's size across sectors, as well as the share of cross-listings since 2003 in their total number.

Three sectors that have enjoyed the highest growth in the number of foreign listings since 2003 are health care, financials, and technology, while telecoms and utilities have recorded the slowest growth. There are also large differences in the average size of foreign listed firms, which can be associated with the economies of scale present in different sectors. The largest foreign listed firms can be found in oil and gas, followed by telecommunications, basic materials, and utilities. By far the smallest are those in technology sector (including computer services, software and hardware, electronic office and telecommunications equipment, and semiconductors).

Table 3.2. Issuers by sector

Sector	Percentage of foreign listed					Percentage of domestically listed					Foreign-listed as percentage of domestically listed	Foreign-listed since the end of 2003 as percentage of total	Median turnover of foreign-listed firms (million €)
	B	R	I	C	Total	B	R	I	C	Total			
Basic Materials	25	24	6	10	14	7	11	11	13	11	7	54	673
Consumer Goods	17	4	12	9	10	13	11	17	12	14	4	64	163
Consumer Services	12	5	8	11	9	10	8	12	12	11	4	68	99
Financials	10	10	19	16	15	30	13	15	6	13	6	80	121
Health Care	0	1	4	8	4	1	2	5	7	5	5	84	82
Industrials	5	9	17	18	14	22	43	30	34	31	2	75	199
Oil & Gas	2	18	5	5	7	1	1	1	1	1	46	66	1235
Technology	0	1	20	16	12	1	1	7	11	6	10	78	33
Telecommunications	12	15	5	5	8	5	2	1	1	1	34	31	788
Utilities	18	13	4	4	8	10	10	1	4	3	13	26	668
Total (percentage)	100	100	100	100	100	100	100	100	100	100	6	64	178

Sources: Author based on data from BNY Mellon, LSE, and BvD.

Important patterns can be identified by comparing the structure of foreign and domestically listed firms. If the share of a sector in foreign listings is high in relation to its share in domestic listings, we can refer to it as well represented, if it is low – as badly represented. The best-represented sectors in foreign listing are oil and gas and telecommunications. They constitute only 2 per cent of domestically listed firms, but as much as 15 per cent of foreign listings. Basic materials category (the extraction of natural resources other than oil and gas) is well represented for Brazil and Russia, but is underrepresented for India and China. Technology firms on the other hand are very well represented for China and particularly India, but not for Brazil and Russia. What could explain these patterns is that Brazil and Russia have internationally established, export-oriented firms in basic materials; China, and particularly India in technology. Such firms may need foreign listings and capital more (to finance international operations) and face lower relative costs (as foreign markets are already familiar with them).

By far the worst represented sector is industrials (including transportation, defence, electrical, and construction industries), with fifty times more domestically listed firms in this category than there are foreign listed firms. Consumer goods and consumer services are well represented in Brazil, but very badly in Russia. While Brazil has internationally successful consumer goods firms, for example, in food industry, there are few such firms in Russia.

In summary, firms in high-growth, capital intensive sectors, such as technology and telecommunications have a stronger propensity to cross-list than those in more stable sectors such as industrials or consumer goods. Thus, a more general feature of stock markets, as particularly suitable to the financing of relatively high-risk and high-return corporate activities, seems to be accentuated in international stock markets (Wójcik 2008). Foreign listings are also common in sectors with internationally oriented firms, in which the home country has a particular competitive advantage.

Table 3.3 shows the structure of the foreign listed firms according to the location of their headquarters. For each country the table presents cities with more than one foreign listed firm, while cities with one foreign listed firm only are classified as the rest of the country. Totals for countries are smaller than those in Table 3.1, since for companies cross-listed on the AIM, operating mainly in the BRIC countries, but incorporated outside of them, we do not have data on headquarter location.

The principal finding is a very strong concentration of foreign listed firms in the leading urban centres. In Brazil and Russia, there were only four cities with more than one cross-listed firm, in India seven, in China eight. Russia exhibited by far the highest geographical concentration of cross-listed firms. Moscow accounted for 63 per cent of cross-listings, with St. Petersburg in the second place with only 5 per cent. Every fifth domestically listed company

Table 3.3. Issuers by city

City/country	Number of foreign-listed firms	Number of domestically listed firms	Foreign-listed as percentage of domestically listed	Median turnover of foreign-listed (million €)	Median turnover of domestically listed (million €)	Foreign-listed since the end of 2003 as percentage of total
Brazil						
São Paulo	30	151	20	1282	200	23
Rio de Janeiro	8	94	9	4688	35	38
Brasilia	3	24	13	399	1047	0
Belo Horizonte	2	21	10	3376	367	50
Rest of Brazil	11	187	6	1543	107	0
Brazil	54	477	11	1642	123	20
Russia						
Moscow	41	301	14	1101	24	56
St. Petersburg	3	60	5	493	35	100
Krasnodar	2	26	8	1538	33	50
Perm	2	24	8	321	71	100
Rest of Russia	23	960	2	572	41	13
Russia	71	1371	5	582	37	45
India						
Mumbai	35	958	4	141	4	66
Delhi	19	429	4	102	8	63
Chennai	12	215	6	31	10	75
Hyderabad	11	161	7	81	6	82
Kolkata	9	219	4	151	10	67
Bangalore	6	118	5	145	18	67
Gurgaon	6	23	26	12	3	100
Rest of India	13	2943	0	131	3	85
India	111	5066	2	97	4	72

(Continued)

Table 3.3. Continued

City/country	Number of foreign-listed firms	Number of domestically listed firms	Foreign-listed as percentage of domestically listed	Median turnover of foreign-listed (million €)	Median turnover of domestically listed (million €)	Foreign-listed since the end of 2003 as percentage of total
China						
Beijing	33	152	22	75	198	67
Shanghai	21	174	12	115	143	52
Shenzhen	9	117	8	78	78	78
Guangzhou	4	38	11	375	170	25
Nanjing	3	37	8	164	165	67
Guixi	2	0	n/a	3768	0	0
Wuxi	2	7	29	470	284	100
Hangzhou	2	41	5	600	170	0
Rest of China	18	1202	1	221	105	78
M. China	94	1768	5	134	113	63

Sources: Author, based on data from BNY Mellon, LSE, and BvD.

from Moscow had a cross-listing, in St. Petersburg only every sixteenth. Next in the order of geographical concentration comes Brazil, with São Paulo overshadowing Rio de Janeiro. A domestically listed company from São Paulo is more than twice more likely to be cross-listed than one from Rio de Janeiro.

In China, Beijing is the centre of the market for foreign listings, even though Shanghai hosts a larger number of domestically listed companies. Domestically listed firms from Beijing are nearly twice more likely to be foreign listed than those from Shanghai. Other major centres of foreign listings are cities in the provinces neighbouring with the municipality of Shanghai (Nanjing, Hangzhou, and Wuxi), as well as Guangzhou and Shenzhen in Guangdong province, bordering with Hong Kong. Further detail, not presented in the table, reveals that there are hardly any cross-listed firms beyond the maritime provinces and the capital region of Beijing. The provinces of Hubei, Sichuan, and the municipality of Chongqing, for example, all representing large industrial centres of inland China, have no foreign listed firms at all.

In India, foreign listings are spread across an elite of seven cities, each with at least six cross-listed firms. Mumbai is in the lead, with nearly a third of cross-listings, followed by Delhi. Other members of the elite are the southern cities of Chennai, Hyderabad, Bangalore, Kolkata, as well as Gurgaon, a recently booming seat of multinational firms, 28 km southwest of Delhi.

Could the concentration of foreign listed firms in the largest urban centres be due to the concentration of the largest firms in these centres? The table does not give a conclusive answer. While in China, and particularly Russia, domestically listed firms from Beijing and Moscow seem larger than those from other centres, this is not the case in Brazil or India. Could this concentration be temporary, whereby firms from the largest urban centres pioneer foreign listing, but with time are followed by firms from other large cities and provinces? Evidence is inconclusive again. In Brazil and Russia, the dominance of São Paulo and Moscow, respectively, was stronger at the end of 2008 than it was in 2003. India and China, on the other hand, have seen many new foreign listing locations.

In Brazil, India, and Russia, the leading centres of cross-listing are the dominant financial centres of these countries (Gritsai 2004; Rossi and Taylor 2005, 2006). Chapter 2 has shown that companies from financial centres are more likely to be listed on a stock market, partly due to the proximity of sophisticated intermediaries, interaction with which is vital in the going public process. It seems that similar forces are at work with regard to foreign listing. The dominance of Beijing on the Chinese foreign listing stage seems exceptional in this respect, as Beijing shares the function of the national financial centre with Shanghai (not to mention Hong Kong), and does not host a stock exchange (these are located in Shanghai and Shenzhen). It is possible that Beijing headquartered firms are favoured in the politically influenced process of listing formerly state-owned enterprises.

To conclude the analysis at the sub-national scale, we compare the sector structure of foreign listed firms by city. An important similarity across countries is that cross-listed firms in consumer services, financials, health care, technology, and telecoms hardly ever come from beyond the top centres of foreign listing. Smaller centres tend to be represented by firms in basic materials, oil and gas, and utilities (Brazil and Russia), industrials (China and India), and consumer goods (India). Thus, smaller cities and provincial areas are not only underrepresented on the map of foreign listings, but their representation, weak as it is, is based mostly on firms in more traditional, less dynamic sectors of the economy.

Intermediaries in the process of foreign listing

An absolute majority of foreign listings from the BRIC countries take the form of DRs. To establish a DR programme, the issuer develops a team of advisors that typically includes an investment bank, lawyers, accountants, and a depositary bank. Investment bankers advise on the type of DRs and the market on which to launch them, advise on the ratio of DRs to ordinary shares, prepare research reports on the issuer, and promote DRs to investors via meetings and road-shows. If foreign listing involves the issuance of new shares and their offering in the form of DRs in the host market (instead of just a conversion of shares circulating in the home market into DRs), investment bankers advise on the size, pricing and marketing of offering, and underwrite it. As there may be more banks involved in underwriting, the one organizing the process is called lead manager. Lawyers prepare contracts between the issuer and other intermediaries, file the required registration statements with the host market regulatory authorities, and manage compliance with the host market laws and regulations. Accountants prepare issuer's financial statements according to the standards required in the host market (JP Morgan 2009).

A depositary bank, also referred to as a sponsor, issues DRs on the basis of issuer's shares held in custody by a custodian bank in the home market of the issuer (appointed by the sponsor), and arranges relationships with market makers and brokers who sell DRs to investors in the host market. A sponsor also plays a key role in day-to-day management of a DR programme. It maintains a register of DR holders, processes dividend payments for them, and keeps them informed about corporate actions of the issuer (Citibank 2007). The relationship between an issuer and a sponsor is exclusive; an issuer may switch between sponsors, but at any point in time it may have only one sponsor for a DR programme. An issuer may choose a different lead manager for each of its offerings.

In this section, we focus on sponsors and lead managers as key intermediaries in foreign listing. We use data on capital raising events (offerings/issues) between the start of 1990 and the end of May 2009, which were conducted with the use of DRs by companies incorporated in the BRIC countries. The latter totals 359 and accounts for 35 per cent of the total number of such events in the world, and 40 per cent of their value.

Table 3.4 presents sponsors and lead managers by the country of issuer. Four sponsors cover 100 per cent of offerings in the sample, with BNYM as a leader. Raw numbers of issues may understate the position of JP Morgan (JPM), as it specializes in offerings of large value. This is related to its weak position in India, where both issuers and offerings are typically smaller than in other BRIC markets. In addition, JPM's customer base in the BRIC countries seems to be growing significantly faster than that of its competitors. The structure of lead managers is much less concentrated than for sponsors. The five investment banks that have managed more than twenty offerings in the BRIC countries since 1990 are (in the order of significance): Merrill Lynch (ML), Credit Suisse (CS), Citigroup (CITI), Morgan Stanley (MS), and Goldman Sachs (GS). Together they were lead managers for 46 per cent of issues. As the average issue size is very similar across banks, their ranking by value of issues is the same. We find some evidence on lead managers' specialization by country. GS has a big market share in China, but has very weak or no presence in Brazil, Russia, and India. ML also has a big market share in China, but weak presence in Russia. CITI in contrast has a relatively equal presence on all markets. CITI and CS are relative newcomers to the business of lead management. Since the end of 2000, they have managed fifteen and seven times more issues, respectively, than they did between 1990 and 2000. The activities of GS, MS, and ML, already established in the 1990s, at best tripled.

Table 3.5 shows the structure of intermediaries by the sector of issuer. While all sponsors are heavily involved in technology firms, there are strong signs of specialization. JPM is a leader in oil and gas, Citibank's focuses on consumer goods and services, DB in financial firms, while BNYM leads in utilities. Specialization seems to apply to lead managers as well. MS leads in oil and gas and industrials, GS in health care, CS in technology, ML in utilities. CITI has hardly any customers in oil and gas and industrials, but otherwise covers all sectors.

Finally, Table 3.6 shows the stock markets on which issues intermediated by particular sponsors and lead managers were launched. The majority of issues sponsored by JPM launch at the New York Stock Exchange (NYSE), which is related to the fact that JPM specializes in serving big issuers. For issues sponsored by DB, the LSE is the main destination, while the Luxembourg Stock

Table 3.4. Sponsors and lead managers by the country of issuer

	Brazil	Russia	India	China	BRIC	Percentage growth in the number of issues since the end of 2000	Median issue value (million €)
Sponsor							
Bank of New York (BNYM)	55	54	48	43	48	223	64
Citibank (CITI)	11	2	21	24	18	210	60
Deutsche Bank (DB)	0	29	24	6	16	222	75
JP Morgan (JPM)	34	15	6	27	17	510	151
All sponsors (percentage)	100	100	100	100	100	250	70
Lead manager							
Citigroup (CITI)	9	10	9	7	8	1400	70
CS First Boston (CSFB)	19	10	2	19	10	640	140
Goldman Sachs (GS)	0	2	4	14	6	210	188
Merrill Lynch (ML)	19	2	12	16	13	200	113
Morgan Stanley (MS)	9	12	4	12	8	140	142
Other	45	63	69	32	54	220	39
All lead managers (percentage)	100	100	100	100	100	250	70
Number of issues	47	41	162	109	359	n/a	n/a
Median issue value (million €)	101	300	39	100	70	n/a	n/a

Sources: Author, based on data from Citibank.

Table 3.5. Sponsors and lead managers by the sector of issuer

	Sponsor				Lead manager						Number of issues
Sector	BNYM	CITI	DB	JPM	CITI	CSFB	GS	ML	MS	Other	
Basic Materials	13	12	9	11	13	13	4	11	14	12	42
Consumer Goods	12	18	12	2	10	13	4	13	0	13	40
Consumer Services	12	15	10	3	10	13	17	11	10	9	38
Financials	9	8	17	13	23	11	9	17	3	8	38
Health Care	6	8	3	13	10	5	22	7	0	7	26
Industrials	9	11	10	10	3	8	4	4	17	12	36
Oil & Gas	3	2	2	13	0	3	4	4	14	4	15
Technology	20	17	29	26	17	29	17	22	21	22	78
Telecommunications	6	9	3	3	10	3	9	0	17	5	21
Utilities	11	2	3	5	3	3	9	11	3	8	25
All sectors (percentage)	100	100	100	100	100	100	100	100	100	100	359

Sources: Author, based on data from Citibank.

Exchange (LUX) gets their foreign issuers mainly via BNYM. Moving to lead managers, ML is by far the most important lead manager for the NYSE, and like GS rarely manages issues launched in Europe. In contrast, CITI and MS are important lead managers for the LSE. There seems to be a significant positive relationship between the median issue value and the share of the top five lead managers. On the LSE, NASDAQ and particularly the NYSE, their share is close

Table 3.6. Sponsors and lead managers by host market

	Sponsors				Lead managers						Number of issues	Average issue value (milion €)
Host market	BNYM	CITI	DB	JPM	CITI	CSFB	GS	ML	MS	Other		
LSE	19	6	14	7	7	4	1	3	7	24	46	270
LUX	23	1	4	1	2	0	1	0	0	27	30	15
NASDAQ	19	18	5	13	5	10	7	7	6	20	55	85
NYSE	39	10	12	32	5	16	10	27	12	23	93	175
OTC	41	19	9	7	6	6	4	7	2	51	76	42
Other	2	2	1	0	0	0	0	0	0	5	5	14
Unavailable	30	10	13	1	5	2	0	2	2	43	54	20
Total	173	66	58	61	30	38	23	46	29	193	359	70

Sources: Author, based on data from Citibank.

to 50 per cent or higher. On the US OTC (Over-The-Counter) markets it is only 30 per cent, and on the LUX almost all issues are managed by investment banks outside of the top five, with Elara Capital from India in the lead. In other words, big investment banks dominate big issues, with small issues left to smaller firms. It is possible that small issuers simply cannot afford the services of the largest investment banks.

In analogy with the LUX and the OTC markets, the AIM segment of the LSE, not covered in Table 3.6, because foreign issuers can list there directly, without DRs, is served mostly by small investment banks. On the AIM they play the role of Nominated Advisors (Nomads) who perform similar functions to lead managers, but on a much smaller scale. In the middle of 2009, 127 issuers from the BRIC countries present on the AIM had as many as forty-three different Nomads, of which only five had five or more clients. All of the top five Nomads are small investment firms, headquartered in London, and some have offices in the BRIC countries (mostly in China).

To summarize, depositary banking and lead management – services key to foreign listing – are dominated by a handful of institutions – the leading investment banks or in the case of CITI and DB, universal banks with strong investment banking arms, all except DB headquartered in New York. CITI actually acts as both one of the leading sponsors and lead managers (for issues sponsored by CITI, CITI is also the most common lead manager). Institutional concentration is higher in depositary banking than in lead management, most likely due to stronger economies of scale. Both services require relationships and expertise in home and host stock markets, but depositary banking, in addition, involves daily processing of huge amounts of transactions and information (Oxford Metrica 2009). Although the leading intermediaries are all international if not global organizations, they exhibit a degree of specialization in terms of the size, sector, and country of the issuers they service, implying that expertise in the intermediation of foreign listing is specific to particular types of issuers, particular sectors, and countries.

The findings of this section are consistent with those on the sub-national geography of issuers undertaking foreign listings. Existing literature demonstrates that the offices of leading investment banks (and other advanced business services firms) are highly concentrated in the leading urban centres, referred to as world cities. In fact, the geography of world cities corresponds well with the centres of foreign listings identified earlier in this chapter. In Brazil and Russia, São Paulo and Moscow are by far the largest concentrations of global investment bank offices, overshadowing Rio and St. Petersburg in this respect (Gritsai 2004; Rossi and Taylor 2005, 2006). In China, Beijing is more prominent as a location of such service providers than Shanghai (Taylor et al. 2009). In India, Mumbai's lead in the world city rankings is stronger than in the market for foreign listing, which can probably be explained by the fact that foreign listings from India rely to a greater degree on the services of smaller investment banks, often of Indian origin, with offices in the high-technology centres beyond Mumbai. Thus, in analogy with the geography of domestic listings being driven to a large extent by the location of investment banks and other relevant services firms, unveiled in Chapter 2, the propensity of firms to list abroad seems to be influenced by the proximity of their decision-making centres to the offices of global investment banks that are instrumental in 'taking' firms to foreign stock markets. In the following section, we will focus on the destination of foreign listings.

Destinations of foreign listings

To recall, our data covers the United States, the United Kingdom, and Luxembourg as the destination markets for cross-listing from the BRIC countries. For the United States, we distinguish between the NYSE, NASDAQ, and OTC markets; for the United Kingdom, between the London Stock Exchange's Main Market (LSE Main) and its AIM set up in 1995 (here aggregated with the more recent Professional Securities Market, with very few foreign issuers and similar regulations to the AIM).

To understand the choice that foreign listing companies face, we need to briefly sketch the regulations and costs prevailing in different markets. The NYSE and the LSE Main are most expensive. The maximum combined listing and annual fee an issuer is charged is capped at the level of approx. $500,000 a year at either exchange, while the corresponding figure for NASDAQ is between $100,000 and $180,000, with costs at the AIM, the LUX, and the US OTC much lower. In addition, the NYSE and the LSE Main Market have explicit requirements in terms of issuer's size. For

NASDAQ and the LUX such requirements are less stringent, while the AIM and the US OTC have no size requirements.

Indirect costs of foreign listing concern reporting and corporate governance requirements. Foreign firms listing on the NYSE or NASDAQ have to register with the Securities and Exchange Commission (SEC) and become subject to US securities laws, exposing them to potential lawsuits by investors. They also need to reconcile their financial statements in accordance with the US Generally Accepted Accounting Principles (GAAP). Foreign firm entering the US OTC markets are exempt from the SEC registration. On the Main Market of the LSE, foreign firms can list their DRs or ordinary shares. Both have to be admitted to listing by the UK Listing Authority before they are admitted to trading by the LSE. Issuers of ordinary shares also need to prepare their financial reports in accordance with the UK or US GAAP or the International Financial Reporting Standards (IFRS). Listing requirements on the AIM are minimal. The requirements of the LUX are stricter than those on the AIM but less strict than those on the US exchanges. The relative stringency of regulation over foreign issuers listing on the US exchanges have been further reinforced in 2002 with the Sarbanes-Oxley Act (SOX), which imposed stricter reporting and corporate governance requirements (Piotroski and Srinivasan 2008; Doidge et al. 2009).

To be sure, the destination markets have major financial centres as their nodes. While it is obvious to refer to a listing on the LSE as a listing in London, we can also refer to a listing in the United States as a listing in New York. Both the NYSE and NASDAQ are headquartered in New York. OTC markets are mostly direct transactions among institutional investors and brokers, but New York is the dominant centre of these institutions.

Overall, as Table 3.7 presents, the US markets (NYSE, NASDAQ, and OTC) have attracted 210 issuers, the UK markets 168, and Luxembourg sixty-eight. The leadership of the United States is not surprising. Foreign listing is about access to foreign capital and investors, and the United States accounts for approximately 40 per cent of global stock market capitalization, and an

Table 3.7. Cross-listings by home and host market

Country	LSE Main	LSE AIM&P	Luxembourg	NYSE	NASDAQ	US OTC
Brazil	0	6	0	30	1	23
Russia	26	23	0	5	0	40
India	9	45	68	11	3	2
China	6	53	0	36	30	29
Total	41	127	68	82	34	94
Foreign-listed since the end of 2003 as percentage of total	63	86	94	40	82	27

Sources: Author, based on data from BNY Mellon and LSE.

unparalleled number of large institutional and individual investors. While the United Kingdom represents a large pool of capital, with the third largest stock market capitalization in the world, the power of London as a magnet for foreign listing, is based on London being a leading location of investment banks, institutional investors, and specialized business services, offering access to capital market expertise, with which only New York can compete (Z/Yen 2010). London is also the centre of a jurisdiction promoting stock market-friendly corporate governance, association with which can boost foreign firms' access to capital (Clark and Wójcik 2007). By comparison, Japan has a stock market capitalization twice bigger than the United Kingdom, but Japanese investors and intermediaries have been rather passive internationally, at least in the last two decades. Foreign listing on the Tokyo Stock Exchange does not seem to offer expertise or prestige relevant to international capital markets.

Luxembourg is the least obvious cross-listing destination. It is a newcomer on this stage, whose stock of cross-listings from the BRIC countries rose nearly from scratch between 2003 and 2008. On the other hand, Luxembourg has had decades of experience in listing foreign bond issues, holding companies, and investment funds. While European Union regulations, which facilitate cross-border equity investment give Luxembourg no particular advantage over London, Luxembourg can offer foreign shares quoted in Euro, and information available to investors in French and German. To be sure, Luxembourg offers relatively low costs of cross-listing.

Analysing the attractiveness of cross-listing destinations, it is important to recognize that stock exchanges and other institutions actively pursue foreign issuers. As foreign listing is one of the fastest growing businesses of stock exchanges, they compete with each other by trying to reach issuers in their home countries (Capaldo et al. 2008). In addition to maintaining offices in Hong Kong, the NYSE, NASDAQ, and the LSE set up offices in Beijing between September 2007 and January 2008. In 2004, NASDAQ appointed a Russian-speaking director at their London office (Baibakov 2004).

In addition, all the destination exchanges considered have been establishing close relationships with their counterparts in the BRIC countries, signing memoranda of understanding, aimed at facilitating investors' access to each other's markets, and a transfer of stock market know-how. Chinese stock exchanges and regulatory authorities, for example, expressed an interest in cooperation with NASDAQ in order to develop a local stock market for high-growth firms. The LSE has been in talks with the exchange in Hong Kong about establishing simultaneous listing for Chinese firms in Hong Kong and London. The NYSE has acquired 5 per cent ownership of the National Stock Exchange of India, and 1 per cent of BOVESPA in Brazil. In the future, we should expect more ownership links between stock exchanges in the BRIC countries and those in the leading stock market centres in Europe and North America.

The significance of foreign listing is also recognized by the authorities of financial centres. The City of London Corporation recently commissioned an international study on the cost of capital, focusing on comparing the cost of raising equity on the LSE with the United States and other European exchanges (Oxera 2006). On the other side of the Atlantic, Mayor Bloomberg and Senator Schumer asked McKinsey to work with the New York City Economic Development Corporation to research the measures needed to sustain New York's and the US leadership in global financial services. The report pays a lot of attention to New York losing the 'battle' for cross-listings (McKinsey 2007). In short, host stock exchanges and financial centres exercise their 'pulling power' towards companies from the BRIC countries with all intent.

Having discussed the power of New York, London, and Luxembourg to attract cross-listings from the BRIC countries treated as a group, we need to stress that their relative attractiveness depends on which of the BRIC countries is concerned. As Table 3.7 shows, while the US markets are the main destination of Chinese, and an almost exclusive destination of Brazilian firms, Russian companies cross-list mainly in the United Kingdom, while Indian companies list in large numbers in Luxembourg. The first factor that can be considered here is proximity between home and host countries in terms of trade links. Presence on a host stock market can support a firm's exports by improving its visibility, and exports can make host market investors more familiar with the firm (Sarkissian and Schill 2004). For Brazilian companies European markets, and for Russian firms US markets are relatively unimportant, which may explain a limited engagement of issuers from these countries with the European and US stock markets, respectively. For China, the United States is a more important export market than Europe, and a more prominent cross-listing market.

Additional insight into the home–host country mosaic of cross-listing can be offered by considering the industrial specialization of host markets, as illustrated in Table 3.8. Host markets tend to specialize in the listing of foreign companies, for which they have expertise built on the listing and trading of domestic firms. NASDAQ has since 1990s been the market of choice for the US high-technology firms. Not surprisingly then, NASDAQ has the majority of its foreign listings from the BRIC countries in technology and consumer services sectors (the latter mostly Internet-based services). The LSE Main Market hosts a large group of foreign issuers in oil and gas, basic materials, and utilities, while the NYSE in telecommunications and health care. Their respective domestic markets boast many large companies in these sectors. Firms are attracted to markets that concentrate other large and leading firms from the same sector, as this is where analysts specializing in the sector are found, and where investors look for companies from the sector to invest in. Presence on such markets is like presence in Paris or Milan for fashion industry.

Table 3.8. Cross-listings by sector and host market

Sector	LSE Main	LSE AIM&P	Luxembourg	NYSE	NASDAQ	US OTC	Total
Basic materials	22	17	7	15	0	14	14
Consumer goods	10	7	16	7	6	13	10
Consumer services	10	6	6	11	24	7	9
Financials	7	29	12	10	3	9	15
Health care	2	2	7	7	6	2	4
Industrials	12	16	16	10	12	14	14
Oil & gas	15	10	4	6	0	5	7
Technology	10	6	24	10	41	5	12
Telecomms	2	2	7	18	9	10	8
Utilities	10	5	0	6	0	21	8
Total (percentage)	100	100	100	100	100	100	100
Median turnover (million €)	703	26	52	1839	68	535	178

Sources: Author, based on data from BNY Mellon, LSE, and BvD.

Corporate size is another important factor affecting the geography of cross-listings. Recall from Table 3.1 that the Brazilian foreign listing firms tend to be the largest and Indian firms the smallest. Thus, it is not surprising to find the Brazilian firms populating the NYSE, while Indian issuers concentrate on the AIM and in Luxembourg.

To extend the analysis, we consider the evolution of home–host market links over time. For Russian firms, the US OTC was the market of choice until 2003. Since then, however, very few companies entered the US markets, while tens listed in London, particularly the AIM. In contrast to Russia, the Chinese corporate sector has continued its engagement with the US markets. Thus, the SOX may have been a major deterrent for Russian companies, but apparently not so for those from China. The path of the Chinese cross-listings on the US stock markets appears particularly intriguing. Until the end of 1996, out of twelve cross-listed Chinese firms, ten were present on the OTC market. Since then, an absolute majority of new cross-listings took place on NASDAQ and the NYSE. This might suggest that companies from a given country as a population make their first steps on less exacting and less visible markets, and then upgrade their cross-listing to higher-level markets.

Finally, Table 3.9 cross-tabulates the headquarter locations of cross-listed firms with their destination markets, classified in two groups: the NYSE, NASDAQ, and the LSE Main with stricter requirements in terms of size, reporting, and corporate governance; and relatively lenient OTC, LUX, and LSE AIM. In Brazil, India, and Russia, out of thirty-nine companies from outside the leading centres of cross-listing, only eight are present on higher-level foreign markets; in the leading centres as many as seventy-seven out of 112. As argued in the preceding section, and documented in Table 3.3, this cannot be explained with the smaller size of firms from outside the leading

Table 3.9. Cross-listings by city and host market

City/country	NYSE, Nasdaq, or LSE Main	LSE AIM&P, LUX, or US OTC
Brazil		
São Paulo	18	12
Rio de Janeiro	5	3
Brasilia	1	1
Belo Horizonte	3	0
Rest of Brazil	4	7
Russia		
Moscow	24	17
St. Petersburg	2	1
Krasnodar	1	1
Perm	1	1
Rest of Russia	3	20
India		
Mumbai	10	25
Delhi	5	14
Chennai	2	10
Hyderabad	2	9
Kolkata	1	8
Bangalore	2	4
Gurgaon	0	6
Rest of India	1	12
China		
Beijing	26	7
Shanghai	13	8
Shenzhen	7	2
Guangzhou	2	2
Nanjing	2	1
Guixi	1	1
Wuxi	2	0
Hangzhou	1	1
Rest of China	14	4

Sources: Author, based on data from BNY Mellon and LSE.

centres. Thus, the urban and regional economic geography matters not only to whether firms engage with foreign stock markets or not, it also matters to their choice of cross-listing destinations. Provincial companies are less likely to cross-list, and when they cross-list they are less likely to enter markets with stricter requirements.

Conclusions and implications

The objective of the chapter was to present an exploratory analysis of the geographical patterns of foreign listing by focusing on companies from Brazil, Russia, India, and China entering the stock markets in the United States, the

United Kingdom, and Luxembourg. Our analysis has mapped the national origins of the foreign listed companies, their sub-national origins in terms of sectors and cities, investment banks dominating as intermediaries in cross-listing, as well as the destinations of foreign listings in terms of host stock exchanges and cities.

At a descriptive level, the cross-listing from each of the BRIC countries can be summarized as follows. In Brazil, it is predominantly about very large companies headquartered in São Paulo listing in New York, representing mostly such industries as basic materials, utilities, and consumer goods and services. They seem to face few political barriers in the process. In Russia, Moscow-based companies active in basic materials, oil and gas industries list mostly in London. The process is politically sensitive as the Russian authorities try to prevent foreign control over strategic industries, and see foreign listing as a threat to the future of Moscow as international financial centre. Typical Indian companies seeking foreign listings are relatively small technology firms, not only from Mumbai or Delhi but also from the technology clusters of Hyderabad, Bangalore, and Chennai. To a larger extent than in other BRIC countries, Indian firms' cross-listing is intermediated by relatively small, domestic investment banks, with London's AIM and Luxembourg as their destinations. Finally, Chinese foreign listing firms are mostly large companies, coming from a variety of sectors, with industrials and financials in the lead, and spread quite evenly between the London and New York markets. Beijing dominates Shanghai as the headquarter location of foreign listed firms. China has the largest population of foreign listed firms in the world, but also the largest potential for further growth.

At a more analytical level, the cross-listing experiences of the BRIC countries exhibit similarities and differences. All four countries have shown a dynamic growth in cross-listing, and considerable resilience of this activity to the global stock market fluctuations. Cross-listing firms are typically large companies that come from fast growth, capital intensive and export-oriented sectors of the economy. The choice of the destination market is affected by trading links between the host and home market and industrial specialization in the host market. There are however important exceptions to these patterns. Cross-listing from Brazil has grown at a much slower pace than from Russia, India, and China. Chinese cross-listing firms are not larger than their counterparts that list only domestically. Luxembourg has attracted hordes of Indian firms without a history of significant trade links with India.

The most important finding of this study is the geographical concentration of foreign listed firms in the leading financial centres of the BRIC countries, which holds even if we account for the size and sector of foreign-listing firms. If foreign listing benefits foreign listed firms but disadvantages domestic firms, then the highly uneven spatial distribution of foreign listings implies the concentration of the benefits of foreign listing in leading urban centres, and the concentration of costs in other cities and provincial areas. In this sense, foreign listing pits New York against London, New York against São Paulo, but also São Paulo against Rio de Janeiro, and maritime China against inland China. The dominance of leading financial centres is much higher in Brazil and Russia than in India and China. Moreover, in Brazil and Russia it has increased, while in India and China it has decreased with time. In addition, we find that cross-listing firms from beyond the leading centres come mostly from traditional, less dynamic sectors of the economy, and tend to list on second-tier host markets, with relatively lenient reporting and governance requirements.

Crucial in linking issuers from the BRIC countries with foreign stock markets is a handful of global investment banks, operating out of global financial centres, with New York and London in the lead, and providing issuers with stock market expertise. Cross-listing is thus a major channel through which the financial practices emanate from these centres to influence corporate sectors in the emerging markets. The level of penetration of the BRIC economies by global investment banks, however, differs not only between countries but also within them. The leading financial centres in the BRIC countries serve as gateways for global investment banks.

There are limits to how much a largely quantitative exploratory study can tell us about the nature of foreign listing. Case studies of foreign listing, covering the interaction between issuers and intermediaries, are one obvious direction for further research. A range of intermediaries relevant to foreign listing should be extended beyond investment banks and include venture capital firms, which may influence listing decisions of high-technology firms. The dynamics of cross-listing activity and its impact on urban and regional economies deserves further research in financial geographies, but also in urban studies and economic geography in general. Concentrated in specific economic sectors, regions, and cities, cross-listing is a factor of uneven economic development. Last but not least, it is a politically charged and contested process. In sum, cross-listing has a multi-dimensional geography, both in its nature and impacts.

The recent financial crisis has a great potential to reshuffle the world of foreign listing. With a drought of capital available for corporations on equity markets in North America and Europe, stock markets in the BRIC countries and other emerging markets may for the first time have a chance of attracting foreign issuers to their own financial centres. Second, the geography of investment banks seems to be changing for good. Their reputation, particularly for the US banks, is severely damaged, and many had to cede significant stakes in their organizations to Asian investors. This may imply more control by the institutions in the BRIC countries and other emerging markets over the market for foreign listing, and possibly more politicization of the process. In particular, considering the abundance of domestic savings in China, the future decisions of the Chinese authorities with regard to foreign listing and the opening of the domestic stock market to foreign investors and issuers will have crucial consequences for the global foreign listing market and the geography of financial centres. One way or another, foreign listing is likely to remain an important factor influencing the map of the world economy.

4

Biased Investors: Proximity in Secondary Markets

Equity is considered a high return – high-risk class of assets. Between 1900 and 2000, the US equity markets yielded an arithmetic average of 8.7 per cent per year above inflation, with the standard deviation of 20.2 per cent, compared to US bonds with real returns of 2.1 per cent per year and standard deviation of 10 per cent (Dimson et al. 2002). While the attraction of investing in equity is obvious, the challenge of managing risks involved in such investments is steep. The most powerful invention that has responded to this challenge, the Modern Portfolio Theory (MPT) tells investors to diversify investments as widely as possible, moving towards a portfolio with equity from individual countries held in proportion to their share in the global equity market capitalization. This prescription, however, is based on the assumption that equity markets are informationally efficient, that is, all information relevant to equity prices is built into them, and consequently it is impossible to beat the market other than by chance and by incurring unnecessarily high risks. Contrary to the assumption of the MPT, information on equity markets is not ubiquitous; it is not available to everybody at negligible cost. This chapter will show that an important way in which investors on equity markets manage their risks is by taking advantage of proximity to the sources of information relevant to equity prices.

The key source of information relevant to equity prices and investigated in this chapter will be equity issuers themselves. The chapter will argue that proximity between investors and corporations (equity issuers) plays an important part in explaining the behaviour and performance of investors in secondary equity markets. By extension it provides a significant insight into the performance of equity markets themselves. It should be made clear from the outset that the chapter does not focus on the role of proximity or closeness between investors themselves or issuers themselves, or between stock exchanges on one side and corporate issuers or investors on the other. Nor it focuses on the position of equity analysts or market makers in relation to other actors and institutions. It goes without saying that investors and issuers are the central actors for whom secondary equity markets actually exist. While actors such as stock exchanges, analysts or market makers provide important infrastructure and services, the key to understanding the secondary equity markets lies in the relationships between investors and equity issuers. To be sure, other types of relationships and proximity will not be ignored. They will be considered to the extent they relate to the proximity between investors and issuers. Readers interested in these other types of proximity in their own right are referred to Lo and Grote (2002).

The role of proximity between investors and issuers on secondary equity markets will be explored by investigating the following issues. How important is proximity in managing risks involved in equity investments? Why is it important? What are the implications of its role for secondary equity markets and beyond these markets? What are the limits to the role of proximity and how is it likely to change in the future? To address these issues I use recent research findings from both financial economics and economic geography. Combining the two bodies of research, I hope to show in detail how and why both global and local factors matter in financial markets, and to uncover some of the intricate relationships between place, proximity, and financial risk management.

Proximity matters – evidence on home bias and local bias

In the first step of exploring the role of proximity in managing equity investment risk, we will focus on two related facets of investors' behaviour – home bias and local bias. There is mounting evidence that investors exhibit a preference for trading and holding domestic shares, issued by companies in their home country, and within the home country they prefer to trade and hold shares of companies that are headquartered close to the location of investors in question. This applies to both institutional and individual investors, who by doing so forgo the potential benefits of portfolio diversification both at the international and domestic level.

Figure 4.1 presents home bias for selected countries and Eurozone (average for years 1997–2005), defined as the difference between the percentage of equity portfolio invested in domestic stocks and the share of domestic stock market in global stock market capitalization. In other words, the figure shows what percentage of equity portfolio should be shifted from domestic to foreign stocks in order to comply with the MPT. The US investors, for example, held approximately 84 per cent of their equity portfolio in domestic equities, while the share of the US equity market in the world equity market capitalization was 45 per cent, resulting in the home bias of 39 per cent. For other countries,

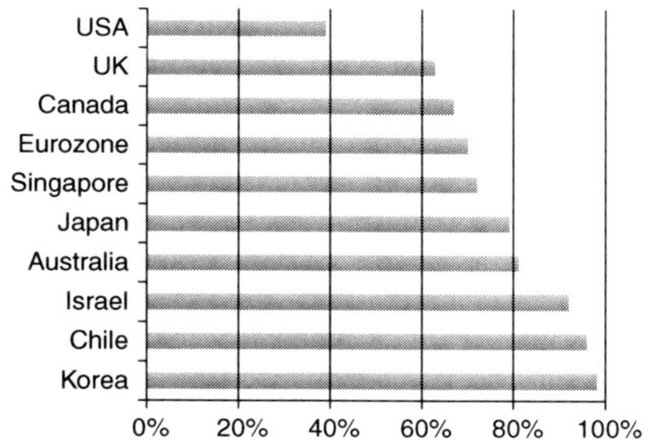

Figure 4.1. Home bias in selected countries (average for 1997–2005)

Notes: Home bias is defined as the difference between the percentage of equity portfolio invested in domestic stocks and the share of domestic stock market in global stock market capitalization (for details, see Bekaert and Wang 2009).

whose stock markets represent a much smaller share of the global stock market, home bias is much larger. In some emerging markets it is larger than 90 per cent. In the small city-state of Singapore, despite all its global connections, home bias exceeds 70 per cent. In Eurozone, with the highest level of international monetary and economic integration, the average home bias is also above 70 per cent, ranging from 46 per cent in the Netherlands to 87 per cent in Portugal. Between 1997 and 2005 in a sample of twenty-seven countries, the home bias decreased, but only at a slow rate of 1.5 per cent a year (for details, see Bekaert and Wang 2009). In short, home bias is large and persistent.

'Local bias' is probably as old as home bias. There is a Danish proverb advising that you should not invest in businesses you cannot see from the tower of your church. Estimating the magnitude of home bias in the United States, Coval and Moskowitz (1999) found that approximately one in ten companies in a fund manager's portfolio is chosen because it is located in the same city as the manager. Ivković and Weisbrenner (2005) document that on average a US individual investor holds approximately 30 per cent of her equity portfolio in the stocks of companies headquartered within 250 miles, while the share of such firms in the total US equity market is on average only approx. 10 per cent. Loughran and Schultz (2004) show that firms in blizzard-struck cities in the United States see a dramatic trading volume drop in their stocks compared to firms in other cities, and that the Yom Kippur holiday dampens trading volumes in companies located in cities with large Jewish populations. While the bulk of research on proximity in secondary equity markets is based on the US data, 'home bias' is well documented across at least developed economies (e.g. Sorensen et al. 2004, cited in Stulz 2005), while countries for which evidence on local bias is available include also China, Germany, Sweden, and Finland.

There are different types of proximity to issuers that seem to matter for investors. Home bias goes beyond simple preference for domestic vis-à-vis foreign stocks. It has been shown that investors are more likely to hold and trade foreign stocks from countries that are closer in terms of physical distance, travel cost, or adjacency. Portes and Rey (2005) show that cross-border equity flows are also related positively to the telephone call traffic between countries, a variable that can represent economic and cultural ties. Hau (2001) documents that traders trading on proprietary accounts in the German blue-chip stocks and located in Germany, Austria, or Switzerland outperform traders located in non-German speaking countries. In a study covering years 1970, 1980, 1990, and 2000, Bhattacharya and Groznik (2008) show that the equity investments of US investors in a foreign country are affected by the size of immigrant population from this country. Thus, all types of fundamentally geographical factors seem to influence home bias.

Most studies on local bias have used administrative boundaries within countries, analysing investors' preference for in-state vis-à-vis out-of-state investments (Huberman 2001) and for investments in firms headquartered within an arbitrarily determined radius from an investor's location (Coval and Moskowitz 2001; Ivković and Weisbrenner 2005). Here, the thresholds of 250 or 100 km have been most commonly used for distinguishing between local and non-local investments. There are however studies that account for other types of proximity than that between investor location and issuer headquarters. Bodnaruk (2004) finds that Swedish investors are more likely to hold shares in companies that have an establishment, but not necessarily the headquarters, located nearby. Grinblatt and Keloharju (2001) demonstrate that Swedish speaking investors living in Finland are more likely to trade stocks in companies that publish their annual financial reports in Swedish in addition to Finnish language, and in those that have Swedish speaking CEOs. Finally, Massa and Simonov (2006) show that Swedish investors are more likely to invest in companies that have the same area of activity as the investor's profession. However, they find that geographical proximity is more important to portfolio composition than professional proximity.

The significance of proximity is also shown in a dynamic context, accounting for the mobility of investors and issuers. Available studies are rare, but provide significant results. For Sweden, Massa and Simonov (2006) show that individual investors who moved recently or changed or lost their job exhibit less local bias. Bodnaruk (2004), however, documents that when individuals move they do sell stocks of companies from their old locations and buy those from new locations. With regard to the issuers, Prinsky and Wang (2006) find that in the United States when a company moves headquarters, the co-movement if its stock market price with companies from old location declines, and that with companies from the new location rises.

Summarizing, research on home and local bias has generated dozens of papers in the leading journals in finance, some of which have received prestigious awards (Coval and Moskowitz 1999; Hau 2001). In short, the evidence on the role of geographical proximity in secondary equity markets is well established and is here to stay. There can be no doubts that home and local bias are fundamentally related to investors' perception and approach to risk, as it is impossible to assume that investors in so many different contexts simply consider domestic and local stocks as those offering higher returns regardless of risk. However, can one really claim that the geographical biases reflect any conscious act of financial risk management that goes beyond mere ignorance and uncertainty about far-away firms? The multiple and often complex ways in which proximity matters to individual as well as institutional investors suggest the operation of real risk management, but to answer this question satisfactorily we need to delve deeper into the issue why home and local bias exist. In what follows we focus on explanations based on information.

Explaining investment bias with information

According to Merton, 'investors buy and hold only those securities about which they have enough information' (1987, cited in Massa and Simonov 2006: 640). But what does 'enough' information mean? And what kind of information? To put it crudely, in order to invest in a security an investor has to know of it and something about it. In other words, she has to be familiar with it. Geographical proximity is without doubt an instrumental factor of familiarity. Investors' knowledge about the world of equity is biased towards local equity, as they consume products and services of local companies, have colleagues who work for local firms, and are exposed to local media that write about local economy. Put differently, firms are more visible to local investors than to remote ones. As Barber and Odean (2008) argue, with approximately 7000 listed companies in the United States alone the world of equity investments is a world of information overload, and investors are bound to use mental shortcuts to make investment decisions. As a result home and local bias could be just behavioural biases.

If home and local bias were nothing more than behavioural biases driven by pure familiarity, they would give investors no edge in relation to non-proximate (foreign or non-local) investors. This contention, however, is unsustainable in the view of evidence that investors can earn superior returns on proximate stocks. Shukla and van Inwegen (1995) find that UK mutual fund managers investing in the United States underperform relative to their US colleagues. In a study of hedge funds investing in Asia, Teo (2009) finds that those with physical presence (head office or a research office) in Asia have superior performance. Coval and Moskowitz (2001) show that mutual funds generate large gains from local investments (defined as holdings within 100 km of the fund headquarters), outperforming distant holdings by as much as 3 per cent per year, and outpacing local stocks not held by 4–5 per cent, on a risk-adjusted basis. Hau (2001) documents that traders proximate to the headquarters of issuers generate superior returns from intraday trading in the stocks of these companies. Ivković and Weisbrenner (2005) show that the US households on average generated an additional annualized return of 3.2 per cent from their local holdings relative to non-local holdings. Superior returns from local investment have also been documented for individual investors in Sweden (Bodnaruk 2004; Massa and Simonov 2006) and China (Feng and Seasholes 2004).

Research testing the performance of actors other than investors also, albeit indirectly, lends support to the role of local informational advantage. Malloy (2005) demonstrates that in the United States, geographically proximate equity analysts produce more accurate forecasts and recommendations than other analysts, while Anand and others (2008) analyse market making in NASDAQ stocks, and find out that market makers located within 100 km of a firm provide more liquidity and contribute more to price discovery than more distant market makers. On an international level, using a sample of thirty-two countries, Bae et al. (2008) document the advantage of domestic over foreign analysts in terms of making more accurate earnings forecasts. The advantage is particularly large for countries with low transparency, and companies with little foreign assets and little participation by foreign investors. Sonney (2009) documents that among US analysts working on European companies, those who specialize in individual countries produce much more accurate earnings forecasts than those who specialize in sectors. Proximity between the analysts and the headquarters of European companies covered by them also contributes to the accuracy of forecasts.

Growing evidence that local investors can outperform remote investors on local stocks, does not imply that familiarity effect does not exist. Rather it suggests that investors can turn familiarity to their own advantage by gaining superior information in relation to non-local investors. In other words, there is an information asymmetry between local and non-local investors. What information then could be available to local investors but is not available to the remote ones? Local investors can talk to employees, managers, and suppliers of the firm; they may obtain information from local media; they may use the company's products and services more often and be better able to judge their quality; and they may have personal ties with corporate executives (Coval and Moskowitz 1999). Geographical proximity may help better understanding of the technical aspects of a firm's operations, as well as lower the cost of evaluating intangible factors such as management ability and corporate culture (Gaspar and Massa 2007). It also improves information about the local business climate. Information with regard to which local investors have an advantage is usually associated with soft (in contrast to hard) and private (in contrast to publicly available) information. The term soft information is usually used interchangeably with tacit information (Gertler 2003) and means information that is hard to communicate to others, let alone capture in written documents. Private information can be defined as that obtained from corporate insiders and not available to the public. Geographical proximity can be crucial in helping investors to access and interpret soft and private information relevant to the value of corporate equity. A remote investor can access public and hard information, for example, by reading local newspapers from far-away places on Internet, but may have difficulty to interpret this information, and may be right to suspect that many local investors will have already had this information for some time.

The role of soft and private information can be corroborated with research showing how different characteristics of stocks affect the existence and degree of local bias and superior performance of local investors. There is evidence that local bias applies particularly to investment in small, highly levered firms that produce non-traded goods, for example firms in the services sector (Coval and Moskowitz 1999). Non-local investors are less likely to be familiar with and possess high-quality information about small firms that do not sell their products or services on a countrywide basis. A similar logic applies to firms with high leverage, which means that firm profitability is particularly sensitive to small changes in revenue and/or costs. It is with regard to such firms that the informational asymmetry between local and non-local investors seems to be the largest. In addition, there is evidence that superior returns realized by local institutional and individual investors are particularly high for investment in smaller companies located in remote areas of the United States (Coval and Moskowitz 2001; Ivković and Weisbrenner 2005). This suggests that barriers experienced by geographical outsiders are more pronounced with regard to firms from small towns and rural areas than those from large urban centres. Importantly, the results on market makers and equity analysts also show that the superior performance of local actors is particularly strong in relation to small firms and firms located outside major metropolitan areas (Malloy 2005; Anand et al. 2008).

What type of local investors would we expect to possess more informational advantage? As individual investors are less sophisticated, that is, they have on average smaller resources and less expertise than institutional investors, we can expect them to exhibit more familiarity bias. Findings by Grinblatt and Keloharju (2001) for Finland, seem to support the role of investor sophistication by showing that local bias is less prominent among investment savvy institutions (corporate, for-profit institutions) than among households and less investment savvy institutions (government and non-profit institutions). The role of investor sophistication is further supported by Massa and Simonov (2006) showing that the degree of local bias in Sweden is related negatively to individual investor's wealth. Further research on Sweden shows that individuals with the strongest home bias are typically male, relatively uneducated, and government employed (with high job security), implying that they are particularly likely to be overconfident and believe in their ability to succeed by investing domestically (Karlsson and Nordén 2007). Bias may also depend on experience and change over the lifetime of an investor. Parwada (2008) shows that in the United States, young investment companies are likely to exhibit more home bias than older ones. To the best of my knowledge, however, there is no research yet that relates the local information premium to investors' sophistication, experience, or wealth.

There is a potential use of information on local issuers that we have not yet mentioned. Investors can buy or sell local stocks based on positive or negative signals, but instead of selling that may also influence the management of the issuer, for example, by communicating the threat to 'walk away' through informal channels like phone calls or meetings with the management. Of course, the power of investors to exercise voice in place of exit would depend on the size of their shareholdings, and as such is likely to be of particular significance for large individual or institutional investors. Consistently with this proposition, Gaspar and Massa (2007) show that firms that have a larger fraction of shares owned by local in relation to remote mutual funds exhibit better corporate governance reflected in lower investment rates and fewer but better acquisitions. Kang and Kim (2008) studying purchases of large blocks of shares (5–50 per cent) in US companies, show that: acquirers prefer geographically proximate targets; local acquirers are more likely to engage in post-acquisition target governance than remote acquirers; and the targets of local acquirers realize higher announcement returns and exhibit better post-acquisition operating performance. This suggests that proximity between investors and issuers could reduce agency problem, that is, the problem of aligning managerial (agents') incentives with investors' (principals') interests. The role of proximity in corporate governance should be highlighted as an important subject for further research.

The last question we need to address in our exposition of theories explaining home and local bias with information is whether the informational advantage of local investors is enhanced by social interaction among investors themselves. In other words, the question is whether social proximity among investors affects their informational advantage and how it relates to proximity between investors and issuers. After all people talk about the prospects of the local economy and local companies as a matter of everyday life. Indeed, Hong et al. (2004) demonstrate that in the United States the more socially active households are more likely to invest in the equity market. Prinsky and Wang (2006) document strong co-movement in the stock returns of firms headquartered in the same area, and attribute this finding to the proposition that physical proximity enables social interaction, which in turn promotes the transmission of investment sentiment and information among members of the community. To be sure, social interaction does not necessitate physical proximity, at least not permanently. Cohen et al. (2008) show that portfolio managers in the United States take bigger positions and earn superior returns on stocks of companies overseen by board members, with whom they used to go to school or university. When the portfolio manager of a fund changes, the new manager shifts to a portfolio influenced by his or her own social network.

While we need to appreciate the role of social interaction among investors, findings by Feng and Seasholes (2004) suggest that proximity among investors plays a secondary part to proximity between investors and issuers. The paper analyses trades of investors in Guangdong in southern China, who for years queue and place their orders at one and the same of a number of brokerage houses, as well as trades of investors from Shanghai, with all trades referring to stocks of firms headquartered in Guangdong. One result is that the correlation of net trades within brokerage houses in Guangdong is not higher at all than the correlation across the brokerage houses in the province. There is, in turn, a significant negative correlation between the net trades of investors in Guangdong and Shanghai. When Guangdong investors are net buyers (sellers), the Shanghai investors tend to be net sellers (buyers), and typically investors from Guangdong time their trades more profitably than their Shanghai counterparts. The authors conclude that these results rule out group psychology as the predominant force driving investment decisions.

Summarizing the section, recent research makes a strong case for the explanation of the home and the local bias based on information. This explanation addresses the major weakness of the Modern Portfolio Theory and the Capital Asset Pricing Model, that is, the assumption of ubiquitous information, and the resulting universal recommendation of portfolio diversification. As Mark Twain put it in his definition of success in 1894: 'Behold, the fool saith, "Put not all thine eggs in the one basket" – which is but a manner of saying, "Scatter your money and your attention"; but the wise man saith, "Put all your eggs in one basket and watch the basket"' (cited in Ivković and Weisbrenner 2005: 267). It appears that proximity is crucial to both choosing and watching the basket.

Alternative explanations of the investment bias

To be sure there are alternative theories that try to explain the investment bias without recourse to information. Let us start with alternative explanations for the home bias. First, international diversification could be hampered by formal restrictions on cross-border equity trading. Available research however suggests that capital controls have been largely removed, at least between developed economies (Kaminsky and Schmuckler 2003). In addition, if formal restrictions were to blame, why would we still find a high degree of home bias within the European Union including Eurozone (Wójcik 2002*a*)? Another alternative is that investors face higher transaction costs, such as brokerage commissions or clearing and settlement costs, in trading equity across borders than in trading domestically. While this is a valid factor, seeing it as a major determinant of the home bias would be inconsistent with findings that cross-border equity trading actually exhibits higher frequency than domestic equity trading (Tesar and Werner 1995). Yet another explanation has been that a large fraction of the capitalization of foreign markets is simply not available on public stock markets, as it is controlled by dominant owners, including home country governments (Stulz 2005). This proposition modifies the recommendation of the Modern Portfolio Theory, whereby investors should diversify their equity portfolio according to the market value of the free-floating equity. This, however, can explain home bias only to a small degree, and in particular, is inconsistent with low shares of US equity in the portfolios of non-US investors (Dahlquist et al. 2003).

Moving to the factors underpinning local bias, there are three groups of explanations competing with the information effects. First, investors may feel more charitable about the familiar and local companies, and feel a desire to invest in them rather than in unfamiliar companies. Second, they may obtain or at least hope to obtain non-investment benefits that will compensate them for the opportunity cost of investing in local companies (Landier et al. 2009). They may be employees who invest in their own companies, hoping that this increases their chances of keeping their jobs. They may be their neighbours, including shopkeepers hoping to contribute to the prevention of high unemployment and all its negative economic and non-economic implications in the community. Finally, according to the third explanation investors could face competition for local resources, such as real estate, labour, and services within their community. If supply of these resources is relatively inelastic, their price goes up with the wealth of the community. Investors may hedge against the risk of local price increases by tilting their portfolio towards local stocks (Bodnaruk 2004; DeMarzo et al. 2004).

It should be noted that the role of charitable motives, non-investment benefits, and local competition in explaining home bias are all about proximity between investors and issuers, represent profoundly economic geographical issues, and as such are extremely valuable directions for future research. Nevertheless, they represent alternatives to the explanations based on information. While they all suggest plausible factors behind local bias (and by extension potentially home bias as well), they cannot explain why investors can obtain superior returns on local investments, and as such do not undermine the explanation based on information.

Implications for investment firms and issuers

So far it has been shown that investors can obtain superior returns on local investments, and that this is most likely due to the use of soft and private information in contrast to hard and public information about issuers. This has significant implications for the size and structure of investment firms, and by extension the whole investment industry. According to a model developed by Stein (2002), 'small firms are at a competitive advantage in evaluating investment projects when the information about these projects is soft and cannot be credibly communicated from one agent in the firm to another. In contrast, large firms do relatively well when information about investment projects can be easily 'hardened' and passed along within the hierarchy' (Berger et al. 2005: 239). This does not rule large firms out altogether, but it means that large firms that want to use soft information effectively need to avoid high levels of centralization and hierarchy. In Stein's words (2002: 1894): 'holding the firm's size and scope fixed, the softness of information will tend to imply that a flatter organizational structure, with fewer layers of management, is more attractive'. What is therefore suggested is an inverse relationship between the degree of centralization and hierarchy in investment firms and the role of soft information in investment projects they deal with. To put it simply, to take advantage of soft information in secondary equity markets you may need to be close to issuers, but you may also need to be small. And if you want to run a large investment institution that is close to many different places, and at the same time enjoys economies of scale, you need to be careful to maintain a relatively decentralized and non-hierarchical organization. In other words geographical proximity can be overcome with organizational proximity but only to a certain extent, and only under certain conditions. Empirical research in both geography and financial economics illustrates the implications of proximity and soft information for investment firms. Jones (2002) shows that branches of international investment banks enjoy a relatively high degree of autonomy in decision-making. Chen et al. (2004)

demonstrate that small mutual funds are not only more likely than their larger counterparts to invest in local stocks, but they also earn superior returns on these investments.

We can also look at the relationship between investment firm size and soft information from the perspective of equity issuers or firms seeking capital in general. If financing a firm involves a relatively large amount of soft information (due to the nature of the projects to be financed and/or the nature of the firm, in particular its smallness) then the suitable sources of finance would be investment firms that are local and small rather than remote and large, or at least large investment firms whose local units have sufficient decision-making power. This resonates with Klagge and Martin (2005: 414) arguing that 'the presence of local critical mass of financial institutions and agents – that is of a regionally identifiable, coherent and functioning market – enables local institutions, small and medium size enterprises, and local investors to exploit the benefits of being in close spatial proximity'. In other words, the spatially limited circulation of soft and private information implies a certain degree of spatial fragmentation of secondary equity markets, limited mobility of capital, and spatially restricted access to capital. Of course, secondary equity markets are not a direct source of capital for firms. Potential for an active and highly liquid secondary market for a security, however, is crucial, as it improves the chances of the security being issued in the first place. If investors tend to trade in local stocks, then rural and provincial firms could find it more difficult to access equity markets, since these areas offer fewer potential investors than large urban centres. Consistently with this proposition, Loughran (2008) finds that rural firms wait longer to go public, are less likely to conduct seasoned equity offerings, and have more debt in their corporate structure than otherwise similar urban firms. Chapter 2 documented that in Europe, the United States, and Japan, large firms from capital cities are more likely to be listed on stock markets than their provincial counterparts. The role of proximity in the circulation of information on secondary equity markets could influence firms' access to capital but also firms' capital structure, as firms facing barriers to access equity market turn to debt financing.

The limits to proximity

Trade-off between proximity and liquidity

If it is so well documented that proximity can improve investors' information about opportunities and risks of equity investment, why are not secondary equity markets exclusively local markets? One important, though not exclusive, explanation involves a trade-off between informational benefits afforded by proximity and liquidity. What is crucial is that an informational advantage to local investors is a disadvantage to non-local investors. The larger the local informational advantage, the less likely non-local investors are to trade a given stock. Local investors can enjoy informational benefits that could improve the risk-return characteristics of their equity investments, but suffer from liquidity risk, the risk of not having a liquid market where they can exit from their investments. At the extreme, with very high local informational advantages, local investors would have nobody but themselves to trade with, and firms would have nowhere but the local pool of investors to draw their equity capital from.

The proximity–liquidity trade-off creates incentives for issuers but also for investors to support the developments that lower the informational disadvantages perceived and experienced by non-local investors. Investors may, for example, support regulatory measures aimed at increasing corporate transparency. Issuers can actively try to overcome the informational disadvantage to non-local investors by increasing their visibility in non-local markets, providing non-local investment communities with more and higher quality information, and introducing measures, such as internal control procedures and external audits, that minimize the leakages of inside information from the company. For small firms, it may be too costly relative to firm's resources to overcome these barriers and they are likely to settle on a combination with high level of proximity-based investment and low level of liquidity. Fortunately in a sense, small firms may also have relatively small needs for equity capital, which can be satisfied on local markets. Firms producing non-tradable goods and services (in contrast to high-technology firms that may obtain high visibility relatively easily) and provincial and rural firms may find themselves in the worst situation. Due to their sectoral and geographical nature, non-local investors may perceive their informational disadvantage as so large, that to overcome these barriers would be too costly for firms. At the same time, there may not be sufficient capital available locally. Consistently with this proposition, Loughran and Schultz (2005) suggest that in the United States, controlling for other factors such as size and sector, rural stocks have lower liquidity than urban stocks. It is possible that this gap can be filled with other sources of finance, such as credit (Loughran and Schultz 2005), but it is also possible that some firms will end up incurring a higher overall cost of capital (see Francis et al. 2007 on higher cost of debt capital in rural US).

There is a further complication of the proximity–liquidity trade-off that appears if we consider that local investors can use voice in addition to exit. This implies that local, that is, informed investors could improve the governance of the issuer and induce shareholder value enhancing decisions such as less over-investment, and fewer but better acquisitions. The benefits of improved governance could then be shared with all investors, including non-local and non-informed ones. To be sure, however, local investors would still have informational advantage with adverse impact on liquidity. Thus, on the one hand the stock price could go up (and the risk premium required by investors go down) due to improvements in governance; on the other it could be reduced (risk premium increased) by adverse impact on liquidity. Research on the net effect is only emerging, with Dass and Massa (2008), suggesting that more local banking relationships of issuers in the United States improve their governance and bring stock market liquidity down, but the net effect on firm value (measured as Tobin's q and stock price appreciation) is positive. Thus, the trade-off between proximity and liquidity is not just about the relationship between local and non-local investors, it is also about the balance of local ownership and monitoring versus liquidity.

Beyond the distinction between soft and hard information

In my view, the main weakness of the existing research in financial economics analysing the role of proximity in secondary equity markets is not its reliance on proximity defined as physical distance (which is considered as an empirical necessity rather than a conceptual statement) but the simplistic and often silent assumptions about the nature of the distinction between soft and hard information. First, soft information, defined as information that cannot be transferred over distance, is by definition local, and consequently soft information *from* individual issuers is as dispersed as the location of their decision-making establishments (or simply headquarters). This, however, does not mean that all soft information *about* issuers is dispersed. Successful assessment of investment opportunities and risks in equity markets requires comparisons between companies, knowledge of whole sectors, comparisons across sectors, and the knowledge of non-local and global business climate.

Information, often of qualitative nature, that allows insights into the global stock market may also be local, but is likely to be concentrated in large urban financial centres, with large institutional and individual investment communities and intensive interaction among them, both inside organizations and between them. Importantly, large urban financial centres are also concentrations of issuers' headquarters. Christoffersen and Sarkissian (2009) show that fund managers in large cities outperform those in small cities in the United States. It is also in large cities, particularly in New York, where the relationship between a managers' experience and his or her performance is the strongest. Large cities and financial centres provide a unique learning environment for finance professionals, not available elsewhere.

Second, soft information in secondary equity markets should not be associated with sophisticated information in contrast to hard information considered unsophisticated. Mathematics and economics involved in equity trading may range from simple ratios such as P/E (market price to earnings) to complex mathematical formulae used in arbitrage and derivative trading, but arguably even the understanding of a P/E ratio is not common among individual investors. Sophistication in the use of hard information, combined with the use of soft information local to large urban financial centres can compensate for the lack of proximity. Corroborating this hypothesis, Malloy (2005) reviews research showing that in Latin America foreign equity analysts outperform local analysts; in the Taiwanese market foreign equity analysts that have a local research group outperform foreigners w/o local presence, and also outperform local analysts; while in Europe home country analysts outperform foreign analysts. These results underscore the significance of investor sophistication and financial literacy. If proximity ruled the world of investment unchallenged, non-local investors could only pursue passive investment strategies, leaving all active investment (stock picking) to locals. In reality, foreign investors can be active and successful.

The relative value of local versus global knowledge may depend on the time horizon of investments. Kalev et al. (2008) show that in Finland, domestic investors have superior short-term returns on all stocks, including Nokia, the largest Finish corporation. In the long-term, domestic investors still have superior returns, however, with the exception of Nokia. It would appear that in the long-run, local knowledge of Nokia is less important than the insights of remote investors. Nokia operates in the technology sector, for which the largest centres of expertise are outside of Finland (mainly in the United States). In the long-run the expertise of foreign traders and their analysts in the valuation of companies in the technology sector is more important than the rumours and information gained by investors and traders in Finland (Albuquerque et al. 2009).

My argument is not about a world of secondary equity markets where local investors use soft information from local issuers and compete against non-local investors who leverage their chances with soft information about markets as a whole and with the sophistication in the use of hard information. This picture would miss a part of the investment industry that is trying to follow both strategies, by combining local information with global information. Combining information and people from different places can help such firms to achieve some degree of cognitive distance between professionals within a firm, which is desirable for innovative investment activity (Boschma 2005). For example, a person from a local branch may recommend buying stocks based on soft information on a specific issuer, but analysts at the headquarters may disagree based on their interpretation of hard information and their judgement of the whole sector or market. Arguably, investment success or indeed innovation in investment can be achieved through such confrontations of different types of information from different sources. As literature suggests, both too much and too little cognitive distance may be bad for innovation. Financial experts, however, use common language and English financial terms, and a common toolbox of financial theories (Clark and Wójcik 2007), which may assure that even combining people with their ideas from different places may not create a too large cognitive dissonance within organizations. To be sure, investment firms trying to combine local with global knowledge face a trade-off between the opportunity cost of not delegating decisions to places where local knowledge is available, and the agency cost associated with delegation (Cashman and Deli 2009).

The argument in favour of the use of information sources that are both local and non-local to specific actors on secondary equity markets resonates with that of Bathelt et al. (2004) who claim that knowledge creation in firms depends on the co-existence of high levels of local buzz and pipelines – channels of communication with non-local actors. The metaphor of local buzz may in fact be very useful in the context of secondary equity markets for yet another reason. Buzz contains both grains and chaff, and it may be difficult to separate one from the other. As such, local information may fuel local herd behaviour. Following DeMarzo et al. (2004) imagine an IT (information technology) engineer in Silicon Valley who decides to invest a lot in IT stocks. His neighbours, who do not work in IT, have a good reason to follow, as their income is less dependent on the IT boom, but their costs of living very much so. While IT engineer may engage in pure speculation, his neighbours hedge their consumption. Thus, consumption motives may aggravate localized herd behaviour. On the other hand, Coval and Moskowitz (2001) use evidence from the United States to argue that fund managers herd most strongly in distant firms and break away from the herd in their local investments. According to the authors, this reveals fund managers' tendency to free ride on the information of others by following the herd in remote stocks.

Thus, we have established that there is a price to pay for exercising proximity in secondary equity markets. One is the cost of lost liquidity. Another is the threat of investors relying on local information at the expense of external pools of knowledge that may also be valuable to investment activities, and central to innovative investment. A related threat is that of local information being too homogeneous and fuelling herd behaviour. In other words, secondary equity markets may be localized or embedded in a locality to the extent that threatens the competitiveness of both local investors and issuers, and consequently that of a local economy (see also Clark and Wójcik 2007).

Changing institutional environment of information circulation

The role of proximity and soft local information in secondary equity markets are not set in stone, as the broader institutional environment in which information on these markets circulates changes. One major trend involves increasing production of hard information but also conversion of what used to be soft information into hard information. Consider, for example, the level of detail that now has to be disclosed by firms in most developed economies on corporate directors, their credentials, remuneration, and shareholdings. What increases is not just the amount but also the frequency and timeliness of information disclosure. Think of transition from annual and half-yearly to quarterly financial reporting by listed companies in many European countries as well as shortened deadlines for preparing and making reports publicly available. Beyond regulatory changes, rating agencies, investment analysts and the rest of the burgeoning sector of financial infomediaries, represent a virtual factory of hard information for investors, and are biting the edges of what used to be reserved as the realm of soft and/or private information.

Another major change in the institutional environment of information circulation involves the international harmonization of accounting and corporate governance standards, with the spread of the International Financial Reporting Standards and the OECD Principles of Corporate Governance in the lead. By making 'the rules of the game' on equity markets (and beyond these markets) more similar across countries, international harmonization may be seen as reducing institutional distance between investors and issuers across national borders, and reducing the role of geographical proximity. In normative terms, however, whether it introduces a more level-playing field between local and remote investors is a contestable issue. As indicated earlier, non-local investors may possess an advantage over local investors due to a higher level of investor sophistication, which outweighs local investors' advantageous access to local information. As such the issues of financial literacy and sophistication should not be overlooked when considering the implications of the international harmonization of equity market regulation.

To be sure, the changing institutional environment of information circulation is not neutral in terms of power relations and involves political processes. It could be in the interest of large investment firms to 'harden' the part of soft information that is local, while guarding the part of soft or sophisticated information, which they are most likely to produce. Consider, for example, patents in financial products and services becoming popular in the United States and contemplated in Europe (Lerner 2001). On the other hand, powerful incumbent local investors as beneficiaries of soft local information may oppose the conversion of soft into hard information. The political economy of information in secondary equity markets should not, however, be reduced to the level of a zero-sum game between large international companies and community-based investment. Advancement in information technology and growing mobility of investors and issuers can in their own right erode the significance and value of geographical proximity. With moving investors and issuers the circuits of soft information exchange are less likely to be geographically localized. Mobile investors and issuers may thus represent a growing constituency that requests a more level-playing field between local and remote investors.

Arguably, the redoubt of the role of proximity in secondary equity markets can be found in the nature of human cognition and behaviour. Even if formal institutions surrounding secondary equity markets converge, will differences in terms of informal institutions such as customs and habits also be reduced? And will not local companies always be more visible to local than to remote investors? Perhaps the evidence on the persistence of local bias in the United States, where there is relatively little institutional diversity, is the ultimate evidence that proximity will remain important?

Final remarks

In this chapter, we have investigated the role of proximity between investors and issuers in secondary equity markets with respect to financial risk management. We have demonstrated that proximity, even if defined narrowly as geographical proximity, has significant implications for investors (in terms of performance and trade-off with liquidity), investment industry as a whole (in terms of size, structure, and strategy), issuers (in terms of access to capital and liquidity), communities (in terms of herd behaviour and competition), and policymakers (in terms of market structure, competition, regulation, and financial literacy). This reminds us that the role of geographical proximity is anything but an outdated or anachronic idea. The consideration for cognitive, social, organizational, and institutional proximity enriches the understanding of secondary equity markets, by complementing the analysis of geographical proximity, but does not make the latter redundant.

What are the implications of these findings for other financial markets? First of all it should be noted that proximity effects are also found beyond secondary equity markets. Evidence is available for primary equity markets, corporate and municipal bond markets, real estate markets, loan markets, as well as markets for corporate cash management and other financial services. In other words, financial agents take advantage of proximity whenever it promises access to valuable information. In fact, the existence of the proximity effects in these markets is mostly explained with soft information, quite along the lines discussed in this chapter. It is not unreasonable to expect that the proximity–liquidity trade-off applies across different financial markets and products. Further research on the role of proximity in markets other than those studied here would be a welcome contribution to the understanding of finance and geography.

In this chapter, I have tried to reverse the order usually found in texts on financial geography. A typical paper starts with arguments from the world of finance, which seem to doom the future of geography, and then uses geographical analysis to prove that 'local' and geography still matter in finance. Here, we started with empirical research in finance arguing in favour of the local, and then used insights from geography to demonstrate the limits of the 'local' and to argue how both 'global' and 'local' matter in finance. This way I hope to contribute to literature that dispels the myth that financial economics is about the ignorance or an attack on the 'local', and geographical research on finance is about the defence of the 'local'. In the times where struck by empirical evidence economics is diversifying into new theories, there is hopefully more room than before for rapprochement between financial economists and economic geographers (Clark 2005). As Huberman (2001: 659) eloquently commented on the existence of home bias: 'investors should soon start gobbling up foreign shares in record numbers. If they do not, economists may have to diversify into other theories.' Geographers could definitely contribute to this process of diversification.

5

Stock Trading in Space and Time: Information and Prices around the Globe

The Efficient Market Hypothesis and the Modern Portfolio Theory assume perfect ubiquitous information. This means that everybody everywhere has complete and identical information. One implication of these theories is that no investor has an advantage in trading financial assets. Another implication is that asset prices should not be affected by the location of trade. Claims on the same set of risky cash flows should be assigned the same value, wherever they are traded.

Chapter 4 has presented research dispelling the myth that no investors have an informational advantage in secondary stock markets. It has shown that proximity to the sources of information relevant to stock prices (whether this is the location of corporate headquarters or an international financial centre) is an important factor that may give investors who are local to these sources an advantage over those who are distant. We should note, however, that this has potential consequences for the role of the location of trade. If the location of the trading platform is related to the composition of investors who use this platform, for example, if investors prefer to use trading platforms in their home country or time-zone, then the location of trade matters for asset prices. Indeed, there is a considerable amount of evidence in financial economic research that for stocks listed in multiple markets, the home market leads price discovery, indicating that investors who trade on home markets have an informational advantage over those trading in foreign markets (Karolyi 2006). The significance of proximity has also been demonstrated in domestic contexts, for single listed stocks, where investors who live close to headquarters of listed companies contribute more to the price discovery of their stocks than do investors who live further away (Anand et al. 2008).

Trading of financial assets is not just an issue of where; it is also a related issue of when, particularly if, we think about financial trading at a global level. As shown by Clark and Thrift (2005), even foreign exchange trading, as one of the most transparent and globalized financial markets, is predicated on time- and space-sensitive processes. It is spread across the three major global time zones, with trading activity peaking at the opening and closing of the foreign exchange markets in Tokyo, London, and New York (in this order). London has a particularly important place in the daily cycle, as its trading hours overlap with those of Tokyo and London. If London did not exist, it would have to be invented at much the same place in time and space between New York and East Asia. In sum, the trading of financial assets can be clustered in space and time, even if technology allows trading from anywhere at any time.

This chapter aims at contributing to our knowledge about the spatiality and temporality of financial trading by asking two general questions. First, where and when does stock price discovery take place? And second, how do general market conditions and sentiment affect the distribution of price discovery? Does price discovery, for example, differ between a bull and bear market? These broad questions will be investigated through a case study of HSBC share prices on stock exchanges in Hong Kong, London, and New York, the leading stock markets of the world, in the years 2006–9. While studies on stock price discovery typically analyse the relationship between two trading venues, this case study addresses stock price discovery around the globe and around the clock. To the best of my knowledge, this is also the first academic analysis of the impact of the recent financial crisis on stock price formation, and the first study assessing the price discovery for HSBC in a tri-market context.

The results show that each of the three markets plays a part in the price discovery of HSBC shares. This is not surprising considering the global presence of the 'world's local bank', and the monopoly on price discovery that each of the three markets enjoys for a part of the twenty-four-hour day. When the trading hours overlap (Hong Kong with London, and London with New York) the price discovery process is amplified, which highlights the role of heterogeneous information. Diversity of perspectives and expectations that come from different markets seem to enrich the market place. Although the twenty-four-hour trading cycle appears like a conveyer belt passing information from Hong Kong to London, on to New York, and then to Hong Kong again, the hierarchy in contribution to price discovery is clear. London – the seat of HSBC's headquarters and regulatory jurisdiction, the locus of its relations with professional service providers, and the home for many of its decision-makers – dominates. Hong Kong – the former headquarter location, and the control centre of HSBC's fast-growing Asian operations – takes the second place. New York, although by far the largest centre of stock market trading in the world, is left with the third place.

The main finding of our analysis of price discovery over time is that while New York was able to compete with London and Hong Kong in the relatively optimistic and stable market conditions in 2006 and the first three quarters of 2007, its significance in price discovery diminished when investors became uncertain and markets more volatile in late 2007. At the peak of the crisis, between September 2008 and February 2009, New York's contribution to price discovery was even lower, and did not fully recover until the end of 2009.

The chapter proceeds as follows. The next section places the research questions in context, by reviewing the theoretical and empirical literature on price discovery in space and time. The following sections introduce the HSBC case study, and propose how to divide the period of study 2006–9 into sub-periods based on general stock market conditions. The analytical core of the chapter presents the distribution of HSBC price changes around the clock, and the transmission of price changes across the three markets. The last section concludes and offers implications for understanding the nature of stock markets.

Price discovery in space and time

There are clear benefits for trading in a given asset to concentrate on a single trading platform accessible to all investors and traders. Sellers benefit from a large number of buyers and vice versa. Trades can be completed more quickly, and the risk of large buy or sell orders raising or lowering the market price is smaller. As the old saying goes, liquidity attracts liquidity (Harris 2003). On the other hand, the concentration of trading on one platform implies a monopoly of the provider of the platform, which in turn points to the benefits of competition between trading platforms, even if it comes at the expense of fragmenting the market. On stock markets, trading individual stocks on multiple trading platforms is common, and typically takes the form of listing and trading a stock on different stock exchanges (cross-listing discussed in Chapter 3). One question that arises as a consequence is that of the relationship between prices of the same stock traded on different exchanges. Of course, there is arbitrage that would quickly restore any significant differences, but the question remains about which market/exchange leads in terms of price change and which follows. Which market discovers the price, thus revealing the possession of superior price-relevant information?

There is a rich body of literature on price discovery in cross-listing. The main conclusion of these studies is that home markets play a dominant part in price discovery. Home market of a company is typically defined as the stock exchange in the country where the company is headquartered. To illustrate the home-market advantage, imagine a German company listed in New York. While both German and US investors can freely trade on either Frankfurt or New York exchanges, the trading of German investors is likely to concentrate in Frankfurt and that of US investors in New York. Even if trading costs in Frankfurt for US investors are not higher than trading at home, US investors would prefer to trade German shares by day, not at night according to US time. As a result, trading in Germany is likely to reflect more price-relevant information. While the cross-listed company would publish a lot of information in English, available around the world, there will always be private (non-public) information available only in Germany. It is Germany where the decision-makers of the company and their families are likely to live and socialize. This is where people they went to school with live. This is where legal, financial, and other advisers and service providers are likely to be. This is where legal and regulatory changes affecting the company most originate and can be best understood. In sum, the home market advantage is not about the location of the trading platform itself. It is about who trades on it, and what access to information they have. A good case in point is a study by Chan et al. (2007) demonstrating that for firms from Mainland China listed in Shanghai or Shenzhen, but traded on two separate segments – A-shares by domestic investors and B-shares by foreigners – A-share market dominates price discovery, as domestic investors possess superior information.

To be sure, proximity between the location of corporate headquarters and investors (and traders) is important also in a domestic context. A study by Anand et al. (2008) on price discovery of US stocks traded on NASDAQ shows that market makers closer to firms' headquarters trade more frequently and contribute more to price discovery than distant market makers. They can predict future prices better. When firms relocate their headquarters, price discovery of formerly local market makers declines and that of newly local market makers increases. Finally, the study shows that market makers that acted as lead underwriters in the firm's initial or later public offerings or advised the firm on mergers and acquisitions (or other investment banking issues) play a particularly prominent part in price discovery. In this sense, the geographical bias that was described in Chapter 2 – the role of proximity between an issuer and its underwriter (-s) – carries over from primary to secondary market.

Anand et al. (2008) thus remind us of the significance of intermediaries in price discovery. In fact, Anand and Subrahmanyan (2008) show that intermediaries account for a greater part of price discovery than other investors. They also point out that intermediaries incur little marginal cost in monitoring the market for the purposes of their proprietary trading (trading on their own rather than clients' account), as they do it for their customers anyway. By extension, financial centres are important for understanding price discovery not only because they represent concentrations of corporate headquarters and investors but also as concentrations of intermediaries, with investment banks in the lead.

The role of proximity between issuers and investors in price discovery depends on the characteristics of the home market, the host market, and the company in question. The advantage of domestic or local investors is less likely with regard to firms from immature, illiquid markets. In immature markets, even if investors have privileged access to stock-specific price-relevant information, they may lack skills to exploit it and/or to combine it with information on relevant international and sector-wide factors. If home market is illiquid, the paucity of trades would slow down the incorporation of new information into the price. The NYSE specialists interviewed by Pascual et al. (2006) agreed that they could only be active in the price discovery of stocks from illiquid and immature markets, and could not compete with liquid home markets. For Spanish companies, traded very actively on the Spanish Stock Exchanges, the paper found that the NYSE contributed little to price discovery, functioning as a mere satellite of the Spanish market.

With regard to the characteristics of the host market, what matters in addition to liquidity is sector-specific expertise. As discussed in Chapter 3, companies like being traded where their peers are traded. In consequence, a host market should have a particular chance to contribute to price discovery if investors and intermediaries trading on it have sector-specific expertise. Research on stock analysts, however, indicates that home-country expertise influences the quality of forecasts more than sector-specific expertise (Sonney 2009). Finally, considering the features of traded companies themselves, the local and home advantage in price discovery should be larger for firms that produce less public information in relation to private information. This would apply to smaller firms, those with less international activity, not included leading stock market indices, but also companies that irrespective of their size and scope are less transparent. Drawing on research from Hupperets and Menkveld (2002), Clark et al. (2006) point out that Dutch companies with poorer transparency and corporate governance have more price discovery in Amsterdam in relation to New York, where they are cross-listed.

Let us move from the question of where to the related issue of when price discovery takes place. Starting with the basics, there are advantages to trading twenty-four hours a day. The whole world never sleeps, and globalization means that events relevant to stock prices may happen any time around the clock. This has implications for competition between trading platforms from different time zones. Research focused on events when foreign markets attempted to capture the stock trading volume from a home market shows that the success of such attempts (if any) is in most cases only transitory, and the trading tends to return to the home market, even with regard to corporations with global scope and brand, like Daimler Chrysler (Karolyi 2003). At the same time, it shows that return to the home market happens to a larger extent if the foreign market is in a time zone near the time zone of the home market (Halling et al. 2008). Thus, competition between trading platforms within time zones is much more severe than between them. It should be stressed, however, that a successful establishment of trading for a stock in a different time zone does not mean that the new location of trading automatically acquires significance in price discovery. A market in a different time zone at least tries to discover the price while the home market is closed, but it may still have very small price impact. Menkveld et al. (2007), for example, show that despite a large and growing market share, the NYSE played a minor role in the price discovery of cross-listed Dutch shares.

Another way to look at the temporality of price discovery is to focus on the distribution of trading activity over the trading hours of a given platform. Here the tendency is for trade to cluster in time, for much the same reason it tends to cluster over trading venues – liquidity. A typical profile of trading activity over the period of trading hours of a stock exchange is high volume and volatility at the open of trading, and another, but much smaller peak of activity right before the close. Market opening seems to be the time when a lot of information is revealed, after it has been accumulated overnight. Close is simply the last opportunity to trade. With cross-listing, the situation gets more interesting, as the trading hours of different exchanges can overlap, creating a period between the opening of the following market and the closure of the preceding. Literature shows that overlaps exhibit particularly high levels of activity (in terms of volume, volatility, and bid-ask spreads) and price discovery (Werner and Kleidon 1996). In overlaps, traders can use either market to trade and big trades can be split to prevent negative price impact (Hupperets and Menkveld 2002). Most importantly, however, overlaps are periods when the clash of price-relevant information from different geographical sources is most intensive. This is when heterogeneous information, based on different expectations hits the market to determine the price (Clark and Wójcik 2001). As a practical reflection of the value of overlapping trading hours many stock exchanges have extended their trading hours. In 1990s, the London Stock Exchange (LSE) traded only between 10:00 and 16:00 hours, at present it trades from 08:00 to 16:30 hours.

In contrast to a substantive body of research being available on the role of time zones and trading overlaps, there is little research investigating how the distribution of price discovery changes over longer periods of time. Moreover, while there is research on how financial crises affect correlations between stock market indices (Markwat et al. 2009; Wang et al. 2009), there is little on how they affect price discovery. One exception is the work of Neumark et al. (1991) showing that for thirty days following the October 1987 stock market crash, the Tokyo and London prices of Japanese and British multiple-listed stocks predicted their New York prices. Otherwise, Tokyo and London were relatively uninformative for New York prices. Although their research covers a period when the costs of arbitrage (trading across markets) were incomparably higher than at present, it does suggest that during market turmoil, home-country markets may become more important. In a recent paper, Clark et al. (2006) analyse the corporate governance crisis at Ahold, the Dutch retail trade corporation, following the revelation of an accounting fraud in 2003, and its impact on price discovery in the Ahold stock price on the Amsterdam and New York stock exchanges. They document that while until 2003, New York had some (albeit minor) contribution to price discovery, its significance faded away under conditions of uncertainty during the corporate crisis. The message is that during market turmoil historical and publicly available information become less relevant. After all, a sudden dramatic drop in price means that old insights failed, alternatives are needed. Lack of confidence in the future of a stock involves distrust in publicly available information about the company. Inside information becomes of particular value.

The objective of this chapter is to advance our understanding of price discovery in time and space via a case study of HSBC share prices on the LSE, the Hong Kong Exchanges and Clearing Ltd (HKEx) and the New York Stock Exchange (NYSE) in the period 2006–9. This case study allows a focus on the role of information in price discovery, as there are few factors that would interfere with the analysis. All three markets are completely accessible to foreign investors and there are no language or regulatory barriers to cross-border arbitrage between them. To be sure, HSBC is traded on the NYSE in the form of American Depositary Receipts. With low arbitrage costs, this should not inhibit the role of the NYSE, and so HSBC ordinary shares traded on the LSE, the HKEx, and ADRs traded on the NYSE can be treated as substitutes (Karolyi 2003). Trading volume in HSBC shares is very high in all three markets. All three markets use continuous trading, so there are no major differences in market structure. In addition, as a bank, HSBC belongs to the sector most implicated in the recent financial crisis.

The HSBC case

This section introduces HSBC with particular attention to three related questions. Where is the home stock market of HSBC? How important are Hong Kong, London, and New York as the loci of information about HSBC? Has the geographical distribution of information about HSBC changed in the period 2006–9? To shed light on these issues, we start with the basics on HSBC's history, size and scope, moving on to its share ownership structure, board of directors, and finishing with changes over the period 2006–9. Figures and other information mentioned in this section are valid for March 2010 unless otherwise stated.

HSBC Holdings Plc, the parent company of the HSBC Group, is incorporated in the United Kingdom, with its head office in London, hosting 8000 staff at eight Canada Square in Canary Wharf. The Group is thus domiciled in the United Kingdom for tax purposes, and the Financial Services

Authority is its lead regulator. Its history started with the founding of Hong Kong Shanghai Banking Corporation in 1865. It was only in 1993, the year following its acquisition of Midland Bank Plc, that HSBC moved its headquarters to London. To promote the Group as a whole, HSBC established a unified brand name in 1999 and in 2002 launched the famous campaign 'The world's local bank'. HSBC offers a full scope of financial services, delivered via 8000 offices in eighty-eight countries, employing over 300,000 people and serving a hundred million customers. With assets of $2400bn at the end of 2009, HSBC was one of the largest corporations in the world.

The share capital of HSBC is divided into approximately 17.5bn ordinary shares. The primary listings of HSBC are in London and Hong Kong. Its American Depositary Receipts (each representing five ordinary shares) are listed in New York, with additional listings on Euronext Paris and the Bermuda Stock Exchange. Trading volumes on the last two, however, are much smaller than in London, Hong Kong, or New York. HSBC has approximately 220,000 shareholders in 119 countries, with two-thirds of shares owned by individual and one-third by institutional investors. While approximately 1000 largest shareholders had 95 per cent of shares, there were only five shareholders with more than 1 per cent of the share capital (with Legal & General in the lead owning 3.16 per cent). As such, the ownership structure of HSBC has to be considered as extremely diluted. The wide ownership of HSBC is not surprising. With a global brand and worldwide operations, the company appeals to investors offering an exposure to emerging markets with a perceived safety of being anchored in the UK regulatory environment. An important implication of the wide ownership base is that there are no shareholders who could be considered insiders just by the virtue of the percentage of share capital they hold. This leaves HSBC's directors and executives as the main insiders.

The Board of Directors has twenty-one members: six executives and fifteen non-executives. The Chairman of the Board of directors, Stephen Green (who was the Group Chief Executive in the years 2003–6) is based in London. The Group Chief Executive (since 2006), Michael Geoghegan was in early 2010 in the process of moving from London to Hong Kong. His Deputy is based in Hong Kong, while the Chairman of HSBC Bank (China) and HSBC Taiwan is based in China. Reflecting HSBC's incorporation in the United Kingdom, the Group Finance Director (responsible i.a. for reporting and compliance) is based in London, and so is the Chief Executive of HSBC Asset Management. The list of top executives completes the Group Managing Director (who is also the Chief Executive of HSBC North America but is not a board member), based in New York. Out of fifteen non-executive directors, seven are based in the United Kingdom, three in Hong Kong, three in the United States, one in France, and one in India. Directors' shareholdings, 6.3m shares in total, are minute in relation to the overall share capital of HSBC, but nevertheless significant. The Chairman, the Group Chief Executive and the Chief Executive of HSBC Asset Management, each with more than 700,000 shares are among the top 1000 shareholders in HSBC.

HSBC went through the recent financial crisis relatively unscathed. It closed its subprime mortgage operations in the United States in 2007, as well as sold and leased back its head office building in Canary Wharf. It did downsize, disposing of approximately 2000 branches in 2008 and 2009, and loosing twenty-five million customers, but its reach in terms of countries actually grew. In 2008, in contrast to the Royal Bank of Scotland, Lloyds, and Barclays, HSBC did not need financial assistance from the British government. In December 2008, the Group injected £750m into the UK subsidiary from its own sources. In 2009, with the reputation of a leading bank relatively unaffected by the crisis, HSBC was awarded as 'Global Bank of the Year' in the Euromoney Awards for Excellence. It raised $18bn from the stock market through a rights issue, and was back in expansion mode, with particular focus on Asia, its most profitable market.

Let us go back on questions posed at the start of the section. The review of the basic facts thus far suggests that London is the main locus of information about the company, with Hong Kong in the second, and New York definitely in the third place. Recently, there is a sense of increasing importance of Hong Kong to HSBC. Not only is the Group Chief Executive moving to Hong Kong, but since 2008 the Annual General Meeting of shareholders held in London is preceded with an informal meeting of shareholders with the Group Chief Executive. Further insight can be gleaned from the geographical breakdown of HSBC's total operating income (Table 5.1). Between 2006 and 2009, the share of Asia-Pacific operations increased from 25 to 30 per cent. The share of North and Latin America dropped from 42 to 34 per cent, while the share of Europe increased from 33 to 35 per cent. These are not dramatic changes, but they may imply an increasing role of Hong Kong and declining role of New York, as the locus of information on HSBC.

Table 5.1. Total operating income of HSBC by region

Region	2009	2008	2007	2006
Europe	35	37	34	33
Hong Kong	17	13	17	15
The rest of Asia	13	13	11	10
North America	21	23	26	31
Latin America	13	13	12	11
Total (percentage)	100	100	100	100

Notes: The rest of Asia includes the Middle East.

Sources: Author based on HSBC Annual Reports.

Table 5.1 summarizes the global character of HSBC. In 2009, the three major time zones had almost equal shares as its sources of income. It is clear then that events affecting HSBC can happen around the clock. In this context, it is worthwhile noting that in 2008 HSBC opened virtual teleconferencing rooms to give its executives scattered around the world 'in-person' meeting experience. These are available in Hong Kong, Dubai, London, New York, Chicago, and Mexico City. This reminds us that HSBC is a really exacting test for price discovery. If the analysis reveals an uneven distribution of information about 'the world's local bank', then the role of geography in stock market trading could hardly be questioned.

Stock markets and the global financial crisis 2007–9

In order to analyse the price discovery for HSBC over time, the period of 2006–9 will be divided into sub-periods based on the prevailing market conditions and sentiment. An alternative would be to identify key dates within the period and observe how price discovery changes within time windows of varying length (ten or thirty days for example) prior and after these dates. This alternative is not pursued because in contrast to the crises of 1929 or 1987, the stock market downturn that accompanied the crisis of 2007–9 did not produce a distinctive 'black' day on stock markets. To be sure, many consider Lehman Brothers' filing for bankruptcy on 15 September 2008 as a turning point, but although major stock market indices fell on the day, they recuperated to their pre-15-September values within a week, before they fell again the following week. This is related to the fact that the recent crisis originated outside of the stock markets, in the sub-prime mortgage sector and the OTC-traded market for Collateralized Debt Obligations.

Figure 5.1 charts stock market performance over the four-year period under consideration. It presents the broadest indices for the stock markets in Hong Kong (Hang Seng Composite Index – HSCI), the United Kingdom (FTSE All-Share – FTSEAS), and the New York Stock Exchange (NYSE Composite – NYSEC). Daily close values are used for all indices. It also shows the trajectory of the HSBC share price as traded on the LSE (using daily close prices in GBP). All data are from Factiva. There is no need at this stage to compare HSBC price across exchanges. Arbitrage is bound to keep these prices close to each other, and whatever differences there are, they are irrelevant to the identification of general stock market trends. Before moving to sub-periods, three general features evident in Figure 5.1 are worth mentioning. First of all, considering a high level of integration of international stock markets, it is not surprising for the major indices (and particularly NYSEC and FTSEAS) to be highly correlated. HSCI moves in tandem with the other two, but with more

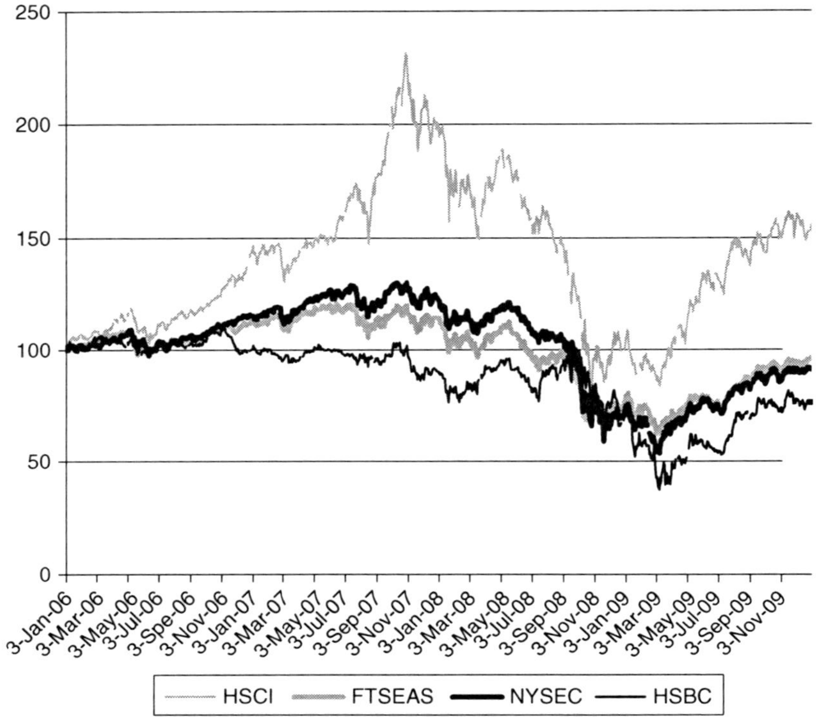

Figure 5.1. Stock market performance, 2006–9

Notes: Hang Seng Composite Index (HSCI), FTSE All Share (FTSEAS), NYSE Composite (NYSEC).

Sources: Author based on data from Factiva.

exaggerated ups and downs. This is typical of emerging stock markets, popular with foreign investors as fast-growth markets in good times, but often abandoned in bad times. Finally, it is not surprising to see HSBC, as a bank, to underperform the all-sector indices.

Four distinctive periods can be identified by analysing market values and their volatility (measured as the standard deviation of daily close-to-close

Table 5.2. Standard deviation of daily returns

Period	HSCI	FTSEAS	NYSEC	HSBC-HK	HSBC-LO	HSBC-NY
Jan06–Oct07	1.21	0.90	0.83	0.79	0.90	0.92
Nov07–Aug08	2.24	1.43	1.33	1.85	1.86	1.70
Sep08–Feb09	3.76	2.90	3.77	4.04	3.99	4.17
Mar09–Dec09	1.83	1.37	1.74	3.32	3.50	3.38

Notes: Standard deviation for HSBC price in Hong Kong (HK), London (LO) and New York (NY) is calculated for prices in HKD, GBP, and USD, respectively.

Sources: Author based on data from Factiva.

returns, as shown in Table 5.2). The first is a period of growth and low volatility, lasting from the start of 2006 until the end of October 2007 when the market indices along with HSBC price peaked. Total growth over the period ranged from 20 per cent for FTSEAS to 130 per cent for HSCI. This was the tail of a bull market that started in 2003. In November 2007, a slow decline starts coupled with a high degree of uncertainty illustrated with standard deviations of daily returns almost double their values from the preceding period. In other words, this is a picture of the stock market waiting for a verdict. Once the severity of the crisis becomes evident in September 2008, the markets crash in a double-dip pattern. The sharp decline of September and October is followed by stagnation in November and slight recovery in December, only to be followed by another crash in January and stagnation in February 2009. This is the peak of the crisis, with volatility twice higher than in the period of slow decline, with markets losing between a third and a half of their value. The green shoots of recovery are seen only in March, marking a return to growth. By the end of 2009, FTSEAS grew by 43 per cent, NYSEC by 56 per cent, and HSCI by 72 per cent, but all of them were far from their record values from 2007. It was also a period of tentative growth, with volatility comparable to that prevailing in the period of slow decline.

HSBC price changes around the clock

Having reviewed the existing research on price discovery, sources of information from HSBC, and divided the four years under investigation into subperiods, its is time to analyse the distribution of price discovery. The analysis will proceed in two stages. First, we will compare price changes for different parts of a twenty-four-hour trading day. The next section will focus on the transmission of daily price changes between the three trading venues.

The opening and closing times of trading in Hong Kong, London, and New York divide a trading day into six parts. Figure 5.2 shows the twenty-four-hour clock for the three exchanges according to GMT time and time differences that prevail for most of the year (late March–late October). For the rest of the year, Hong Kong opens and closes one hour earlier (in relation to London) due to daylight time saving in London. The interaction of the latter with daylight time saving in New York, in turn, produces short spells in March and October, when New York opens and closes one hour earlier (in relation to London).

The following two-part question is asked. What is the role of each part of the twenty-four-hour cycle in moving the stock price of HSBC, and how does this role change over time? To answer this question, the absolute price change is calculated for each part of the day on each day (when there is trading on all three exchanges), and then average absolute price change is calculated for

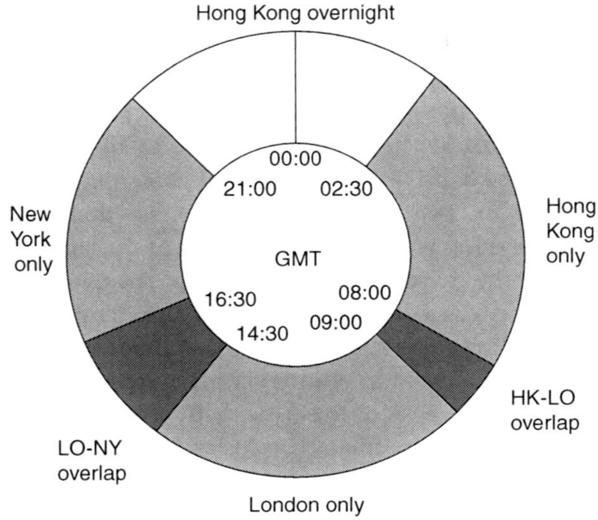

Figure 5.2. The twenty-four-hour clock of trading HSBC shares
Sources: Author.

each part of the day for the whole four-year period and each sub-period. The data used are the open and close HSBC stock prices from the NYSE (ADR price divided by 5), the LSE (converted into USD), and the HKEx (also converted into USD). All data were obtained from Factiva. For example, the absolute price change for the overlap between Hong Kong and London is that between the London open and the Hong Kong close price. To summarize this method, absolute price changes are used as an indication of the use of price-relevant information during different parts of the day, building on the method first developed by Barclay and Warner (1993).

Table 5.3 summarizes the results showing the share of each day-part in the sum of mean absolute price changes for each period, as well as the mean absolute price change per hour. Over the whole four-year period, the time between Hong Kong close and New York open, when only London trades HSBC shares, contributes most to price changes – 22 per cent. The second largest contribution – 18 per cent – happens between Hong Kong open and London open, when Hong Kong has monopoly over trading. The time of New York's monopoly over trading (from London close to New York close) contributes 15 per cent of price changes. London holds the first position and Hong Kong holds the second position in price changes throughout the four periods. This seems to confirm our expectations about the role of the three trading locations in the price discovery for HSBC shares. London trading is most likely and New York least likely to incorporate private information about HSBC into its share price, with Hong Kong in the middle.

Table 5.3. Share in absolute price changes and mean absolute price change per hour according to the phase of trading

	HK overnight	HK only	HK-LO overlap	LO only	LO-NY overlap	NY only
Share in absolute price changes						
Jan06–Oct07	16	18	15	19	15	17
Nov07–Aug08	15	18	14	23	16	14
Sep08–Feb09	14	17	14	24	16	15
Mar09–Dec09	11	19	15	24	17	14
Jan06–Dec09	14	18	14	22	16	15
Mean absolute price change per hour						
Jan06–Oct07	0.02	0.02	0.15	0.02	0.04	0.02
Nov07–Aug08	0.02	0.02	0.19	0.03	0.06	0.02
Sep08–Feb09	0.03	0.03	0.30	0.04	0.09	0.04
Mar09–Dec09	0.01	0.02	0.20	0.03	0.05	0.02
Jan06–Dec09	0.02	0.02	0.19	0.02	0.05	0.02

Sources: Author based on data from Factiva.

Significant price changes take place during the two trading overlaps, one between Hong Kong and London, the other between London and New York. Together they contribute as much as 30 per cent of price changes. This is even more impressive if we consider how short these overlaps are. On average, throughout the year the overlap between Hong Kong and London lasts only half an hour, and that of London with New York two hours, compared to the periods of six hours, six hours, and 4.5 hours when Hong Kong, London, and New York, respectively, hold monopoly over price discovery. This finding seems to confirm our expectations about the role of heterogeneous information driving the market during trading overlaps. Price discovery appears particularly intensive when Hong Kong and London overlap, adding to the significance of these trading locations.

There is a significant fluctuation in the contribution to price changes over the four sub-periods. The price changes on HSBC's core home market – London – are particularly large in the run-up to and at the peak of the crisis. Trading overlaps have the largest contribution to price changes at the peak of the crisis. It appears that private information, and heterogeneous information plays a particularly important role in the conditions of uncertainty. In contrast, New York contributed most to price changes in the period of growth and relatively low volatility. It seems that the optimistic and stable market made those trading in New York confident in the public information available to them, and unconcerned about their poor access to private information in relation to Hong Kong, and particularly London. They lost some of this confidence, however, when the markets turned from a bull to a bear. Although New York investors and traders had better access to information about the unfolding financial crisis (being the primary origin of the crisis), what mattered for the HSBC stock price was information specific to HSBC.

Transmission of daily price changes

The preceding section took the simplest possible approach to analyse contribution to price discovery. While price changes are important in identifying periods of time and trading venues that bring new information to the marketplace, comparing absolute price changes is a static method that does not inform us whether price changes in one market actually influence those on other markets. Put differently, it tells us about the potential of a market to influence others but not the actual influence. To extend the analysis, this section evaluates the transmission of daily price changes from one trading venue to another, by regressing the daily return on HSBC shares on each of the three markets on the daily returns on HSBC shares on the preceding markets. The following three regressions are estimated:

$$r_t^{\mathrm{HK}} = \alpha_1 + \beta^{\mathrm{NY}} \cdot r_{t-1}^{\mathrm{NY}} + \gamma^{\mathrm{LO}} \cdot r_{t-1}^{LO} + \epsilon_1$$

$$r_t^{\mathrm{L}O} = \alpha_2 + \beta^{\mathrm{HK}} \cdot r_t^{\mathrm{HK}} + \gamma^{\mathrm{NY}} \cdot r_{t-1}^{\mathrm{NY}} + \epsilon_2$$

$$r_t^{\mathrm{NY}} = \alpha_3 + \beta^{\mathrm{LO}} \cdot r_t^{\mathrm{LO}} + \gamma^{\mathrm{HK}} \cdot r_t^{\mathrm{HK}} + \epsilon_3$$

Rate of return r on day t in Hong Kong, for example, is calculated as the difference between the close price on day t and the close price on day $t - 1$, expressed as a percentage of the close price on day $t - 1$. Rate of return on day $t - 1$ is calculated with the close price on day $t - 1$ and day $t - 2$. Hong Kong returns are estimated as a function of New York and London returns from the preceding day. London returns are estimated as a function of Hong Kong returns from the same day, and New York returns from the preceding day. Finally, as New York opens and closes last, its returns are estimated as a function of London and Hong Kong returns from the same day. The coefficients of most interest in the equations are betas, as they reflect the extent to which return on a given trading venue influences the return on the following venue. The regressions are estimated for each of the four sub-periods.

Figure 5.3 shows beta coefficients for the three exchanges. There are no gamma coefficients significant at 1 per cent level, while all betas are significant at 0.1 per cent level. London has by far the strongest influence on the following market (i.e. New York) throughout the period. Hong Kong comes as a strong second; New York comes third. Consistently with the results of the preceding

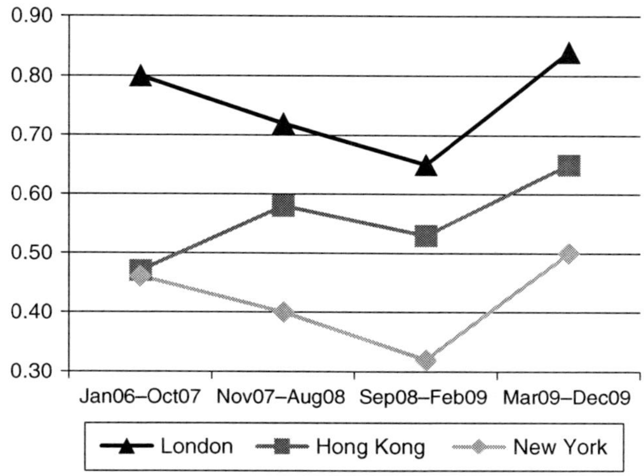

Figure 5.3. Price impact on the next market

Notes: The figure presents beta coefficients from regressing the daily return on HSBC shares on each of the three markets on the daily returns on HSBC shares on the preceding markets.

section, the influence of New York is strongest in the relatively bullish market of the first period, Jan06–Oct07, when it rivals the influence of Hong Kong. In the period of heightened uncertainty (Nov07–Aug08) and during the crisis itself (Sep08–Feb09), New York, however, falls far behind Hong Kong.

It is not surprising to see beta coefficients fall during the crisis. High uncertainty and volatility mean that prices are likely to change in the opposite direction than those on the preceding market. This gives a V-shaped pattern of coefficients for London and New York over time. Hong Kong however does not follow this pattern. Its impact on the following market (London) actually increased in Nov07–Aug08, and then fell less than the impact of New York and London in Sep08–Feb09. This implies that while the absolute price changes in Hong Kong did not grow nearly as much in Nov07–Feb09 as they did in London (see the shrinking share of Hong Kong in Figure 5.3), they had a larger influence on London than in Jan06–Oct07. Overall, between 2006 and 2009, Hong Kong was the market the influence of which increased most. It seems that in the run-up to and during the crisis Hong Kong, the second home of HSBC, joins London's efforts in price discovery, while the role of New York recedes. These findings may also reflect the growing significance of Hong Kong as the hub of HSBC's expanding operations in Asia.

Before we close the analysis, let us relate the results on price discovery to data on trading volumes for HSBC shares across the three markets and the four sub-periods. As Table 5.4 shows, on average, over the whole period of 2006–9,

Table 5.4. Average daily trading volume (in millions of shares)

Period	Hong Kong (HKEx)	London (LSE)	New York (NYSE)
Jan06–Oct07	22.1	56.8	3.3
Nov07–Aug08	28.6	56.4	9.9
Sep08–Feb09	33.3	57.3	14.6
Mar09–Dec09	35.3	52.7	14.4
Jan06–Dec09	27.6	55.9	8.4

Sources: Author based on data from Factiva.

London traded twice as many HSBC shares as Hong Kong, and seven times as many as New York. Thus, the order of significance in trading volumes is the same as that for price discovery. In addition, consistently with the results on price discovery, we see the share of Hong Kong in trading volume increasing gradually over time, from 40 per cent of London's in Jan06–Oct07, to nearly 70 per cent in period Mar09–Dec09. For New York, however, the declining position in price discovery during the crisis is accompanied by impressive increases in trading volumes. While the analysis of the relationships between price discovery and liquidity is beyond the scope of this study, the results suggest that the structure and dynamics of trading volumes can but does not have to be correlated with the structure and dynamics of price discovery. While being the smallest market for HSBC, New York still trades millions of HSBC shares a day, which is not a level of liquidity that could in its own right significantly inhibit price discovery in New York.

One last consideration worth posing for is the role that HSBC shares play on each of the three exchanges. In Hong Kong, HSBC is the most traded share and the biggest component of the Hang Seng Index. In London, it is one of the most traded shares, and an important component of FTSE100. In New York, as an ADR, HSBC would be considered as average in its market capitalization and trading values, and is not a part of the elite Dow Jones Industrial Average. In theory, while HSBC is the same company wherever its shares are traded, the role it plays on different markets may influence the distribution of price discovery. As research in behavioural finance has shown, the largest and most visible stocks are more likely to attract investors' and traders' attention and effort (Barber Odean 2008). While this should not make a big difference for price discovery between London and Hong Kong, the relative insignificance of HSBC for the US stock market may contribute to weak price discovery for HSBC in New York.

Conclusions and implications

The objective of this chapter was to document and account for the circulation of information on secondary stock markets. Specifically, we have analysed the distribution of price discovery for HSBC shares across three of the leading stock exchanges in the world: the NYSE, the LSE, and the HKEx. The distribution of price discovery has also been investigated over time, within a twenty-four-hour cycle of trading, and in the four-year period between 2006 and 2009, straddling the recent financial crisis. HSBC is one of the world's largest corporations, with global scope of operations as well as a global image. HSBC shares are traded by exchanges in the leading global financial centres, and their trading between these exchanges (arbitrage) is subject to minimal costs. Thus, the challenge of the chapter was the following. If one can show that the distribution of price relevant information across the three exchanges and financial centres is important for price-discovery of HSBC shares, then one could only expect the geographical distribution of information to be more important for nearly any other company.

We found that there is a clear hierarchy of markets in terms of their contribution to the discovery of HSBC stock price. This hierarchy is consistent with the expected distribution of price-relevant information across the three global financial centres. London dominates. It is the seat of HSBC headquarters, home to most of its top decision-makers, and home to its relations with key service providers, such as investment banks, security analysts, law and accountancy firms. Hong Kong comes second. It is the hub of HSBC's operations in Asia; it is essential to its identity and the claim to being the leading bank for emerging markets. It is also home to many of its decision-makers. In addition, HSBC is the single most important stock traded on the HKEx, the main driver of the Hang Seng Index. New York comes last, despite being the largest stock market trading centre of the world (in terms of total trading and the trading of foreign stocks). New York is also the centre of expertise in security analysis, ahead of Hong Kong, and possibly ahead of London as well. Hence, it is not its ability to process publicly available information about HSBC that limits New York's contribution to price discovery. The only explanation is that although HSBC has large operations in North America, New York cannot rival Hong Kong's and particularly London's access to private information with regard to HSBC.

The chapter demonstrates that the value of private information in relation to public information on stock markets depends on market conditions. With a bull market still in place in 2006 and early 2007, New York was confident in information it was receiving about HSBC and its power to interpret this information. It was in late 2007 that the problems building up in the financial sector (in the United States first and then spreading internationally) turned public information about banks much less valuable, and eventually (at the peak of the crisis in the months following September 2008) worthless. It was exactly in the period that the advantage of London and Hong Kong over New York increased. Importantly, however, in response to growing uncertainty and pessimism, price discovery did not simply concentrate in London. Rather, the crisis increased the significance of collaboration between London and Hong Kong, searching for the right price.

The increasing role of Hong Kong during the crisis and in the period of fragile recovery of 2009 seems to reflect the growing emphasis of HSBC on Asian operations as the main driver of the Bank's income and profits. Related to that is an increasing role of Hong Kong as the Bank's decision-making structure. Recall the move of the Chief Executive Officer from London to Hong Kong in 2010, and informal shareholder meetings organized in Hong Kong prior to Annual General Meetings in London. In this context, it is interesting to compare my results with those of Agarwal et al. (2007), who showed that in 1996 Hong Kong contributed more to price discovery of HSBC than London. This was three years after HSBC moved its headquarters from Hong Kong to London, which suggests that shifts in the locus of price discovery may be slow and subject to considerable inertia. After all, crucial private information is located within a social circle of a company's key decision-makers and those who interact with them on a regular basis. Michael Geoghegan may move to Hong Kong, but a large part of his social network will remain in London. After 1993, it took several years for HSBC price discovery to move to London. Even if price discovery moves back to Hong Kong, it is unlikely to happen quickly.

The results have implications for understanding the relationships between financial centres. In his tour-de-force of international financial centres, Youssef Cassis (2005) remarked that herd-behaviour on financial markets is related to the concentration of investors and traders in few financial centres. While I agree with this remark, I would stress that even if there are few dominant sources of information, expertise, and expectations, combining them can still make a big difference. Clark and Wójcik (2001), analysing the Asian crisis of 1997–8, documented a less pessimistic attitude in New York than in London about the impact of the crisis, which was proved correct by the subsequent performance of the stock markets. They suggested that this advantage of New York was based on more heterogeneous sources of information in New York (coming among others from the high-technology centres of Sillicon Valley and Boston, as well as other large US financial centres like Chicago and Philadelphia). This chapter reinforces this point, showing that the role of heterogeneous information is particularly important during market turmoil. Witness the stronger role of the London–Hong Kong duo and trading overlaps between late 2007 and early 2009.

Interpreting the results, we should not yet jump to conclusions about the role of the location of stock exchanges themselves. London dominates and New York lags behind in price discovery for HSBC, not because the LSE is closer to HSBC's headquarters but because investors trading on the LSE have better access to private information about HSBC. Those who trade on the HKEx have the second best, and those on the NYSE the worst access. Location of the exchange is still closely related to the location of those using it. Despite the fact that the HKEx is fully open to foreign traders, the latter still represent only 40 per cent of trading activity. The US combined with the UK-based investors contribute twice less trading than do Hong Kong-based investors. In other words, this chapter, like the preceding one, is about proximity between investors and issuers. It brings us close, however, to the question whether proximity between stock exchanges on the one side and investors, issuers and other intermediaries on the other side matters for the operation of stock markets. This issue will be explored in Chapters 6 and 7.

6

An Embedded Exchange: Between Real and Virtual Space

Stock exchanges are probably one of the favourite types of financial institutions referred to in the literature on globalization. This may be due to the hybrid nature of stock exchanges. On the one hand, they are described as symbols of market economy and agents of shareholder capitalism (Dore 2000). On the other hand, they are considered central parts of national economic infrastructures, and symbols of national financial centres or even national identity. An additional reason for the popularity of stock exchanges in research might be the fact that while global finance is difficult to follow in quantitative terms, data on and from stock exchanges are relatively easy to obtain. In particular, data on stock exchanges are one of very few easily available types of financial data that can be assigned to cities. But can they really be so clearly assigned? Say one considers market capitalization of companies traded on the London Stock Exchange (LSE). Is it clear what these figures really have to do with London? And what places does one assign to figures on the NYSE-Euronext or NASDAQ-OMX? Where are traders, investors, issuers, or computers matching orders? Where will stock exchanges be in the future? Can we observe or expect the fate of stock exchanges to be divorced from the fate of financial centres?

The main objective of this chapter is to provide an empirical, detail-rich account of the geographical nature of stock exchange activities and then use this account to draw some general implications about the relationship between geography of stock exchange activities and geography of financial centres. This relationship is significant not only for academics but also for finance practitioners and public policymakers trying to understand the factors affecting the interrelated futures of finance and economic development in space (O'Brien 1992; Budd 1995; Leyshon 1995, 1997). Due to the scarcity of geographically focused research on how stock exchanges actually go about their business (Laulajainen 2001, 2003), the chapter takes an empirical, bottom-up approach,

and is based on the case study of the Warsaw Stock Exchange (referred to as the WSE or the Exchange). With a booming stock market in one of fastest growing and soon to be one of the largest economies in Europe, the paramount role of foreign ownership in the financial sector of Poland, and continued independence of the WSE, Warsaw is a hotly debated spot on the map of European stock exchanges (Claessens et al. 2003).

In this chapter, I use insights gained through a total of twenty interviews with members of the Exchange Management Board, Supervisory Board, Directors and employees of individual departments, devoted to both strategic issues as well as everyday activities of the Exchange. Interviews with insiders were complemented with over twenty interviews with the executives of other institutions on the capital market such as issuers, banks, brokerages, pension and investment fund management companies, and were focused on these organizations' relationships with the WSE. All interviews were conducted in March and June 2005. These insights were updated and complemented with a review of documents available on the website of the WSE and other relevant data on the Polish stock market conducted in 2010.

The next section defines stock exchanges and their activities as well as identifies the literature relevant for analysing the geographical nature of these activities. The following three sections introduce the WSE, its position in the Polish capital market, and outline the development of the Polish stock market in an international context, as well as its basic geographical structure. The core empirical sections investigate the geographical coordinates and characteristics of various activities of the WSE, starting with the trading system and relationships with exchange members, through relationships with issuers, to interactions with investors. The last section draws some implications from the case study for the debate on the future geography of stock exchanges and its continued or discontinued links with the future geography of financial centres.

Geography of stock exchanges

A stock exchange can be defined as 'an organised market for the buying and selling of securities' (Moles and Terry 1999: 520). In order to organize the market, the business of exchanges precedes the instant of trade order execution and extends beyond. The World Federation of Exchanges (WFE) lists the following major stock exchange activities: writing the rules for market activity and their enforcement, admitting intermediaries, admitting securities to listing, assuring disclosure of corporate information, setting up information technology (IT) and communication systems facilities, diffusing market information to a wide public, trading, assuring prompt and final clearing and settlement of orders, providing for securities registry, transfer agent, and depositary activities (WFE

2003: 3). To be sure, the scope of activities varies from one exchange to another. Moreover, there is a heated debate whether stock exchanges should be required by law or regulation to perform certain functions, for example admission to listing, or whether they should be allowed to focus as closely as possible on trading itself (Lee 1998; Steil 2001).

Research on the geography of stock exchanges has to consider the fundamental concepts of economies of scale, scope, and agglomeration. There is a large body of literature in financial economics and economic geography that demonstrates the significance of these economies in the financial services sector (Kindleberger 1974; Davis 1990; Porteous 1999; Gehrig 2000). It explains the vertical (across products and services) and horizontal (across places) consolidation of financial services firms, and their concentration in financial centres, based mainly on the sharing of wide and deep labour pools, sets of suppliers of advanced services (including law and IT firms), telecommunications infrastructure, and information spillovers.

Economies of scale, scope, and agglomeration are all relevant for stock exchanges. Their core functions, that is, the matching of buy and sell orders and price discovery involve large fixed expenditure on technology, leading to significant economies of scale (Pirrong 1999). Economies of scope are significant as well, with the trading of equities, for example, creating opportunities for the creation and trading of derivative financial instruments based on individual equities and equity indices. The existence of economies of scale and scope in stock exchange activities has been proven by empirical research (Hasan and Malkamäki 2000). In particular, Malkamäki's analysis (2000) covering thirty-eight exchanges between 1996 and 1998 suggests that while significant scale economies exist with respect to trading, the scale advantages in activities involving issuer specific information are not clear. Based on these findings, Malkamäki argued for the benefits of centralization of the electronic trading function and continued realization of other functions on a decentralized basis.

While there is rich evidence on the significance of proximity between issuers, investors, and traders (as presented in the preceding chapters), the literature remains silent about the role of a stock exchange. In an attempt to fill this gap Lo and Grote (2002) suggest that in contrast to the mutual proximity of traders, investors, and issuers, which remains important, the location of the stock exchange will lose significance in the future. This is however a partial answer, as Lo and Grote restrict their analysis to the trading function of a stock exchange, a virtual space in which sell and buy orders are matched. In order to test the proneness of stock exchange activities to concentration in financial centres, another important question needs to be tackled. How does a stock exchange, as an operator of the trading system, make companies enter their securities into the system, and make investors and traders use the system? In later work, Grote (2007) remarks on the proximity between a stock exchange and traders potentially contributing to innovation in the trading system. A wide-scope, systematic geographical analysis of the relationships of a stock exchange with issuers, investors, and traders, however, has not as yet been conducted.

There are many aspects of relationships between stock exchanges and issuers, investors, and traders that can affect the location of a stock exchange. These include the sharing of infrastructure, labour pool, suppliers, and customers. The strategy of this chapter is to focus on the role of face-to-face contact between a stock exchange on one side and traders, issuers, and investors on the other. It is well established in literature that business organizations in financial centres are sociable, with contacts being 'crucially important in generating and maintaining a flow of business and information about business' (Thrift 1994: 333). While these organizations spend huge resources on communications technology, the technical connectivity does not lessen but rather adds to their hunger for social connectivity (Lee and Schmidt-Marwede 1993; Gaspar and Glaeser 1998; Sassen 2005). Thus, one way to analyse the proneness of stock exchange activities to concentration in financial centres is to document the nature of their external contacts, and the relative role of technical versus social connectivity. Another major observation from this literature is that financial centres must not be reduced to sites of a myriad of financial and related businesses engaging in relationships with each other. What must be added to this picture is the increasing role if not dominance of a handful of international financial corporations spanning various financial centres (Amin and Thrift 1992; Clark 2002). The lesson for this chapter is that following the contacts between a stock exchange on one side and the traders, issuers, and investors on the other, it must be remembered that all of these actors, including the stock exchange itself, can be members of international networks based on ownership, strategic collaboration or other links. It should be added that while the network approach has been applied to study financial centres (Taylor et al. 2002; Beaverstock et al. 2003; Faulconbridge 2004), no existing work focuses on stock exchanges.

Research questions addressed in this chapter refer to the proneness of stock exchange activities to concentrate in financial centres. The term 'stock exchange activities', not 'stock exchange' is used, as the chapter focuses on the location of people and equipment carrying out stock exchange functions, not on the location of the headquarters of a stock exchange. In other words, the emphasis is on where and how stock exchanges operate, not on their ownership structures. This distinction is particularly important given the existence of international stock exchange structures such as the NYSE-Euronext, integrating stock exchange activities in many places.

A review of relevant literature could be extended in at least three directions: one concerned with liquidity in stock trading, another stressing the political nature of stock exchange business, its relationships with the state, including legal and regulatory issues (Tickell 2000; Majury 2005); and yet another focusing on the labour markets of financial centres (Leyshon et al. 1993). These themes, though addressed where most relevant, are not the main focus of this chapter. To summarize, the intended contribution of the chapter is first to 'animate' stock exchanges as actors in relation to other major actors on the stock market, that is, members, issuers, and investors, by focusing on stock exchange activities that involve these actors. Second, the chapter analyses the geographical nature of stock exchange activities by describing where and how they take place in virtual or real space. Third, stock exchange activities are put in the context of location of other actors on the stock market, recognizing that the latter can be part of international networks. As this contribution is offered mainly through a case study of the WSE, the following section introduces the WSE, presenting its origins and position within the structure of the Polish capital market.

The Warsaw Stock Exchange in the Polish stock market

The WSE was first created in 1817, ceased its operations in 1939, and was recreated after the fall of communism in 1991. The establishment of the WSE was assisted by experts from the stock exchanges in Paris and Lyon, subject to an international agreement between Poland and France. Trading on the WSE started with shares of five formerly state-owned companies. While in the first half of the 1990s the Exchange was admitting mostly privatized companies, in the second half of the 1990s, companies that were private from their inception started to dominate the market, at least in terms of numbers. The WSE has been founded and until recently fully controlled by the State Treasury. In November 2010 the Exchange conducted an IPO of its shares, which reduced the state ownership to 35 per cent (representing 51.4 per cent of voting rights). Minority shareholders consist mainly of banks, brokerage houses, investment funds, and listed companies. The highest decision-making body of the Exchange is the General Meeting of Shareholders, which among other powers can amend the WSE Articles of Association, and elects the members of the Exchange Supervisory Board as well as the President of the Exchange Management Board. While the Supervisory Board, consisting of representatives of banks, brokerage houses, issuers, and other financial institutions, oversees exchange operations, the Management Board coordinates the day-to-day operations, grants and evokes exchange membership, admits securities to trading, and supervises the trading activity of members (WSE 2009).

The WSE owns one-third of the share capital of the National Depository for Securities (NDS), with the National Bank of Poland and the State Treasury owning one-third each as well. The NDS handles clearing and settlement for securities and maintains securities in the form of computer records. Only institutions admitted by the Exchange, called exchange members, mainly brokerage houses and banks, may operate on the Exchange. This means that investors and intermediaries (e.g. brokerage houses which are not members) must send their orders to the Exchange via an exchange member. Exchange members use custodian banks to handle the records of securities on their proprietary accounts and the accounts of their customers. The overall supervision of capital market institutions is conducted by a state administration agency – the Polish Financial Supervision Authority (PFSA). The supervision is intended to ensure universal access to reliable information on the securities market and observance of fair-trading and competition rules by entities operating on that market.

The WSE conducts trading in financial instruments on three markets:

- The Main List (in operation since 1991) supervised by the PFSA, recognized by the European Commission as a regulated market, and trading equities, bonds, pre-emptive rights, rights to shares, investment certificates, structured instruments and derivatives, including futures contracts and options.
- NewConnect (launched in 2007) organized and maintained by the WSE as an alternative trading system, and recognized by the European Commission as a Multilateral Trading Facility (see a detailed discussion on them in Chapter 7). It is used for trading equity and other equity-based instruments, and was designed for start-ups and developing companies, particularly from the sector of new technologies.
- Catalyst (launched in 2009) trading debt instruments including corporate and municipal bonds.

In summary, the WSE is the only regulated exchange for trading financial instruments in Poland, the owner of the only alternative trading system (NewConnect) in the country, and the co-owner of the only clearing and settlement organization. In addition, it has significant regulatory powers over companies listing their securities and trading members. It is one of the central institutions of the Polish capital market. In 2009, the WSE had approximately 200 employees, and in 2008 it earned revenues of €44m.

The Polish stock market in an international context

Poland has the largest stock market in Central and Eastern Europe, and one of the fastest growing stock markets in the world. Table 6.1 presents some basic measures of stock market development in Poland and other major countries in the region: Austria, the Czech Republic, and Hungary. Poland has a similar

Table 6.1. Stock market development in Austria, Czech Republic, Hungary, and Poland

	2009	2001
The number of domestic listed companies		
Austria	97	99
Czech Republic	16	47
Hungary	42	55
Poland	470	216
Market capitalization of domestic listed companies (in billion €)		
Austria	79.5	28.3
Czech Republic	31.3	9.0
Hungary	20.9	11.6
Poland	105.2	28.8
Stock trading value (in billion €)		
Austria	36.4	8.6
Czech Republic	17.6	3.6
Hungary	18.4	5.4
Poland	41.4	10.8

Source: Author, based on data from the Federation of European Stock Exchanges.

stock market history as Hungary and the Czech Republic. In all three countries stock exchanges were first established in the nineteenth century, and were re-established between 1990 and 1992. Recently, however, while Wiener Börse has acquired majority stakes in the Budapest (in 2004) and Prague exchanges (in 2008), the WSE has remained state-controlled, and stayed out of the Central European Stock Exchange Group, controlled by Wiener Börse and launched in 2009. Poland has enjoyed a much more dynamic stock market development than Hungary or the Czech Republic. This has been explained with stricter enforcement of the securities law, underpinned with a high level of investor protection, extensive information disclosure by issuers, and an independent and highly motivated regulator. Enforcement of the securities law in the Czech Republic has been evaluated as more lax, with Hungary exhibiting an intermediate level of enforcement (Glaeser et al. 2001). While the number of domestic listed companies (including those traded on NewConnect) in Poland more than doubled between 2001 and 2009, in the Czech Republic and Hungary the number of issuers present on the public equity market declined.

The growth of the Polish stock market was the strongest with regard to primary markets. No other European country has recorded such a large increase in the number of listed companies in the last decade. In fact, as Table 6.2 shows the WSE was the European leader in the number of IPOs in 2008 and 2009 (as well the first half of 2010). Even before the start of the recent global financial crisis, in 2007, the WSE was second only to the LSE in primary stock market activity. As shown in Table 1.2, the level of stock market participation of companies in Poland was higher than in the Czech Republic

Table 6.2. The number of initial public offerings

	2007	2008	2009
Deutsche Börse	2	0	0
LSE	32	1	7
NYSE-Euronext	8	2	6
WSE	13	11	9
Europe	72	22	33

Note: Figure for Europe represents the total for all exchanges reporting to the Federation of European Stock Exchanges (FESE).

Source: Author, based on data from the FESE.

and Hungary, and comparable to Austria. The growth of the secondary markets, however, was also strong. The percentage increase in market capitalization between 2001 and 2009 in Poland was the highest in Europe, and by 2009 the ratio of market capitalization to GDP for Poland was higher than that of the Czech Republic, Hungary, as well as Austria (Table 1.1). In addition, in 2009 the WSE had the fourth position in Europe in the volume of trading stock market index-based derivatives. In this respect, the WSE followed Eurex (operated jointly by the Deutsche Börse and the SIX Swiss Exchanges), Euronext Liffe (part of the NYSE-Euronext group), and OMX (part of NASDAQ-OMX), but it was ahead of the Spanish Exchanges and Borsa Italiana.

Geographical structure of the Polish stock market

To complete the background for the analysis of the activities of the WSE, Table 6.3 presents data for major institutions involved in the Polish stock market according to the location of their headquarters. Regarding domestic institutions, Warsaw, which accounts for approximately 5 per cent of Poland's population, is the seat of approximately 26 per cent of companies listed on the Main Market, and between 69 and 100 per cent of stock market intermediaries. To be sure, the NDS, and the PFSA are also located in Warsaw. The results presented in the table should be interpreted with caution. First, if the size of the analysed institutions or some measure of their activity were considered (e.g. revenues), the concentration of capital market functions in Warsaw would be even larger. On the other hand, many domestic institutions covered in the table have branches spread throughout the country. Finally, a majority of institutions counted as domestic is controlled by foreign owners (Rogowski 2005). While a study of the branch networks as well as the ownership and control links of Polish capital market institutions is beyond the scope of this chapter, Table 6.3 offers a valuable quantitative background for a qualitative

Table 6.3. Major institutions on the Polish stock market according to the location of headquarters

Type of institution	Warsaw	Total domestic	Foreign	Warsaw/total domestic
Issuers	99	385	25	0.26
Members of the WSE	21	28	19	0.75
Brokerages	41	53	12	0.77
Custodian banks	9	13	n/a	0.69
Investment funds	39	48	n/a	0.81
Pension funds	14	14	0	1.00

Note: The number of issuers refers to firms listed on the Main Market only. The data for investment and pension funds refer to management companies of these funds. All data are valid for the end of 2009.

Source: Author, based on data from the www.gpw.pl and www.knf.gov.pl

analysis of the relationships of the WSE with both domestic and foreign actors on the capital market.

The trading system and relationships with members

Since November 2000, trading on the WSE has taken place using the WARSET trading system. The system was based on technology purchased from the Paris Bourse, which in late 1990s was one of the most successful trading technologies used by exchanges around the world. A simplified description of the architecture of WARSET starts with an investor placing an order at a brokerage house (or a bank offering brokerage services). Since 2004, the majority of transactions were placed via Internet, with the rest placed at a customer service point of a brokerage house. Next, the order is forwarded via interface software to the central computer TANDEM, which is the heart of WARSET receiving all orders, checking their validity and matching them. Order matching is subject to one of two systems. In the first system, called a single price auction and applied to shares and other instruments for which liquidity is relatively low, all transactions are executed at a single price determined on the basis of all orders entered into the system. The procedure of price determination and transaction execution takes place twice a day. In the second system called continuous trading, and applied to instruments that sustain higher liquidity, an order can be executed any time during a trading session between 10:00 and 16:00, once there is an appropriate opposite order in the system. In addition, on an ongoing basis TANDEM calculates the value of indices, including WIG20 index based on the stock prices for twenty largest companies listed on the WSE in terms of market capitalization and liquidity. Information about executed transactions is sent by TANDEM to the NDS, which ensures clearing and settlement. Information about executed transactions and indices is sent by TANDEM to a satellite market data distribution system, whereby it is forwarded to brokerage houses, the PFSA, and information vendors including Reuters and Bloomberg, the Polish Press Agency (PPA), as well as Internet portals.

Thus far, the technical aspects of the connections between the building blocks of the WSE trading system have been described. The question is whether any social connectivity is needed on the top of technical connectivity for the trading system to function properly. In order to tackle this issue, we will focus on the relationships that are central to the architecture of the trading system – those between the Exchange as the system operator and Exchange members. Recall that only Exchange members can operate on the WSE, that is, only they can trade on their own or their clients' accounts. Recall also that a typical Exchange member is a brokerage house or a bank offering brokerage services. In 2004, however, the list of entities entitled to become members has been extended to include banks not offering brokerage services as well as foreign investment firms conducting brokerage business in Poland from abroad using remote communications systems without obligation to have a branch in Poland. While the former have been admitted to membership only to engage in the trading of one specific type of instrument – treasury notes futures, the access of remote members to trading is in legal terms equal to the access of Polish brokerage houses. One other category of members, which is important for our analysis, is that of market makers, which undertake to place sell and buy orders for a given security on their own account with a view to maintain and increase its liquidity.

Remote membership represents an important step in the adoption of the EU regulation on the single passport for investment services firms, and is of particular significance for the WSE. The pool of domestic members is limited, with the ensuing consolidation of brokerage industry driving down the number of brokerage houses as well as banks offering brokerage services. Regulatory issues aside, the consolidation trend implies a growing potential for an individual member or a group of members to match sell and buy orders internally, without using the services of the Exchange. Given the pressure to acquire remote members, the WSE does not simply wait until foreign investment firms knock at its door. Instead, the Exchange seeks remote members among other means by approaching foreign investment firms during road shows and financial trade fairs, for example, in the City of London. In the process of remote members' acquisition, the role of facilitators may be performed by Polish banks that render custodian services to foreign investment firms active on the Polish stock market. By 2009, there were almost as many foreign (remote) as domestic exchange members (Table 6.3). The share of remote members in total equity trading in 2008 was only 10 per cent but it was growing (www.wgpw.pl).

Interactions between the WSE and current Exchange members refer to both day-to-day and routine operations as well as business development. Every day a team at the WSE oversees the trading session and has to react quickly to any technical issues or procedural irregularities. Their decisions, for example, about the suspension of trading in a particular instrument have to be communicated instantaneously to members. Another team is a help desk, which communicates with members in order to resolve issues regarding the interface between TANDEM and members' software as well as any problems regarding the distribution of information from the WSE to members. Again, the speed of problem resolution is of paramount importance, and if a WSE employee knows a member employee well, it can be helpful. Other, not day-to-day, but still routine activities include the renewal of contracts between the WSE on one side and members and market makers on the other, as well as involvement in the training and examination of licensed brokers. In addition, there are regular quarterly and extraordinary meetings of the Committee for Market Indices, gathering mainly stock market analysts and investment advisors employed by Exchange members, in order to advise the WSE on such issues as index methodology and changes in the composition of financial instruments in an index.

Summarizing, while remote membership implies that foreign investment firms do not need to set up branches or subsidiaries in Poland in order to trade at the WSE, it does not automatically lessen the need for social connectivity between members and the Exchange. In a sense, domestic members of the WSE could also be called remote members, because they do not need to be physically present at the WSE in order to trade. Social connectivity between the Exchange and members plays a particularly large role with regard to activities aimed at business development of the WSE. While the acquisition of new members has already been discussed one should also consider activities related to the design of information products, derivative instruments, and the operations of the WSE team responsible for the general development of the trading system. It has been stressed in interviews that for these activities to be effective, people in those units have to know the needs of the market, and to recognize these needs they need good relationships with all users of the Exchange services including members and market makers.

Relationships with issuers

This section describes the relationships of the WSE with companies that issue securities traded on the Exchange. It starts with the acquisition of new issuers, discusses the process of admitting new securities to listing on the WSE, and finally analyses relationships with issuers whose securities are already listed.

To attract new business the Exchange actively searches for potential issuers. The Exchange maintains two databases, one with companies that have expressed their interest in listing but have not yet applied for it, the other with firms that have not expressed such interest but due to their size and/or other characteristics are recognized as potential issuers. Both of these groups, totalling hundreds of firms, are contacted by the WSE on a regular basis with promotional materials, including success stories about recent issuers, as well as invitations to events organized by the WSE. Apart from correspondence, the WSE advertises itself to potential issuers through media, including trade press, both national and regional in coverage. Together with trade press, associations of entrepreneurs or independently, the Exchange organizes conferences and meetings with potential issuers. In 2004 alone, under names including 'Road to capital' and 'Small and medium firms in EU', such events numbered over twenty and took place in ten cities around Poland. The acquisition of new issuers is a long-term process, and at the end of the day a company has to be convinced that the benefits of listing on the WSE exceed the costs. Considering that each case is specific, meetings of experts from the WSE with key representatives of a potential issuer, including the chief executives, board members, controlling owners, and influential advisors, are crucial and indispensable. It may take many meetings spread over a couple of years before a company decides to list if at all. The Listing Department holds on average three meetings with potential issuers weekly, with an absolute majority of these meetings taking place in Warsaw.

Admission of a company and its securities to listing at the WSE is a process that involves a number of legal and other formal requirements as well as various intermediaries. Here a simplified picture of the process is presented focusing on the relationships between the issuer and the WSE. First, to have its securities traded on the WSE, a company must prepare a prospectus, including the presentation of its financial situation and risk factors for potential public investors, and apply to the PFSA, which makes the decision regarding admission to public trading. The WSE receives the draft prospectus from the PFSA and takes part in a meeting convened by the PFSA with representatives of the applicant, its advisors including a brokerage house that assists the company in the going-public project, the NDS, and other relevant regulatory authorities, with the objective to discuss any issues the applicant should address before the PFSA makes their final decision. Provided the decision of the PFSA is positive, the company can apply to the WSE for admission to listing. An application is available online but a firm usually has numerous questions to the WSE before its submission. Next, the Listing and the Legal Departments of the WSE prepare opinions, which are considered along with the prospectus and company's application by the Exchange Management Board at a meeting usually gathering the President of the Management Board of the applicant, its advisors, Chief Financial Officer, and representatives of the relevant brokerage house. To reach the decision, the Exchange Management Board considers such factors as the financial position and prospects of the company, and the experience and qualifications of its executives. If the decision is positive, a company can make a debut on the WSE. The first day when a company's shares are traded on the WSE can be a colourful event, with new issuers celebrating their first step in the world of 'high finance', not least for marketing purposes. Some executives are reported to say that the debut of their company on the WSE is the happiest day of their life.

After the debut, interactions between the issuer and the Exchange revolve around further capital market activities of the issuer as well as reporting. The former may involve the issue of new shares or corporate bonds, a merger with a different company or the launch of an employee share ownership plan. Email communication is sufficient to assist standard operations such as the division of the nominal value of shares. With non-standard tasks such as the division of a company into parts, numerous meetings between the WSE experts, company representatives, as well as financial and legal advisors may be necessary. Moving on to reporting, the WSE receives all reports from issuers via a special purpose electronic mail system called ESPI. Issuers are obliged to submit periodic financial reports as well reports on relevant events, for example significant changes in ownership, changes in the composition of the decision-making bodies or large contracts signed by the company. In the first five months of 2005, the WSE received over 8000 reports. Every employee of the Listing Department is assigned between twenty and thirty companies and is responsible for reading all reports coming from these companies, as well as deciding whether any action should be considered in response to new information. Since the time allowed to make a decision, for example to suspend the trading in some shares so that the public has time to learn the news, is only a matter of minutes, it is crucial that the respective employee of the Listing Department knows their companies well. The same news may trigger different decision depending on the context. For example, if a company signs a large sales contract relative to its size the suspension of trading may be in order, unless the contract is a part of a series of contracts that has been announced by the company earlier.

Reacting to corporate news may require consulting the source of information. Every issuer has a person assigned as the contact person for the WSE. As the contact person needs to be not only competent but also needs to have some decision-making power, the role is usually performed by a member of the management board or a person in charge of investor relations. The first-hand knowledge of issuers acquired by the WSE in the process of listing and through ongoing communication is also key to the role of the WSE as a reputation intermediary. In 2009, for example, the WSE has conducted a survey of corporate social responsibility in listed companies, which led to the creation of the Respect Index. In addition, the WSE has led the design of the code of best practices in corporate governance for listed companies. This activity involves conferences and meetings with issuers, as well as the largest Internet service dedicated to the issues of corporate governance in Poland (at www.corp-gov.gpw.pl).

Moving on to another aspect of the relationship between the WSE and current issuers, special treatment is afforded to the largest twenty of them, constituents of the WIG20 index, also referred to as the 'golden corporations'. Each of these companies has a contact person in the Listing Department, referred to as a carer; has free of charge Internet access to real-time quotations; and can organize a quarterly conference with analysts and investors free of charge on the premises of the Exchange. Some other companies also organize their conferences with analysts and investors at the WSE, and the latter organizes seminars and conferences open to all issuers on such topics as the International Financial Reporting Standards or the EU capital market regulations. Some of these conferences and seminars are organized jointly with the Association of Issuers.

On the other side of the corporate spectrum, the NewConnect market launched in 2007 gives smaller and younger firms an opportunity to enter the stock market via procedures simpler than admission to the Main Market. The simplest option is private placement, aimed at a maximum of ninety-nine investors (individual and institutional). In this cased admission to trading on NewConnect is granted on the basis of a document prepared by an authorized advisor. The NewConnect market to a large extent follows the model of the Alternative Investment Market of the LSE, described in Chapter 3. Simplified listing does not however imply a process in any sense devoid of human interaction. In order to support the access of young and dynamic firms to the stock market, the WSE has initiated an Internet-based social network 'NewConnect All the People', but also the NewConnect Club which holds regular meetings of entrepreneurs and financial intermediaries, hosted by the WSE.

Summarizing the section, the WSE is definitely not a passive provider of a trading system for equity. Instead, it takes an active part in the creation of equity, thus creating demand for its own services. Lowering the price of listing is not a sufficient tool to increase demand. In fact, one of my interviewees cited a study according to which many companies stated the cost of listing as the factor preventing them from approaching the WSE, but when asked about their estimates of these costs, most companies did not have a clue. In a similar vein, other interviews stressed that many potential issuers fear an entry into 'high-finance' associated with the 'aggressive' world of scrutiny and professional advisors. In this context, the WSE needs to reach to potential issuers and communicate with them as directly as possible. In addition, the WSE attempts to ease the capital market entry by facilitating relationships between companies and capital market intermediaries. In 2005, the Exchange introduced a programme called WSE IPO Partners aimed at supporting intermediaries (including brokerage houses, certified auditors, legal and investment firms) that assist issuers in raising equity via the WSE. In 2010, the programme had tens of domestic participants as well as twenty-three foreign-based WSE IPO Partners from nine countries.

The analysis of relationships with firms applying for listing as well as those that already have their securities traded on the WSE points to an indispensable role of direct communication, combined with but not substituted by the use of technology. To be sure, one must not forget the international factors affecting the relationships of the Exchange with issuers. At the end of 2009, the WSE listed twenty-five foreign companies, including three from Austria, the Czech Republic, and the Netherlands each. In 2008, the WSE became the first foreign exchange to open an office in Kiev, the capital of Ukraine, the activities of which are centred on attracting Ukrainian issuers to the Polish stock market. On the other hand, a number of large Polish companies listed on the WSE had portions of shares listed and traded abroad, mainly in the United States and the United Kingdom. Not surprisingly, the Exchange pays particular attention to tightening its relationships with the largest issuers, and as it turns out this involves intensified contact in both virtual and real space.

Relationships with investors

Prior to an analysis of the relationships between the WSE and investors, we need to explain the structure of investors. In the period 2002–7 the shares of foreign, domestic individual, and domestic institutional investors in the total value of stock trading fluctuated between 25 and 40 per cent each (www.gpw.com.pl). There seems to be a trend towards a declining share of domestic individual investors and an increasing role of foreign investors. With large fluctuations over time, however, it is not unambiguous. In addition, domestic individuals accounted for a majority of trading on NewConnect as well as in the trading of futures and options contracts. The UK-based brokers accounted for approximately 70 per cent on equity trading conducted by remote members. Regarding domestic individual investors, the total number of individual investment accounts rose from approximately 0.8m in 2004 to over one million in 2008, out of which approximately 20 per cent record any transactions in any given quarter, and as such are considered active. Among institutional investors, management companies investing the assets of pension funds play the largest role, and at the end of 2009 were estimated to hold at least €10bn Euro worth of Polish shares listed at the WSE. Their assets are not only growing, but are also captured in Poland, as foreign investments are not allowed to exceed 5 per cent of managed assets. Other institutional investors or individuals do not face any major regulatory restrictions on their foreign investment.

Day-to-day interaction between the WSE and investors involves the flow of stock market information. To be sure, information needs vary from one investor to another. Many individual investors are content with end of day summaries of price levels and indices. Sophisticated investors, including most institutional investors need to evaluate their portfolios on an intra-day basis, minute by minute. Investors can obtain information directly from the WSE or from one of the information vendors, to whom the WSE sells their information. A considerable amount of information about all aspects of the WSE activities including trading is available on its website, which in 2005 contained approximately 700 web pages with between 2000 and 3000 A4 pages of text and graphics. In 2004 and 2005, the website had on average 500,000 visits a month. Together with the PPA, the WSE has created an open and free-of-charge economic newswire service called WSEInfoSpace covering firms listed on the WSE but also other markets in Central and Eastern Europe.

While the flow of information products is mediated by telecommunications technology, certain less day-to-day activities bring investors and the Exchange closer to each other in real terms. On some occasions representatives of the WSE go to meet investors, for example, by attending outside conferences and trade fairs for financial products or organizing road-show conferences abroad. The latter had the general objective of promoting the Polish capital market and in 2004 took place twice in London and once in Boston. On a regular basis, investors come to the premises of the WSE, whether to take part in conferences, seminars, workshops on such issues as new financial instruments or taxation of capital gains, or to attend an open day dedicated mostly to beginning investors. The Exchange also offers its premises for meetings of investors themselves as well as meetings of investors and issuers. Examples include meetings co-organized by the WSE for the Association of Individual Investors, or for the issuers' conferences with investors and analysts. Regarding the latter, the WSE has created the WSEInfoEngine, which offers investors an online real-time access to broadcasts of issuers' annual general meetings as well as issuers' meetings with analysts. Thus, whether in virtual or real space the WSE offers a contact point between issuers and investors.

Another side of the WSE activities with regard to investors concerns education, which is particularly important in the context of a country where stock market did not exist for over half a century before 1991. The educational strategy targets mainly young people, and is conducted partly via a separate, though wholly owned by the WSE entity called the Foundation for Capital

Market Education. The largest ongoing project is the Exchange School, a series of courses on the basics of capital market and investing, modelled partly on the French L'École de la Bourse. In 2004, over sixty courses were organized around Poland, for approximately 1600 participating students, with course materials also available on Internet. In addition, on a daily basis the WSE hosted at their premises groups of high school students totalling approximately 18,000 in 2004. Other educational activities include publications, lectures at universities, Internet-based stock market games and competitions, and input into the design of economics curricula for high schools.

Summarizing the relationships between the WSE and investors, at the first glance one notices the flow of market information from the Exchange to investors, which does not require proximity. At a closer look however, one needs to appreciate the significance of information that flows from investors back to the Exchange concerning their feedback on services received as well as needs for new information products or investment instruments. To be sure, some feedback is obtained at a distance. For example, the Exchange's website features surveys on such issues as the timing of trading sessions or the popularity of various indices. Such surveys, however useful, can only cover standardized issues and are targeted at individual, geographically dispersed investors. In contrast, to gain insight into opinions and ideas of institutional investors, the WSE is likely to engage with them on a more personal, face-to-face level. It is also likely that formal contacts between the WSE and institutional investors at conferences or seminars are only the visible top of an iceberg of informal relationships. In this context, it may be useful to mention that the Exchange is located in the very heart of Warsaw, within a short distance to bars, restaurants, and other meeting places of the Warsaw financial sector elite. It is also relevant that a significant portion of the financial sector employees, including those working at the WSE, graduated from the leading, and until several years ago one of the few, institutions offering economics education in Poland – Szkoła Główna Handlowa (the Warsaw School of Economics).

Conclusions and implications

On the completion of our tour of the WSE activities, it is time to return to the question of the relationship between stock exchange activities and financial centres. Figure 6.1 summarizes different activities of the WSE, indicating the degree to which they depend on close social contacts for the sake of exchange and interpretation of information. This classification is not meant to be complete or strict, but rather illustrative in indicating three types of activities. On the one side, there are facilities for trading and distribution of standard information, which require state-of-the-art technical connectivity but little in

	Trading system and relationships with members	Relationships with issuers	Relationships with investors
High dependence on close social contacts	Communication with market makers and other members needed for the development of the trading system	Acquisition and admission of new issuers Complex capital market activities of current issuers Reacting to news from issuers Facilitating issuers' relationships with other intermediaries including legal and financial advisers, brokerage houses, PR firms	Communication with investors, including analysts and investment advisors, needed for the development of information products, for example indices, and the development of the trading system
	Acquisition of new members Communication with members needed for a smooth conduct of a trading session Renewal of contracts with members Training for brokers, market makers, and other members	Simple capital market operations of current issuers Organizing training, conferences, and seminars for issuers	Sale of advanced information products to investors Investor education Facilitating relationships between investors and issuers
Low dependence on close social contacts	Trading system and back office IT	Flow of standard information from issuers to the exchange	Flow of standard information to investors, including Internet-based information

Figure 6.1. Activities of the Warsaw Stock Exchange according to their dependence on close social contacts

Source: Author.

terms of social connectivity. Consequently, people running these activities could be located anywhere in relation to members, issuers, or investors. Other groups of activities, which were not the focus of the WSE case study, but can be classified as requiring little in terms of close social contact, are clearing and settlement of securities transactions. On the other side, activities that require a high degree of face-to-face contact make an exchange gravitate towards a place where members, issuers, and investors concentrate. Many of these activities cluster within the category of relationships with issuers, which require not only close social contacts but also expert knowledge in terms of the local regulation and local corporate law. This is consistent with the analysis of Malkamäki (2000), suggesting that listing and surveillance of issuers are labour intensive and involve complex information. Nevertheless, among relationships with members and investors, there are also activities that require close social contact. These concern communications needed for the development of the trading system and information products. It is typical for the financial services sector that innovation occurs through close interaction with customers, and stock exchanges seem to be no exception in this regard.

Thus far, it is suggested that stock exchange activities are prone to concentrate in a financial centre depending on the degree to which they rely on close social contacts with members, issuers, and investors. It should be added that the proximity factor in the relationships between an exchange and other key players on the stock market is asymmetric. While for an exchange, the relationships with members, issuers, and investors constitute raison d'etre, for the latter relationships with an exchange in most cases represent a small part of their overall business portfolio. In consequence, if a stock exchange wants to cultivate non-standard relationships with key players on the stock market, it needs to adjust to their location.

To be sure, we have to be cautious when generalizing the results of a specific case study. As discussed, the WSE has enjoyed a monopoly on the Polish secondary stock market, granting it also a considerable power in primary stock market activities. It would be a mistake, however, to compare it to the monopoly enjoyed until recently by stock exchanges in Western Europe, where there have been mature investment banks and other stock market intermediaries ready, if only allowed to do so, to step in, compete with the incumbent exchange, and fulfil some of its functions. The Polish stock market was built from scratch in early 1990s. Banks had absolutely no experience with stock markets; neither were there any other stock market intermediaries present. The WSE was the first actor on the stock market of modern Poland. Wiesław Rozłucki led the establishment of the WSE in 1990–1 as the director of the Department for Capital Market Development, a division of the Polish central government.

Since its foundation, the WSE has contributed to the dynamic development of the Polish stock market, as an exchange that is well embedded in the Polish economy and adopts a long-term developmental perspective. It has been embedded by establishing multiple connections with a broad array of actors on the stock market, and through efforts to build an inclusive marketplace. This is exemplified by the success of the listing and trading platform for small and medium sized companies (NewConnect), and by a proactive stance in reaching potential issuers in all parts of the country. The latter has resulted in a very low bias towards companies from the capital, as illustrated in Chapter 2. The WSE has exhibited a long-term orientation by engaging in activities that do not bring direct revenues but are key for developing the marketplace, including the advancement of corporate governance practices and financial literacy. To appreciate this embeddedness and long-termism, it is important to know that Wiesław Rozłucki was the CEO of the WSE between 1991 and 2006, probably the longest serving CEO of an exchange in the world, and has a Ph.D. in economic geography. At the entrance of his office, I saw a large wall map of Poland, with pins of one colour indicating the headquarter locations of companies already listed on the WSE, and pins of a different colour indicating companies identified as those that could potentially become listed, for example, by the virtue of their size.

The position of the WSE on the European stock exchange landscape is uncertain. For the time being the Exchange, even after an IPO, remains state-controlled. In the mid-2000s, the WSE attempted to buy ownership stakes in exchanges in Lithuania, Hungary, and the Czech Republic, but the attempts failed, arguably due to the state-ownership of the WSE. In 2007 and 2008, however, the WSE managed to acquire stakes in secondary exchanges in

Ukraine and Romania. The WSE has stayed away from regional consolidation led by Wiener Börse, which established the Central European Stock Exchange Group in 2009, including exchanges in Prague, Budapest, and Ljubljana. In late 2009, an invitation to bid for a majority stake in the WSE, issued by the State Treasury, was answered only by Deutsche Börse, and the bid was rejected. In July 2010, came a potential breakthrough in the international relations of the WSE, as it announced a strategic partnership with the NYSE-Euronext. In this way, the WSE confirms its 'French connection', twenty years after the French experts helped to establish the WSE, and ten years after the trading system was purchased from France. Whether the partnership will be limited to the migration of the WSE trading to the NYSE-Euronext platform (as announced) or will result in the WSE joining the NYSE-Euronext corporate group remains to be seen.

If the WSE does turn into a branch of the NYSE-Euronext group, it will be important to see how this will affect its embeddedness in the Polish economy and long-termism. Pessimists will say that these virtues will be sacrificed on the altar of efficiency and short-term profitability. Optimists will argue that the Polish stock market is now developed enough, and needs an internationally competitive exchange using state-of-the-art technology, rather than an exchange that tries to perform all stock market functions, and acts as a monopolistic public utility company. The message of this chapter is that one important way to establish the future impact of stock exchange consolidation on the Polish stock market and Warsaw as a financial centre would be to analyse its performance in the context of relationships with different actors on the stock market, taking seriously the geographical nature and footprint of these relationships. It is the competition and consolidation in the stock exchange industry that the book turns to in the following chapter.

7

Revolution in the Exchange Industry: Battle for Liquidity and Financial Centres

In his book *Capitals of Capital*, Youssef Cassis states that stock exchanges set the pulse of financial centres (2006: 6). Out of the top ten financial centres in the world according to the Global Financial Centre Index (Z/Yen 2010), only Geneva does not have stock exchange headquarters (although it has an office of the Swiss Exchange). In Canada, Brazil, and Australia, which witnessed domestic battles for financial centre primacy in the twentieth century, winners – Toronto, São Paulo, and Sydney – host the national stock exchange. This coincidence between financial centre and exchange location can be found also at the intra-urban level. The relocation of JSE Securities Exchange from downtown Johannesburg to Sandton in 2000, for example, marked the rise of Sandton as the city's new financial district. It is difficult to think of a single country, where the only or the main exchange is not located in the country's primary financial centre. While a financial centre can function without a stock exchange (think of Geneva, Boston, or San Francisco), stock exchanges certainly contribute to financial centres in tangible (employment, infrastructure) and intangible ways (image, brand, reputation).

The last decade has shaken the stock exchange landscape, particularly in the United States and Europe. While the words of the former CEO of the New York Stock Exchange (NYSE) John Thain – 'every country has a flag, an army, and an exchange' (Biglari 2007: 5) – were true to reality in 2000, ten years later we have international stock exchange groups such as the NYSE-Euronext, the London Stock Exchange (LSE) Group (including Borsa Italiana – BIT), and the NASDAQ-OMX Group (with operations in at least sixteen countries). All of them are self-listed, have diluted ownership structures, and feature state-controlled institutions from Dubai and Qatar among major investors. A special report of the *Financial Times* in 2007 entitled *nomen omen* 'World Financial Centres and Exchanges' hints at the fate of exchanges becoming divorced from the fate of financial centres. In the lead article John Authers (1) claims: 'The on-going soap opera of consolidation matters greatly to shareholders of the exchanges involved. But it has little relevance for the balance of power between the world's financial centres'.

In my view, the stress on nationality in the debate on the relationship between exchanges and financial centres is misplaced. Financial centres, particularly in the twenty-first century, are about location rather than nationality. A stock exchange, like any company, may have a difficulty to discern nationality, but its decision-makers, employees, and hardware must be somewhere, and where they are is an integral part of corporate strategy. There is much more to geography than nationality. Confusing geography with nationality reminds me of the airline analogy, which I have heard many times interviewing experts at stock exchanges. It goes as follows. People and governments used to care about the nationality of airlines, but now they only care about cheap tickets and good service. Likewise, they should and will stop caring about the nationality of exchanges. What the story does not mention is that competition among airlines (including an open market for their ownership) makes geography of airline industry more interesting than ever before, as companies can develop fewer but bigger airline hubs involving jobs, research and development, and attracting related services. Witness, for example, the development of aviation finance in Ireland. Nationality may influence location (think of Ryan Air), but what matters more directly is competition and business strategy.

The objective of this chapter is to investigate competition in the stock exchange industry and its relationship with the development of financial centres. Empirically, the emphasis is on Europe, particularly since the introduction of the Markets in Financial Instruments Directive (MiFID) in 2007. Comparisons will nevertheless be made between Europe and the United States, and some implications drawn at the global scale. The main source of material for the chapter is previous work on the evolution of stock exchanges and markets (Michie 2006; Casey and Lannoo 2009) and data on equity trading from the Federation of European Stock Exchanges (FESE). In addition, the author has conducted tens of interviews with stock market experts in financial centres around Europe, which have helped to gain an insight into the practices of stock exchanges and related institutions.

The analysis takes the following steps. First, I sketch the main forces that have transformed the stock exchange industry in the last quarter century, with particular focus on the last decade in Europe. The following section analyses the impact of these forces on the business models of new entrants and established players in the industry. It shows how the changes in the environment of exchanges have revolutionized the way these institutions conduct their business. Next, I introduce the main actors on the European stock exchange stage and interpret the battle for liquidity between 2000 and

2010. The final part of the analysis presents the footprint of the revolution in the stock exchange industry, interrogating the location of stock exchange operations for both new and established exchanges, as well as its relationship with financial centres. The last section concludes, drawing some implications for the global stock exchange industry and stock markets in general.

The central argument can be previewed as follows. In the 2000s, regulation in the United States and subsequently in Europe responded to the needs of investors and traders, allowing them to take advantage of modern technology, and unleashing a competition that was never before witnessed in the stock exchange industry, with a singular focus on liquidity. By 2010, new exchanges in the United States and Europe proved successful in the battle for liquidity. Essential to their success was the adoption of a simple and efficient business model of two-sided platforms, which contrasts with and threatens the model of diversification and vertical integration embraced by incumbent exchanges. The increased competition and network effects in the industry have been accompanied by its continued concentration in the New York City area in the United States, and emerging dominance of London in Europe, driven primarily by the value of proximity between exchanges and their major customers in terms of computers and human relations. While the NYSE-Euronext and the LSE Group may suffer, revolution in the stock exchange industry benefits New York City and London as financial centres.

The winds and waves of change

This section provides a historical background and conceptual framework for the analysis of competition in the stock exchange industry, by identifying the winds and waves of change. The winds of change are the major forces operating on the stock exchange industry: technology, the nature of demand for stock exchange services, and regulation. Waves are the major historical events, milestones in the history of the industry in Europe, starting with the Big Bang of 1986, which reformed the LSE and precipitated a series of stock exchange deregulation in Europe; followed by the Investment Services Directive, in force since 1996, and replaced by the MiFID directive in 2007. There are many detailed accounts of change in the environment of stock exchanges (see e.g. Ferrarini 1998 or Casey and Lannoo 2009 for focus on regulation, and Lee 1998 on technology and governance). Compared to them this section is bound to look sketchy, nevertheless it is necessary to contextualize change in the exchange business model, competition for liquidity, and location.

Prior to the mid-1980s, European stock exchanges were mutual organizations owned by members trading on a physical trading floor (open outcry pit) and earning statutorily fixed commissions on executed orders sent to them by customers who, at least as far as retail trades are concerned, were obliged to send their orders to the stock exchange. This picture of stock exchanges functioning like national monopolies was in place at least since the Second World War, but was to change in 1986 with the financial reform referred to as the Big Bang in the United Kingdom. The core reforms involved the abolition of fixed fees and opening the membership of the LSE to banks and investment firms, including the admission of foreign members (Michie 1999). The reform coincided with the replacement of the open outcry pit with screen-based electronic trading. What had the most direct impact on other stock exchanges in Europe in the aftermath of the reform in London was the Stock Exchange Automated Quotation-International (SEAQ-I), a computerized quote-driven trading system (modelled after the NASDAQ in the United States), which after 1986 attracted a substantial amount of trading in stocks from Continental Europe. The first to respond to this challenge was the Paris Bourse, which lost a significant amount of trading to SEAQ-I, and underwent a reform between 1986 and 1989. In the early 1990s, other exchanges followed, including Madrid, Milan, Brussels, Amsterdam, and the German exchanges (Pagano 1998). The common themes in this wave of deregulation were the liberalization of commissions, introduction of screen-based trading, and broadening access to stock exchange membership. The reforms lowered the costs of trading, speeded up execution, made trades more transparent, and increased the liquidity of the market.

The next major reform came with the ISD in 1996, the main objective of which was to introduce an EU passport for investment services firms, whereby firms once authorized by their home country regulators could operate in any other Member State. A major implication was that authorized investment firms that wanted to become members of a foreign stock exchange, did not need to be physically present in the home country of that stock exchange. Stock exchanges had to accept remote members and provide them with trading screens. The ISD, however, did not introduce direct competition between stock exchanges, as it recognized existing stock exchanges as regulated markets and allowed Member States to maintain concentration rules, whereby national authorities could require that at least retail investor orders are executed only on the domestic regulated market (Ferrarini 1998). Thus, the privileges of exchanges were maintained and competition between them was restricted.

This changed only in 2007 when MiFID came into force. The concentration rules were abolished, allowing regulated markets (incumbent exchanges) and investment firms to set up Multilateral Trading Facilities (MTFs), which can trade any equities that are eligible for trading on regulated markets. In addition, subject to trade transparency rules, investment firms can internalize retail investor orders in the capacity of systemic internalizers (with the investment firm as a counterparty to each trade). Stock exchanges lost their monopoly on trading, but also on market data, as trades taking place outside of regulated markets can be reported to an MTF or a specialized data vendor like Bloomberg or Reuters, and not necessarily to the incumbent exchange (Davies 2008; Casey and Lannoo 2009). Finally, MiFID requires investment firms to have a best execution policy – procedures to ensure that their customers' orders are sent to the trading venue that offers best execution (affected by a combination of stock price, speed, fraction of order executed, costs).

MiFID is the centrepiece of the Financial Services Action Plan initiated in the EU in 1999, following recognition that ISD was insufficient for the development of an integrated European capital market. Other directives most relevant to the stock market are the Prospectus Directive, Transparency Directive, and Market Abuse Directive. With the Prospectus Directive in force since 2005, once a company gets its prospectus authorized by the home country authority, its shares can be listed anywhere in Member States or traded unlisted on an MTF, without the latter needing to ask the issuer for permission. The Transparency and Market Abuse directives regulate the ongoing disclosure and reporting requirements of issuers.

A major wind of change, thus far silent in this account, is the nature of demand for stock exchange services. Over the last quarter century we have witnessed a growing demand from issuers, driven i.a. by privatizations of formerly state-owned companies; and from investors, driven mainly by the rise of private pension funds. In terms of structure, investors' demand has been dominated by institutional investors, mainly pension, mutual, and insurance funds, as well as institutional traders, with hedge funds and investment banks in the lead. Large traders acting on behalf of institutional investors and on their own account demand speed and cheap execution much more effectively than retail (individual) investors ever could. Large institutional investors want to diversify their equity holdings internationally and are interested in quick and cheap buying and selling across national markets, treating the global or at least the European equity market as one world of investment opportunities. Over the last twenty-five years, this demand and way of viewing equity markets grew increasingly out of match with the European stock exchange infrastructure. Large investment funds and their brokers want to trade European stocks without the cost of being members of ten to twenty different exchanges, each with its own rules for membership, trading, clearing, and settlement.

The direction of the wind of change affecting the European exchange industry has been mostly eastwards, blowing from the United States, with the world's largest and most liquid stock market, and the seat of the largest institutional investors and investment firms. All waves of change in Europe have been affected by events in the United States, with NASDAQ and deregulation in the United States stimulating Big Bang (via the pressure of the US investment banks present in the City of London); and the Regulation National Market System reform of 2005 in the United States inspiring MiFID, as the EU has considered the lack of an integrated European stock market as a major obstacle to lower cost of capital for European firms and better access to investment opportunities for investors. It should be noted that the fragmentation of European stock markets along national borders presented a major barrier to the expansion of US investors and intermediaries. The Sarbanes-Oxley Act of 2002, contributing to a wave of de-listings in the United States, restricted domestic revenue potential for the US exchanges and other stock market intermediaries, and became one of the motives for them decisively entering the battle for liquidity in Europe in the mid-2000s. Likewise, the US investors and intermediaries are a major source of demand for European exchanges and intermediaries.

The impact of technology on the evolution of stock exchanges is closely related to the issues of demand as well as regulation. Prior to the 1980s, traders would meet on a physical trading floor and orders from their customers would be collected via telephone. Starting in the mid-1980s, open outcry pits were gradually replaced by computers displaying and matching orders, with traders sending their orders via computer networks from the dealing rooms of investment firms within the financial centre where the stock exchange was located. Traders themselves would collect orders from their customers still mostly via telephone. In the mid-1990s, with Internet and remote access, the connections between exchange order matching and display engines could extend across borders, and investors themselves could send their orders to trading firms via computer networks. Since the late 2000s, with the MiFID and best execution rules, traders and intermediaries need to be connected to multiple venues. A parallel innovation in this field has been the Financial Information eXchange (FIX) Protocol developed by investment banks and firms, which has standardized the format of trade-related messages, becoming a global language for the automated trading of financial instruments. The history of stock exchange technology is thus a story of increasing connectivity achieved through a network of physical infrastructure and rules.

The 2000s witnessed yet another technological revolution. As computing power and the speed of data transmission grows exponentially, an increasing part of trading is generated by trading firms writing and installing algorithms on computers which generate orders automatically. While in the mid-1980s it was an achievement for SEAQ in London to execute up to ten trades a second (Michie 1999), in 2010 computers can generate thousands of orders per second each, putting an enormous pressure on stock exchanges to process these huge numbers of transactions quickly. The fastest matching engines offer a round trip (from receiving an order to sending a message confirming its execution) measured in microseconds. As the speed of message transmission approaches the speed of light, there is demand from the trading firms to locate their order-generating computers as close as possible to the matching engines of exchanges, referred to as co-location services or proximity to liquidity. In stock trading, the notion that time is money has been taken to a new level.

In summary, we have shown that the exchange industry has been transformed over the last quarter century by forces that can be classified under the broad headings of demand, technology, and regulation. While regulation provides clear milestones in the history of stock exchanges, in a sense it has responded, arguably with considerable delay, to the demands of modern investors and intermediaries, allowing them to take advantage of available technologies. In Europe, changes in the exchange industry have been greatly affected by earlier changes in the US stock markets, channelled to large degree via the City of London. The United States as a continental size economy with the world's largest stock market has been influential as a major source of business for European exchange industry, and treated in many respects as a benchmark for European regulation. As I shall argue in the next section, these macro-changes in the environment of stock exchanges have had huge consequences for how stock exchanges formulate their strategies.

Revolution in the exchange business model

This section will explain how the changes in demand, technology, and regulation have revolutionized the very business model of a stock exchange. The starting point of my argument is the increasing separation of trading from listing, services to traders from services to issuers, or more generally secondary from primary stock markets. This separation has created an opportunity for the emergence of a stock exchange business model focused exclusively on trading, which in Europe has materialized in the form of MTFs. Specifically, it will be shown that MTFs treat the secondary stock market as a two-sided network, with liquidity makers on one side and liquidity takers on the other, and consequently have developed their business as the provision of two-sided platforms. The concept of two-sided networks and platforms, inspired by network economics and business studies, will also allow me to compare the strategy of MTFs with the behaviour of incumbent exchanges, and draw implications about competition in the exchange industry.

The winds of change identified in the previous section are very useful in explaining the growing separation of trading from listing. In terms of demand, we have noted a shift to markets dominated by large, internationally oriented investors. These investors' interest in the number of listed companies in the

United States growing from say 7000 to 7050 or in bringing another small size issuer to the German stock market is minute compared to their interest in easy and cheap cross-border trading of large capitalization stocks. Their interest in small capitalization stocks is limited, because trading such stock involves high risk of adversely influencing price (liquidity risk). Alternatively, large investors would have to split their portfolio and attention into minute fractions. In the field of technology, algorithmic trading and ultra-speed connections reflect the fact that trading becomes more technology driven, while listing and other issuer services remain relationship-based. This enlarges the gulf between the two activities in terms of procedures and skill sets. Finally, regulation allows (and in some respects and contexts requires) issuers services to migrate from stock exchanges to regulatory authorities and companies other than stock exchanges (including rating agencies or media companies). The recent EU directives harmonize core procedures related to prospectus authorization and issuer reporting, handing them over to regulatory authorities, and allow stock trading without listing by MTFs. The separation of issuer services from trading happens also at the level of national regulation. In the United Kingdom, listing and delisting of stocks was transferred to the Financial Services Authority before the EU directives were in place (Macey and O'Hara 2002). As a result, the relationships with issuers matter less for the stock exchange business, and trading – the production of liquidity – becomes ever more critical and their raison d'être. In a sense, stock exchanges become more like derivatives exchanges, with few or none direct relationships with the issuers of traded securities.

In Europe, MTFs epitomize this shift to a singular emphasis on liquidity production, by treating the secondary stock market as a two-sided network and focus their business on providing two-sided platforms to service this market. It should come as no surprise that stock markets operate like networks. A trader/investor on a stock market benefits from the presence of other traders/investors. Buy/sell orders are attracted to the market where they can find the maximum number of other sell/buy orders. Liquidity attracts liquidity. Even in a physical sense, we have illustrated the development of trading as a network of connected traders, investors, and exchanges. Secondary stock market however, is not any type of network – it is a two-sided network, with liquidity makers on one side and liquidity takers on the other. Liquidity makers are traders (institutional or individual) who send both sell and buy orders for the same stocks in order to make a profit on the difference (spread). As the spreads are typically small, the volume and speed of trading is paramount. Liquidity takers are investors (institutional and individual) who buy and sell stocks to build and rebuild their portfolios. The recognition of these two distinctive sides is key to the strategy and success of businesses providing platforms connecting the two sides.

Some of the most successful companies of the last ten to twenty years have based their business model on two-sided networks. Web search engines like Google, for example, connect searchers and advertisers. Windows and Mac operating systems connect consumers with application developers. While concentrated in information technology (IT) and media, and very much enabled by the development of Internet, two-sided platforms are also present in more traditional sectors. Shopping malls, for example, are two-sided platforms connecting shoppers and retailers. A crucial feature of two-sided networks is the impossibility of identifying the cost and revenues side of business. A steel plant buys iron ore and sells steel to customers. A web search engine does not have a simple value chain; both searchers and advertisers are its customers. Analysing exchanges as two-sided networks is thus consistent with the recognition that they are being transformed from monopolistic public utilities to competitive financial companies with strong features of IT and media sectors.

The application of the concept of two-sided networks and platforms to stock exchanges is new. Eisenmann et al. (2009) actually give stock trading as an example of one-sided networks, as they see stock traders selling and buying, thus playing double roles in the market. Evans and Schmalensee (2007), however, classify financial exchanges as two-sided platforms. Here I obviously side with the Evans and Schmalensee. My analysis of MTFs as two-sided platforms is inspired by the brilliant account of strategies for two-sided platforms in the *Harvard Business Review* by Eisenmann et al. (2006). To the best of my knowledge, this is the first study that describes secondary stock markets as two-sided networks, and MTFs as two-sided platforms.

The basic logic of an exchange as a two-sided platform is that the more liquidity makers there are using a platform, the more attractive the platform is to liquidity takers and vice versa. In addition there are positive same-side effects. Liquidity makers benefit from the presence of other liquidity makers, and liquidity takers from the presence of other liquidity takers. The business of the platform provider is to offer the technology (with order matching engine in the centre) and rules (types of orders, rules for matching them, transparency). The distinction between the two-sides of the network is critical to pricing strategy. Here, the key to success is the decision on which side to subsidize and which to charge. Adobe Acrobat, for example, charges document producers (people who want to convert their documents into pdf have to buy Adobe Acrobat writer software), while document readers can download and use Adobe Acrobat reader software free of charge. Without the subsidy and revenue side defined in this way, the product would not work. The side that should be subsidized is one that is more sensitive to price and quality. In the exchange business, these are the liquidity makers rather than takers. Simplifying, ultimate investors have to invest their cash somewhere. Liquidity makers, mostly high frequency (HF) traders, make money on trading itself, and the speed and reliability of trading procedures affects the core of their business. As a reflection of this logic MTFs, while charging traders for connecting to the platform, actually pay money (give rebates) to liquidity providers and charge liquidity takers, retaining the difference. They recognize liquidity makers as those who post orders in the order book and takers as those who use existing orders. Chi-X, a leading European MTF, for example, uses the maker–taker fee structure, charging takers 0.3 bp and giving rebates of 0.2 bp to makers. Effectively, rebates to liquidity makers allow them to post sell and buy order with narrower spreads, improving the prices obtained by liquidity takers, and increasing the volume of transactions.

Next to pricing, the second major strategic issue for two-sided platforms is winner-take-all dynamics. Can the whole market eventually be served by a single platform? In secondary stock markets economies of scale related to positive network externalities are immense. There are no capacity constraints either. Technology is available for a single platform to serve the total volume of stock trading for the whole of Europe. There are, however, two major reasons why European (or the United States) market is unlikely to be served by a single platform. Liquidity demanded by traders and investors comes in different forms and shapes, which in turn stimulates demand for special features that may be difficult to satisfy by a single platform. The basic characteristics of a stock trade include stock price, cost of transaction (including clearing and settlement), speed, and discretion/transparency. Discretion is particularly important for large traders and investors who do not want their order to be seen by others. Such orders are often executed in dark pools of liquidity, where order book is invisible to traders. Firms running algorithmic trading care about speed, while retail traders and investors care most about the best available stock price and the cost of transaction. The second factor is the level of government intervention, which in the exchange industry probably surpasses anything seen in the IT or media sectors, where two-sided platforms are common. The objective of regulation in both the United States and EU is to enhance competition for trading and exchange services. Concentration of trading on one platform or a set of platforms controlled by one company would be an anathema to regulators. In addition, best execution means that brokers channelling orders on behalf of their customers cannot simply connect to one platform (which they may have an incentive to do if they co-own the platform), sit back and watch other platforms lose business. They are obliged to ensure that they send orders to the platform offering best execution. Best execution may mean different things to different customers, and the right venue for it may change every day. As a consequence, it is difficult for platform providers to secure exclusive participation of big 'marquee' users in their platform.

How does the embrace of the logic of two-sided platforms by MTFs affect incumbent exchanges? In general, incumbent exchanges in Europe have over the last decade chosen the path of business diversification, covering issuer services, post-trade services, data and IT services, in addition to trading. Listing fees, representing the bulk of issuer services, have been a secure source of revenue, as European issuers rarely list their shares outside their home country. Thus, competition for listings is limited to listing of non-EU companies. However, as the activity on primary stock markets in the last decade has been low, listing revenues have stagnated, and their share in total revenues of stock exchanges has fallen from 18 per cent in 1998 to 6 per cent in 2008 (based on aggregate figures for all members of the World Federation of Exchanges). Some stock exchanges have extended their post-trade services to include clearing and settlement (e.g. the Deutsche Börse Group owning Clearstream). Trading services have been extended as well with mergers of stock exchanges with derivatives exchanges (e.g. LIFFE is a part of the NYSE-Euronext Group, and Eurex a part of the Deutsche Börse Group). In addition, some stock exchanges have opened their own MTFs, developed their IT operations specializing in trading technology (e.g. NASDAQ-OMX Group) or purchased firms with expertise in his field (e.g. the recent acquisition of Millenium IT by the LSE Group).

In addition to vertical integration, stock exchanges have pursued a strategy of horizontal integration via cross-border mergers and acquisitions (M&A), leading to the creation of widely-held and self-listed international exchange groups, discussed in more detail in the following section. Hardly a month goes by without an M&A event in the exchange industry. With all the restructuring, and generally positive conditions in international financial markets, the early and mid-2000s has been a period of financial success for stock exchanges, with revenues and profits having multiplied. The Dow Jones Global Exchanges Index rose from a hundred at the start of 2000 to 1200 at the end of 2007. Revenues per employee in the exchange industry have been spectacular, much higher than for banks or insurance companies (Capaldo et al. 2008).

Notwithstanding the expansion and financial success of incumbent exchanges, the pure liquidity-focused two-sided platform model of MTFs poses a major new threat to them. MTFs are small and flexible organizations, which are both more IT-driven and closer to liquidity makers and takers than incumbent stock exchanges. The former is reflected in incomparably higher speed of trading MTFs offer and the role of IT expertise in the biographies of their executives. The latter is underpinned by the fact that they are closely held by major liquidity takers and makers themselves. The ultimate arbiter of competition between incumbent exchanges and MTFs will be the battle for liquidity. Stock exchange groups, however diversified, will struggle if their share in trading falls substantially. When an exchange loses the majority of trading volume in a stock, the issuer may consider whether it is still the right primary market for it. Falling shares in trading would also put pressure on the exchange's ability to charge for trading data – MTFs give it away for free. Thus, in 2010, it is possible to see the threat of the incumbent stock exchange model to crumble, as in a domino effect, where falling trading takes down with it other parts of the business. An option for incumbent exchanges may be to introduce the maker–taker fee model to their own trading activities. One problem with it is that as a result some large customers would have to pay more and could migrate to MTFs. Another problem is that it would make the prices of exchanges directly comparable to those of MTFs, leading to the ultimate challenge of whether the incumbents can beat MTFs at their own game, offering quicker and cheaper trading. Incumbent exchanges are unlikely to get rid of competition by taking over MTFs, as this would raise opposition from regulators as well as investment bank and traders. These strategies in the parlance of two-sided networks are called platform envelopment, whereby a big multi-platform provider takes over other successful platforms. Platform envelopment is unlikely to succeed in the exchange industry. MTFs are here to stay and threaten the model of the incumbents.

The battle for liquidity

Having explained the factors operating in the environment of stock exchanges, and generic changes they have undergone internally, the stage is set to introduce the major actors by name. Thus, this section presents the battle for liquidity in stock trading in the last decade in Europe, with references to the situation in the United States. This will also give us an opportunity to provide examples of strategies pursued by both incumbent exchanges and MTFs. In the first part of the section, our attention will concentrate on the interpretation of data on the value of trading executed in the electronic order books of European stock trading venues, as presented in Table 7.1.

To start with, let us introduce the trading venues that resulted from recent M&As of exchanges. BIT merged with the LSE in 2007, giving rise to the LSE Group. Trading migrated from Italy to the LSE trading platform in 2009. The Central and Eastern European Stock Exchange Group (CEESEG) is a holding company launched officially in 2009 with stock exchanges in Budapest, Ljubljana, Prague, and Vienna as subsidiaries, with the management of the Vienna Stock Exchange at the steer. The latter is the controlling owner of stock exchanges in Ljubljana and Prague, and together with a consortium of Austrian banks controls the Budapest Stock Exchange. The NASDAQ-OMX Nordic and Baltic includes stock exchanges in Stockholm, Copenhagen, Helsinki, Iceland, Vilnius, Riga, and Tallinn, and is part of the NASDAQ-OMX Group,

Table 7.1. The percentage shares of exchanges in European trading value

	2000	2005	2006	2007	2008	2009	I–VI 2010
Athens Exchange	1.6	0.6	0.7	0.6	0.5	0.6	0.4
BME (Spanish Exchanges)	7.2	11.9	11.0	11.2	9.8	11.2	9.9
Borsa Italiana	15.2	13.4	11.0	10.6	8.1	8.4	n/a
CEESEG	n/a	n/a	n/a	n/a	n/a	n/a	0.8
Deutsche Börse	15.2	15.8	15.3	16.5	17.3	13.5	13.1
London SE	13.8	21.6	21.2	21.1	20.5	15.8	21.8
Copenhagen SE	0.5	n/a	n/a	n/a	n/a	n/a	n/a
Helsinki SE	2.4	n/a	n/a	n/a	n/a	n/a	n/a
Stockholm SE	6.2	n/a	n/a	n/a	n/a	n/a	n/a
NASDAQ-OMX (Nordic and Baltic)	n/a	7.6	7.4	7.0	6.4	6.2	5.7
NYSE Euronext	27.8	25.0	22.8	22.2	20.5	17.2	15.9
Oslo Børs	0.7	2.0	2.4	2.2	2.2	2.0	2.0
SIX Swiss Exchange	8.7	0.7	6.6	6.8	7.5	6.6	6.0
Warsaw SE	0.2	0.3	0.4	0.4	0.4	0.5	0.5
Other incumbent exchanges	0.6	1.0	1.3	1.3	1.2	1.0	0.1
Total incumbent exchanges	100.0	100.0	100.0	100.0	94.3	83.1	76.2
BATS Europe	n/a	n/a	n/a	n/a	0.0	2.3	4.6
Burgundy	n/a	n/a	n/a	n/a	n/a	0.1	0.2
Chi-X	n/a	n/a	n/a	n/a	5.2	10.7	15.6
NASDAQ-OMX (Europe)	n/a	n/a	n/a	n/a	0.0	0.5	0.5
NYSE Arca Europe	n/a	n/a	n/a	n/a	n/a	0.0	0.2
Turquoise	n/a	n/a	n/a	n/a	0.5	3.3	2.7
Total MTFs	n/a	n/a	n/a	n/a	5.7	16.9	23.8

Source: Author, based on data from the Federation of European Stock Exchanges.

the product of the merger of OMX with the US-based NASDAQ in 2008. OMX dates back to the early 2000s and itself was preceded by the Norex Alliance that started in the 1990s. Joint trading platform was introduced by OMX in 2004. The NYSE-Euronext is the product of the merger of Euronext with the NYSE in 2007. Euronext started with a merger of stock exchanges in Paris, Amsterdam, and Brussels in 2000, with Lisbon joining in 2002.

Before analysing trading values, let us consider briefly the pattern of the current stock exchange groupings. First, there is a regional element. This is obvious for the CEESEG. Here the strong position of Austrian banks in the financial markets of the Czech Republic, Hungary, and Slovenia was instrumental in the creation of the group. Neither the Bratislava Stock Exchange nor the Warsaw Stock Exchange, however, has joined. Regional logic obviously also underpins the development of the NASDAQ-OMX Nordic and Baltic, again with an important exception of Norway, which enjoys a vibrant corporate sector and community of domestic investors.

Compatibility of traditions, strategic objectives and expertise matters as well, as indicated by the shape of European and transatlantic mergers. The NASDAQ-OMX Group is a marriage of markets specializing in relatively small firms and dynamic sectors, including IT and biotechnology. Nordic countries are prominent in these industries. Euronext markets of France, Netherlands, Belgium, and Portugal are all in relatively centralized financial systems, with little significance of regional stock exchanges or regional banks (Verdier 2002). This may be one of the factors that facilitated the creation of Euronext as the very first successful international merger in the industry. Second, the economies of these countries are dominated by large companies, with telecommunications and utilities sectors in the lead (including energy and water companies, often formerly state owned), which makes their markets quite compatible with the focus of the NYSE. To be sure, simple generalizations must be avoided, as there is a lot of contingency in the history of M&As in the stock exchange industry. When the NOREX alliance was formed in 1998–9, Oslo Børs had just implemented a new trading system while Copenhagen urgently needed a new one. This was clearly an important reason for Copenhagen to join the Alliance, and for Oslo to stay out. NASDAQ attempted to buy the LSE in 2006, Deutsche Börse tried to merge with it a couple of times. Personalities and particular circumstances can matter as much as structural economic and business issues.

Moving to the analysis of trading values, we will focus on the share of each exchange in the total European trading value. To be sure, the total trading value fluctuated widely in the considered period (Figure 7.1). It stagnated between 2000 and 2004, grew by 140 per cent between 2004 and 2007, and fell subsequently by 15 per cent in 2008 and by nearly 40 per cent in 2009. The first half of 2010 promised a recovery to the levels of trading from 2006. Another caveat is that the share of an exchange in the total European trading value cannot be interpreted strictly as a market share, since until 2008 trading was limited almost entirely to domestic companies (or companies domestic to one of the countries of an exchange group). In 2007, trading of non-domestic firms accounted only for 3 per cent of the total European trading value. In other words, until 2008 the shares of exchanges in the European trading value express the relative size of their trading rather than market shares as such.

Euronext, the pioneer of stock exchange consolidation, entered the twenty-first century as by far the largest stock exchange in Europe, with BIT, Deutsche Börse (DB) and the LSE in the second, and the Spanish Exchanges (Bolsas y Mercados Españoles – BME), Stockholm and Swiss exchanges in the third league. Between 2000 and 2007, the growth of trading on Euronext lagged behind the DB, and particularly the LSE. BIT grew at a slower pace as well. As a result, at the peak of the trading boom in 2007, DB and the LSE closed the gap to Euronext. BME become the fourth largest market. Figure for the SIX Swiss

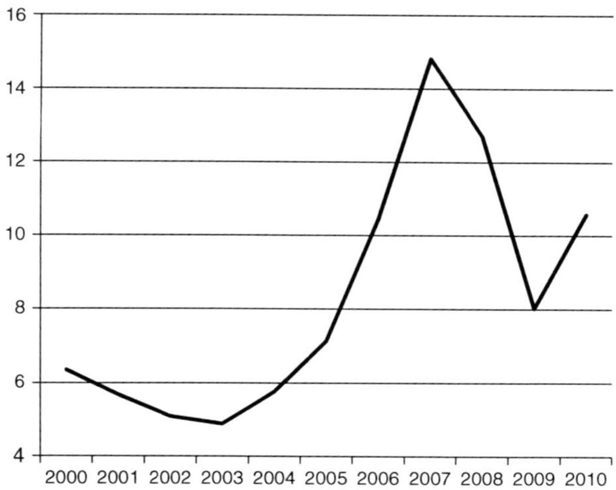

Figure 7.1. The value of stock trading on European exchanges (in trillion €)
Note: The figure for 2010 is based on data for the first half of the year multiplied by 2.
Source: Author, based on data from the Federation of European Stock Exchanges.

Exchange (SIX) in 2005 is very low due to the migration of trading in blue chip stocks to Virt-X, a London-based subsidiary of the SIX, not included in the FESE data.

In 2008, the stage entered MTFs. Chi-X launched trading in March 2007, before MiFID came into force, as part of Instinet (headquartered in the United States and owned by the Japanese investment bank Nomura). BATS Europe, a subsidiary of BATS Global Markets (incorporated and headquartered in the United States), launched in 2008. Turquoise launched in 2007 by a consortium of investment banks (Citigroup, Credit Suisse, Deutsche Bank, Goldman Sachs, Merrill Lynch, Morgan Stanley, UBS, with BNP Paribas and Société Générale joining later). In February 2008, it was taken over by the LSE Group. Burgundy launched in June 2009, set up by investment banks and firms from the Nordic countries. NYSE Euronext and NASDAQ-OMX launched their own MTFs – NYSE Arca Europe and NASDAQ-OMX Europe (known as NEURO), respectively. In July 2010, the trading from NEURO was migrating to Equiduct Systems, a London-based MTF, hitherto without significant trading activity.

Chi-X launched very successfully, becoming the eighth largest European exchange in the first year of operation. By 2010, it tripled its share in trading, becoming Europe's third largest exchange. BATS Europe captured approximately 4 per cent of trading value, becoming number eight in 2010, while Turquoise claimed the ninth spot. Together by June 2010, they controlled a quarter of European trading value, which is all the more remarkable given the general slump in stock market activity. Comparing the changes in trading values in the last three years, it is obvious that MTFs attracted trading from the LSE, Euronext, and to a lesser extent the DB.

It is only with the entrance of the MTFs that we can talk about real competition for market shares, as MTFs trade stocks traded on incumbent exchanges. All MTFs focus on the largest and most liquid stocks. In June 2010, Chi-X traded approximately 1000 stocks from fifteen countries (the United Kingdom, Ireland, France, Germany, the Netherlands, Belgium, Switzerland, Austria, Italy, Spain, Portugal, Norway, Sweden, Finland, and Denmark), covering top stock market indices from each of these countries plus mid-cap indices for the largest markets. BATS Europe traded a similar number of stocks from exactly the same markets. Turquoise traded approximately 1800 stocks from seventeen countries (the same as Chi-X and BATS plus Hungary and the Czech Republic). The coverage is similar for NYSE Arca and NEURO. Burgundy in contrast, only trades stocks listed in Stockholm, Helsinki, Copenhagen, and Oslo. In short, in 2010, any of the top 1000 European stocks could probably be traded on six venues: the home exchange (also referred to as the primary market), Chi-X, BATS Europe, Turquoise, NEURO, and NYSE Arca Europe.

Figure 7.2 presents the real market shares, defined as the share of different venues in the trading value of stocks according to their primary market (where they are listed; in almost all cases this is also the country where the issuer is headquartered). The figure shows the average share of each venue in the last five trading days of June 2010. Primary/home markets dominate, but the share of the three top MTFs is significant. The large share of category 'other markets' for Dublin, results from the fact that Irish stocks are traded mostly on the LSE; for Oslo there is a significant share of trading on NASDAQ-OMX. Chi-X is ahead of BATS Europe in every single market.

The market share of MTFs differs greatly from one home market to another. Reasons for this variation can be traced to the familiar categories of demand, technology, and regulation. The main customers of MTFs are institutional traders and investors, interested mainly in trading large cap, liquid stocks. These stocks are more prevalent in the United Kigdom, the Netherlands, France, and Switzerland than in Austria, Norway, Denmark, or Italy. Finland is the home to the largest Nordic company – Nokia – which boosts the share of MTFs in the Finnish market. In terms of technology, trading on MTFs requires infrastructure that connects traders, investors, and their intermediaries to MTFs. This infrastructure, including Smart Order Routing (SOR), which automatically searches for the best trading venue for a given order and sends the order to this venue, is not yet available widely or evenly across Europe. Brokers and dealers are still to a large extent wired to incumbent exchanges. Although no data is available, based on interviews I would speculate that the availability of infrastructure, including SOR, is particularly good in London, Amsterdam,

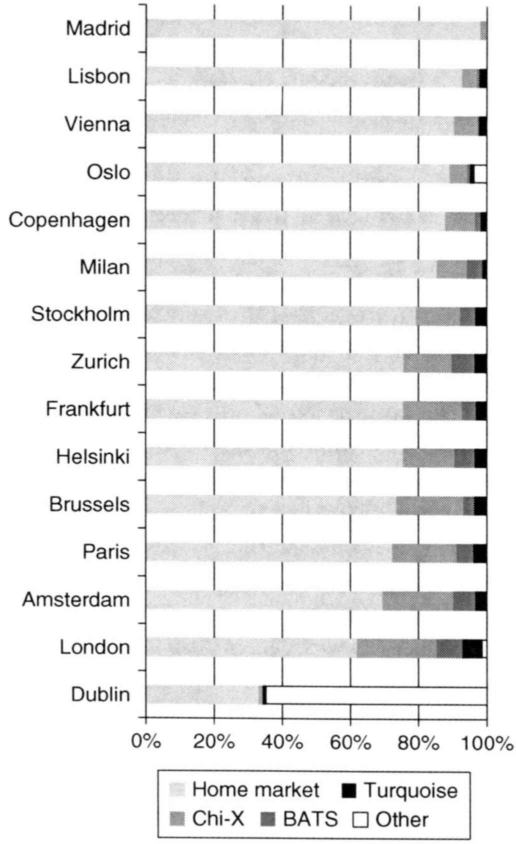

Figure 7.2. The share of exchanges in the trading value of stocks according to the home market of the issuer

Source: Author, based on data from BATS Europe for the last five days of June 2010.

and Paris. Finally, with regard to regulation MiFID is *de facto* not yet fully implemented. In Spain, for example, because of complex clearing and settlement requirements, it is still difficult for traders to bypass BME when trading Spanish stocks.

As we saw in the preceding section, positive network externalities in the secondary stock markets shape the strategy of MTFs. The challenge for any new MTF is to gain a sizeable trading volume as quickly as possible, which will then attract more liquidity. For that reason the strategy is not to start with small stocks and small customers, learn, and then move on to large stocks and large customers. Rather they start with the largest stocks in the largest markets (the United Kingdom is number one in Europe in that respect). This strategy is related to the ownership structure of MTFs. Large traders are the main owners of MTFs and they can redirect their orders from incumbent exchanges to MTFs. MTFs can also reward their most active traders with ownership stakes to further induce them to move trading. Hengelbrock and Theissen (2009), for example, documented a positive correlation between the share of investment banks from the Turquoise consortium in the ownership of a company, and the share of trading in this company's stocks conducted on the Turquoise platform.

The competitive landscape in European stock trading in June 2010 can thus be summarized as follows. The fastest growing part is made of two large MTFs independent from incumbent exchanges. There are three major international stock exchange groups: the LSE Group, NYSE-Euronext, and NASDAQ-OMX and three large stock exchange groups with a lesser international presence: the DB, SIX, and BME. The lower tier is made of a small regional stock exchange group CEESEG, Oslo Børs, a handful of independent exchanges in Central and Eastern Europe, and Burgundy – testing a unique strategy of developing a regional MTF. By comparison, in the United States there are four stock exchanges: NYSE, NASDAQ, BATS, and Direct Edge, out of which the first three and largest are already present in Europe. To be sure, the data for trading analysed in this section is not complete. It does not include systemic internalizers, dark pools and OTC trades among investment banks and other traders. The estimates of FESE for 2010 imply that approx. 40 per cent of trading in Europe is not included in the data used in this chapter. Unfortunately details on these trading activities are unavailable. This large hole in available data, however, does not undermine the arguments of this chapter. It just underscores the level of competition in the industry and the role of investment banks and other trading firms.

The battle for liquidity in Europe is intensifying, but arguably it is still in its infancy. While the fact that one can trade almost any of the large European stocks on as many as six different venues raises concerns about excessive fragmentation; in practice, only two MTFs have significant market shares. These two, Chi-X and BATS-Europe, has thus far succeeded in the face of the adversity of general market conditions, stirring a revolution in European trading, and becoming probably too large to be swallowed by competitors. If the current trends continue, before the end of 2010, Chi-X may become the second largest European exchange, and the total market share of MTFs in trading value may exceed 30 per cent.

A very geographical revolution

What is the geographical dimension of the recent transformation in the business model of stock exchanges? Where do MTFS – the new stars of the trading industry – operate from? How does the competitive landscape of the European stock trading industry relate to the geography of European financial centres? This section will address these questions and argue that the revolution we have witnessed in the stock exchange industry is a very geographical revolution. This is not because everyone, even a stock exchange or a stock trader, has to be somewhere, but because location really matters in the modern trading industry. It is an integral part of business strategy, affecting competition and its outcomes.

Let us first go back to Table 7.1. It is relatively simple to assign incumbent stock exchanges to places, as their names usually indicate headquarter locations. To complete the picture, BME is headquartered in Madrid, BIT in Milan (now a part of the LSE Group headquartered in London), DB in Frankfurt am Main, NASDAQ-OMX Nordic in Stockholm, with the European headquarters of NYSE Euronext in Paris. The global headquarters of NYSE Euronext and NASDAQ-OMX are in New York City. MTFs require more explanation, as their names do not contain names of cities or countries, though they often contain the word Europe. This is not surprising, given that typically they have a pan-European strategy. It would not serve their marketing well to be associated with a particular national market. Notwithstanding the somewhat anonymous and pan-European labels, the geographical reality of MTFs is quite simple. Out of six MTFs with significant trading, the largest four are headquartered in London (and actually in the square mile of the City of London!). NYSE Arca Europe (a part of NYSE Euronext) and Burgundy are headquartered in Paris and Stockholm, respectively. In other words, London headquartered exchanges in 2010 controlled 44 per cent of European stock trading activity.

Apart from headquarters we need to consider the location of matching engines on which trades are executed. The matching engines of the LSE Group, Chi-X, BATS, Turquoise, and NEURO, are all located in London or its vicinity, with the European trading of NYSE Euronext in the process of moving to a data centre in Basildon in 2010. This implies no less than 66 per cent of European stock trading value executed on matching engines within 30 miles from the centre of London. If we consider that the bulk of systemic internalization and OTC trading executed by investment banks also happens in London, the percentage of trading concentrated in London could be even higher than 66 per cent. This is a level of dominance comparable to that in foreign exchange trading, where London also accounts for approximately two-thirds of the European total (Bank for International Settlements 2010). What are the reasons for such a high level of concentration of stock trading in London? Why MTFs in particular locate their decision-making and hardware in London, thus contributing to its dominance?

The foremost factor affecting the geographical concentration of the stock trading industry is the value of proximity, which takes two principal forms:

proximity between exchange professionals and marquee customers, and that between the matching engines of exchanges and computers generating orders used by marquee customers. On the side of liquidity takers, the marquee customers of exchanges are institutional investors and investment banks. As a dominant headquarter location for the British financial institutions as well as the leading location for European institutions with international operations and American institutions with European operations, London is the decision-making centre for the largest pool of money in Europe. On the liquidity making side, marquee customers are HF traders, operating as departments of investment banks or as independent specialized firms. The latter are mostly US-based firms (such as Getco, Tradebot, and Infinium), for whom trading in London affords a familiar legal environment, as well as offers the neighbourhood of other US financial firms and a great pool of specialized labour for their offices. It should be added here that MTF employees and executives are mostly former traders and IT professionals. Thus, proximity between people facilitates interactions that help marketing, product development, and market surveillance of exchanges, and benefit them indirectly via access to a specialized labour pool.

Proximity between computers is important because of latency – the speed with which an order can reach the matching engine of the exchange, be executed, and the confirmation of its execution return to the computer from which it was sent. Latency is particularly important to HF traders, who use computer algorithms that constantly compare prices of tradable instruments, identify anomalies in relation to past statistical relationships between prices, and generate orders bidding for securities deemed underpriced and offering those deemed overpriced. For these orders to succeed every microsecond counts. It is estimated that algorithmic trading accounts for approx. 60 per cent of stock trading in the United States, and 30–40 per cent in the United Kingdom. Chi-X, for example, is currently upgrading its system to handle 1 million messages per second. The Forbes magazine estimated that in 2008 HF traders in the United States made $21bn in gross profits (Moyer and Lambert 2009).

The role of speed has led both MTFs and incumbent exchanges to offer co-location services, whereby trading firms can co-locate their computers with the matching engine of the exchange. Co-location takes place in data centres (big buildings full of compartments and racks filled with servers connected by ultra-high speed cables) usually run by independent data centre companies, from which exchanges lease space (matching engines themselves can be leased as well). There are different degrees of co-location. A computer can be in the same room as the matching engine, in the same building or in a separate data centre run by the same company as the data centre hosting the matching engine. Distance is critical, as the race for speed approaches its natural limit – the speed of light. Leading MTFs offer a round-trip time for an order of less than 250 microseconds. If the matching engine is in Stockholm, as is the case for Burgundy, the trip of light from and back to London takes approximately ten milliseconds. Hence London-based traders who do not want to be at a disadvantage to Stockholm-based ones need to co-locate their computers in Stockholm. When, after the merger with BIT, the LSE moved trading in Italian stocks to the matching engine in London, traders based in Italy suddenly lost advantage over those in London. Even if a customer does not use co-location services, proximity to the matching engine still helps the quick execution of trades. There are obviously advantages in putting matching engines close to each other. Customers can then cheaply connect with different exchanges, and exchanges have the option of re-routing orders they cannot fulfil themselves to other exchanges, thus attracting additional order flow.

The value of proximity between people and computers combined creates a virtuous circle of network externalities; whereby customers attract matching engines, matching engines attract more customers and more matching engines. This virtuous circle has clearly taken root in London. The main locations for data centres housing matching engines include Central London, Park Royal, Docklands, Slough, and Basildon. London is by far the leading data centre location in Europe (serving all types of industries and firms beyond exchanges, see SAMI 2009), but the supply of data centres has to be seen as a beneficiary, not the driver of the concentration of exchange industry in London. Frankfurt, Amsterdam, and Paris offer high-quality data centres, and cheaper IT experts, but they have not succeeded in attracting new exchanges.

Regulation has also played a part in the concentration of trading industry in London. First of all, even before MiFID, the United Kingdom had no concentration rules, which allowed initiatives (led mostly by investment banks) to set up trading platforms trying to compete with the LSE. Chi-X and Turquoise may be the first successful movers, but were by no means the first that tried. Second, the UK authorities were among the fastest in Europe in implementing MiFID, conducting extensive consultation with industry. By contrast, in Germany, for example, regulators offered little feedback or advice to firms on how to prepare for MiFID, and Spain simply declared at the outset that it would not implement it on time (Casey and Lannoo 2009). By June 2010, there were 137 registered MTFs, out of which seventy-one were registered in the United Kingdom. Eventually, countries slow at implementation can do little to stop firms from other Member States from providing services within their territory, while their domestic firms are left incapable of doing the same (Lannoo 2007).

I do not have detailed data for the United States, but it is safe to say that geographical concentration of the exchange industry has also taken place across the Atlantic. The New York-headquartered NASDAQ took over exchanges in Boston and Philadelphia, while NYSE took over Archipelago (which earlier bought the Pacific Stock Exchange based in California). The only other full-status stock exchanges in the United States – BATS Exchange and Direct Edge – are headquartered in Kansas City and Jersey City, respectively. NYSE, NASDAQ, BATS Exchange, and Direct Edge all have matching engines in the area of Jersey City in New Jersey (just across the Hudson River from Manhattan). BATS Exchange in Kansas City is located close to Tradebot, one of its marquee customers.

While the logic of co-location and proximity to marquee customers applies to incumbent exchanges as well as to MTFs, the strategy of business diversification, horizontal and vertical, practiced by some of the leading incumbent exchanges, has a specific footprint – one of extensive spatial network of operations. NASDAQ-OMX is probably the best example, illustrated in Table 7.2. With global headquarters in New York City and European headquarters in Stockholm, NASDAQ has offices, exchanges, or subsidiaries in twenty- nine locations, excluding the location of matching engines and disaster preparation facilities (precise information on which is not publicly available). The geographical spread of its offices reflects the significance of proximity to its trading technology users (other exchanges including Singapore Exchange, Tokyo Commodity Exchange, and Australian Exchange), and issuers (Beijing and Silicon Valley). Subsidiaries reflect diversification into new issuer services and media. To be sure, while MTFs focus solely on trading, they have emerging international structures as well. BATS Europe is a subsidiary of BATS Holding which owns BATS Exchange in the United States. Nomura – the controlling owner Chi-X Europe is also a 100 per cent owner of Chi-X Global with a trading platform in Toronto, and Chi-X APAC with fledgling operations in Hong Kong, Tokyo, and Singapore.

In summary, stock trading has become a much more competitive, technology driven and efficient industry, but it has not become people-less or dissolved in virtual space. People, hardware, and physical infrastructure matter no less than ever before. With their sole focus on trading, MTFs employ staggeringly small numbers of people. With more than forty employees, Chi-X is the third largest exchange in Europe, with more than seventy employees BATS Exchange is the third largest in the United States. These figures are comparable to employment at the Malta and Cyprus stock exchanges, respectively, while Deutsche Börse, for example, has approximately 3000 employees, and NASDAQ-OMX Nordic employs nearly 1000. With their scope of activities much broader than that of MTFs, incumbent exchanges remain large financial institutions. In the United States between 1998 and 2006, employment in the exchange industry as a whole increased from approximately 7000 to 9000. The significance of the exchange industry, however, cannot be captured with employment figures. Exchanges play a

Table 7.2. The geographical network of NASDAQ-OMX

	Americas	Europe and Middle East	Asia Pacific
HQs and Exchanges	New York	Stockholm	
Exchanges	Boston, MA	Copenhagen	
	Philadelphia, PA	Helsinki	
		Oslo	
		Riga	
		Tallinn	
		Vilnius	
		Reykjavik	
		Yerevan	
		Dubai	
Offices	Menlo Park, CA	London	Beijing
	Chicago, IL	Milan	Sydney
	Rockville, MD		Hong Kong
	Washington, DC		Tokyo
	Eugene, OR		Singapore
	Calgary (Canada)		
Subsidiaries	Maynard, MA		
	Spokane, WA		
	Los Angeles, CA		

Note: Does not include the locations of matching engines and disaster preparedness facilities in the United States.
Source: Author's compilation based on www.nasdaqomx.com

central part in the creation of a network connecting traders and investors. The geography of the exchange industry implies that this network has nodes in large financial centres.

Conclusions and implications

The objective of this chapter was to investigate competition in the stock exchange industry and its relationship with the development of financial centres. It is an irony that while trading corporate ownership rights in a way epitomizes capitalism, the institutional architecture of the stock exchange industry in Europe until recently – made of national monopolies operating like public utilities – could hardly be further from a model of free competitive markets. Over the last quarter century, but particularly in the last decade, the stock exchange industry has undergone a transformation at an accelerating rate. The chapter has tried to document and interpret this transformation starting from a synthesis of changes in the environment of exchanges, explaining a revolution in their business model, analysing the battle for liquidity, and finishing by discussing its footprint in terms of location of exchange activities.

I have argued that changes in demand, technology, and regulation transformed the exchanges, triggering the development of a networked structure of the exchange industry and unleashing economies of scale. These changes have brought to life new exchanges, which have focused solely on the production of liquidity, and have embraced the business model of two-sided platforms, while incumbent exchanges have pursued horizontal and vertical integration. While the expansion and financial success of the incumbent exchanges is a fact, new exchanges, gaining market shares at a spectacular rate, threaten the core business of the incumbents. The revolution in the exchange industry in Europe has fortified the position of London as the dominant European financial centre. New exchanges, the paragons of the revolution, operate out of the Square Mile of the City of London, and two-thirds of the value of European stock trades are executed on the matching engines located no further than 30 miles from the City. London is the central node of the European stock exchange network just as New York City has maintained an equivalent role in the United States. Exchange professionals and major liquidity makers and takers benefit from mutual interactions, while the matching engines of exchanges are attracted to the computers of major traders and vice versa.

The revolution in the exchange industry came from the United States, took hold of Europe but is yet to reach other parts of the world. Internationally, the revolution seems to reinforce the New York City – London axis of global financial centres. The European headquarters of NYSE Euronext are in Paris, and NASDAQ-OMX has promised to support Stockholm as a financial centre, but the European matching engines and major customers of both institutions are in London. There are first signs of consolidation of stock exchanges in Africa, where stock exchange in Johannesburg has ambitions to develop a pan-African stock exchange, and Asia, where NYSE Euronext is developing software to link exchanges and brokers in all ASEAN countries (with a pilot to link Kuala Lumpur and Bangkok in 2011). NASDAQ-OMX has ownership links with the stock exchange in Dubai; NYSE Euronext has links in Doha. New Exchanges such as Chi-X and BATS also have emerging intercontinental structures.

In the ongoing saga of M&As and the battle for liquidity, it is difficult to predict winners and losers in terms of particular stock exchange groups. In terms of their footprint, however, the trend seems less ambiguous. Even if the stock exchange revolution harms the LSE and the NYSE as its icons, it benefits New York City and London as financial centres. Notably, no offshore stock exchange centres have succeeded either in Europe or in North America, although some have tried (Young and Theys 1999). This is in contrast to the successes of offshore centres in some other parts of the financial sector, such as banking or fund management. To use a metaphor, the stock exchange industry is not divorcing financial centres, although in the process of integration it is concentrating on fewer spouses. It is not the first time we can witness a decline of stock exchange industry centres. Rio de Janeiro, Geneva, and Otago hosted the first stock exchange in Brazil, Switzerland, and New Zealand, respectively, but no longer have any.

Apart from financial centres, who are the major winners and losers of the stock exchange revolution? The winners are investment banks and firms that can capture a share of the booming trading activity stimulated by the revolution. Hopefully the winners are also investors for whom building and rebuilding their portfolios should become cheaper. The winners could also be issuers, benefiting from better access to stock markets and lower cost of capital. The benefits of the stock exchange revolution may however be uncertain for small- and medium-sized companies (SMEs). Nielsson (2009), for example, shows that following the Euronext merger in the early 2000s, liquidity increased only for big capitalization stocks. The merger seemed to have no impact on the liquidity of SMEs or the number of new listings. Witness that with the exception of Burgundy, no MTFs trade small capitalization stocks. Perhaps the two-sided platform model, so successful with large capitalization stocks, does not work for small caps? Or perhaps a subsidy is in order to develop a pan-European MTF for SMEs?

To be sure, with the revolution in the stock exchange industry in Europe still in its infancy, research thereon can hardly be conclusive. One of the interesting directions for future studies would be to analyse the impact of stock exchange M&As on financial centres through a series of case studies, for example, comparing Paris with Brussels and Amsterdam or Stockholm with Helsinki and Copenhagen. How do their financial sectors adapt to the loss of certain stock exchange institutions and functions? How does it affect traders, investors, and issuers in those centres? Engelen and Grote (2009) made the first foray in this direction, indicating the slow decline of Amsterdam and Frankfurt as second-tier financial centres as a result of trading moving to London. Another pertinent question concerns the limits of international integration in the stock exchange industry. Given that algorithms do not distinguish between day and night, could there be one global trading platform for the world's largest stocks?

8

The Map of the Global Stock Market Redrawn: Stock Market Centres and their Future

The objective of this book has been to explore and explain the spatial organization of stock markets, by studying the significance of geography for the behaviour of different players constituting stock markets and relationships among those players, focusing in turn on issuers, investors, and intermediaries. Geography has been understood broadly as the significance of place and space, taking diverse forms including the role of proximity, agglomeration economies, flows of information in space, and institutional characteristics of places. The geographical approach has also manifested itself in attention to scale at which stock market processes operate, from global, through supranational and national, to regional, urban, and intra-urban. We have presented statistical evidence and case studies, documenting the footprint of stock market development, but also the recent trends affecting it, including the boom in emerging markets, the impact of the financial crisis 2007–9, high-frequency trading, and the regulatory revolution in Europe.

This chapter presents a synthesis of some of the key findings of the book, by proposing a theory of stock market centres, understood as concentrations of stock market intermediaries, investors, and issuers' headquarters, connected and operating through a global network. This theory, stressing the mutual constitution of stock markets and cities, is built on the existing theory of global cities. We start by proposing the theory supported with evidence already presented on the preceding pages of the book. To support and illustrate the theory further, the theoretical section is followed with new empirical evidence on the size and evolution of stock market centres in the six largest economies of the world: the United States, China, Japan, Germany, France, and the United Kingdom. In this way, the book will complete the journey from the map of stock markets focused on countries (as presented in Chapter 1) to a more complex, but also more true map on which cities play a key part. The chapter finishes with a discussion and speculations about the implications of the theory of stock market centres, as well as other theoretical and empirical findings of the book, for the future of financial markets, the corporate sector, and cities.

The theory of stock markets centres and their network

The starting point for the theory of stock market centres are the ideas of Saskia Sassen, referred to as the global city theory, first published in her book 'The Global City: New York, London, Tokyo' in 1991, and later refined in the new edition of 2001. The theory consists of a sequence of seven hypotheses, out of which we will focus on the first five, leaving aside the issues of social and economic polarization within global cities. The first hypothesis is that globalization makes central/coordinating functions of firms grow in significance. With more and more firms operating internationally, or at least increasingly affected by events and competitors from far-away places, it becomes ever more complicated for firms to make decisions on their supplies, production, distribution, and marketing. With diminishing geographical barriers to sourcing supplies, locating production, moving goods and services, and communication, making the right choice and revising it on a regular basis is vital for the survival of companies in a global marketplace. Second, as these central functions grow in complexity, having to incorporate huge amounts of information and decision-making variables, they are increasingly outsourced to specialized services firms, instead of being conducted in-house, at the corporate headquarters. This gives firms access to external expertise and flexibility in terms of costs and the choice of particular advisors. Specialized services encompass a wide range of firms including financial services, legal services, human resources, accountancy, tax advisory, information technology consultancy, management consultancy, marketing, and public relations agencies. These are also often referred to as advanced or knowledge intensive business services (Wood 2002).

With the third hypothesis, the theory moves to the spatial organization of the specialized services providers. It is claimed that they benefit from locating close to each other, forming agglomerations, thus giving rise to global cities. This helps them interact with each other and share a common labour pool and infrastructure. Consider, for example, a company intending to expand in a new country by taking over an existing firm operating in that market. Such a project would involve advice on financial, legal, marketing, technological, and managerial issues, and would require different types of advisors to act in a coordinated way. Fourth, as corporate headquarters outsource their coordinating functions, they become freer to follow other location factors, whether this is a source of inputs or employees specific to the needs of a particular company or simply an attractive environment away from large crowded cities. In other words, specialized service providers concentrate in global cities on behalf of corporations, reducing the necessity of the corporations themselves to follow suit. Finally, according to the fifth hypothesis, specialized service providers need to develop international presence, ideally maintaining global networks of offices. This helps them access knowledge local to different places, and at the same time build global expertise, crucial in their services to customers, the essence of which is to help companies navigate in the globalized world. International activity also helps specialized services providers attain economies of scale. With their global networks, they act as spanners connecting places, giving rise to a network of global cities.

Saskia Sassen's book and its new edition are one of the most cited works on the broad topic of globalization, and the concept of global city is influential in policy circles as well (Dicken 2004). Witness, for example, websites debating the prospects of Shanghai or Dubai as global cities. While Sassen's original work on global cities focuses on New York, London, and Tokyo, others, with the Global and World City research network in the lead, have considered a more general notion of 'global citiness', measuring the position of hundreds of cities in the corporate networks of leading specialized services providers (Taylor 2004). Yet others have investigated the role of specific types of specialized services in global cities (Faulconbridge 2008; Faulconbridge et al. 2008). Surely, the global city is a big theory that considers the processes of globalization, urbanization, and the growth of the services sector within one stream of reasoning. In the context of urban research, one of its contributions is to shift attention from cities as decision-making centres of manufacturing companies to cities as centres of financial and other advanced business services. An exclusive focus on business services providers, however, involves the risk of neglecting their relationships with customers, without which services companies would not exist in the first place. Consequently, by studying service providers only, we may gain knowledge about this particular economic sector and their impact on the life of cities, but not about globalization in general. Here we avoid falling into this trap, by applying and testing the logic of the global city theory on the stock market. As a market, by definition, stock market has sellers and buyers, customers and providers.

Let us formulate a sequence of propositions, equivalent to those of the global city theory, but using stock markets rather than globalization as a starting point. First, the emergence and development of stock markets involve an institutional and geographical dispersion of corporate ownership. As described in Chapter 1, the very essence of a stock market is the creation of more or less uniform ownership stakes and spreading them across a multitude of investors. As there are limits to how many investors can be found in any one place, spreading ownership across places becomes crucial. Stock market development is thus an essential ingredient of financial globalization. In other words, spatial expansion is in the DNA of stock markets.

One direct consequence of stock market development is growing demand for intermediaries connecting an increasing number of investors from an increasing number of places with each other (to make secondary markets work), and with issuers (in primary markets). Intermediaries to whom we can refer as the stock market industry satisfy this demand. This includes investment banks, playing a key part in linking issuers and investors on primary markets, and focusing on wholesale investors. Stock exchanges and brokerage companies, in turn, link investors to each other on secondary markets, and investors to secondary markets, respectively, focusing on retail investors. Linking investors and issuers is more than just helping them find each other, matching supply and demand. It also gives rise to an industry that addresses problems amplified by institutional and geographical dispersion. The first of these problems is information asymmetry, whereby the stock issuer knows better what they intend to use the money for than an investor does. The second problem is agency, whereby corporate managers can act in their own interest and against the interest of investors as owners of stocks. Investors, particularly if small and/or remote do not have their own means to assure themselves that particular stocks are worth owning and buying. They need assurance on the integrity of information on the issuers and the actions of corporate managers. This leads to demand for activities including: investment advice and portfolio management, corporate governance rating agencies and consultancies, audit and due diligence by accountancy firms, investor relations firms, equity analysis and research, and securities law. Thus we have arrived at proposition 2: stock market development feeds the growth of the stock market industry. We have seen examples of the prominence of this industry, with investment banks in the lead, throughout the book.

The third proposition is that stock market intermediaries benefit from co-location. On primary stock markets, we have shown that equity issuance involves a large number of intermediaries; at least one investment bank, a law firm, an accountancy firm, a brokerage company, and a stock exchange, which need to cooperate and thus can benefit from proximity (see Chapters 2 and 6). For secondary markets, we have shown that proximity between stock exchanges and other intermediaries matters not only in terms of human relations but also in terms of computers, with the trend to co-locate computers generating orders with the matching engine of the trading venue (Chapters 6 and 7). Benefits of co-location are also of indirect nature related to the access to a shared specialized labour market (Chapter 2) and infrastructure, including ultra-high speed computer connections (Chapter 7).

Translating the fourth proposition of the global city theory is more difficult. Can corporate headquarters, as the strategic and financial decision-making centres of companies, ignore the location of the stock market industry and vice versa? It can be argued that proximity not only between securities firms and corporate headquarters but also between them and major institutional investors, such as pension and mutual funds, continues to matter. In fact, institutional investors such as mutual and pension funds may be considered a part of the securities industry as they serve retail investors as their customers, and intermediate between them on one side and issuers, and the rest of the securities industry, for example, investment managers and consultants on the other (Clark 2000). Transactions on primary stock markets require frequent interactions, and trust between issuers and securities firms (Chapter 2). Firms from the centres of stock market industry are more likely to go public, even in countries with the most developed stock markets. Once they are public, firms from the centres of stock market industry are more likely to list on foreign stock markets (Chapter 3). On secondary markets, institutional investors have been shown to skew their investments towards the stocks of local issuers, and to time their trades in these stocks better than remote investors (Chapter 4). Proximity to corporate headquarters and decision-makers also helps investors discover the stock price for even the most globalized of companies (Chapter 5).

Apart from their direct interactions, stock market intermediaries and issuers' headquarters benefit from co-location by sharing a large and deep labour market offering stock market-oriented skills, including financial executives, non-executive directors, investor relations experts, as well as accountants skilled in financial reporting required from publicly listed firms (Burton et al. 2006). The argument here, supported with literature on financialization, is that corporate headquarters cannot fully outsource stock market-related functions. Stock market development involves the priority of shareholder value maximization in corporate activities, and sensitivity to how stock markets react to corporate decisions (Clark and Wójcik 2007). As such, stock market development transforms corporations themselves, and increases their internal demand for stock market-related and general financial expertise (Froud et al. 2006). As a result, there is no reason to expect that proximity between stock market intermediaries and corporate headquarters would diminish over time. Thus, the fourth proposition is that stock market industry centres would also constitute important centres of corporate headquarters, and that with time this relationship would not weaken. This point is a major challenge to the global city theory. Later in this chapter it will be supported with further empirical evidence.

The fifth proposition is that global presence and expertise are of utmost importance to stock market intermediaries. A global network may indeed be more important in stock market industry than in any other type of specialized services. Opportunities for raising capital for companies are global as are opportunities for investing money on the stock market. Chapter 3 has shown how intermediaries with global presence, with investment banks in the lead, connect issuers from emerging market economies to foreign investors and global capital markets. Chapter 4 has stressed how stock market intermediaries combine local and global knowledge, placing their analysts close to companies and economies concerned, while maintaining centralized research teams processing information and comparing prices across sectors and countries on a global scale. As demonstrated in Chapter 7, global investment banks have been major players revolutionizing the stock exchange industry, acting as sources of high-frequency trading, intermediaries of institutional investors and owners of new trading venues. The networked character of stock market intermediaries and stock market centres affects the circulation of information and the formation of stock prices. As concluded in Chapter 5, stock market centres constantly (albeit not without friction) pass information from each other. Price discovery is most efficient in the overlapping trading hours, when information from different sources and places is combined.

The networked nature of stock market industry reflects the fact that stock market is a network. As argued in Chapter 7, secondary stock markets are two-sided networks connecting liquidity providers with liquidity takers. Stock exchanges provide platforms (with technology and rules) to connect these sides. Primary stock markets are networks connecting issuers with investors, with investment banks acting as the major providers of platforms making these connections. As a result, the stock markets arise as a multi-sided network, in which the connecting platforms may be electronic, but their providers (investment banks, stock exchanges, and others) benefit from proximity to each other, investors, issuers, and other specialized services providers. Given the strong network externalities and scale economies in these networks, they evolve towards a global scope. These processes give rise to stock market centres and their global network.

Before we conclude our application of the global city theory to stock markets, more elaboration is required on the category of 'stock market industry'. After all, investment banks, brokerages, and even stock exchanges deal not only with stocks but also with securities in general. Stock market industry is an integral and central part of securities industry, with corporate stock remaining the largest class of financial assets in the world (Bank of England 2007). Analysing the relationship between stock and securities markets further, we propose that stock market development could be seen as securitization of corporate ownership. This is inconsistent with the definition of securitization in financial economics textbooks. According to Mishkin, securitization 'is the process of transforming otherwise illiquid financial assets (such as residential mortgages, auto loans, and credit card receivables), which have typically been the bread and butter of banking institutions, into marketable capital market securities' (2007: 255). The mainstream definition of securitization is, however, too narrow, limiting our understanding of its implications. Arguably, the essence of securitization is making an asset more liquid, that is, easier and cheaper to buy and sell, which necessitates the development of primary markets (i.e. changing the characteristics of an asset so that it could be offered to a large number of investors), as well as the development of secondary markets, where assets can be traded among investors. A broadened definition covers securitization of corporate ownership, as well as securitization of corporate, household, and government debt.

Consequently, the theory of stock market centres could be translated into a theory of securities market centres. Securitization leads to an institutional and geographical dispersion of financial asset ownership. The process gives rise to the development of securities industry. Securities firms benefit not only from proximity to each other but also from proximity to the issuers of securities and investors, thus giving rise to securities market centres. Finally, securities firms operate global networks, and act as spanners in the global network of securities market centres. This key contribution of securitization to the development of the network of global cities and globalization in general cannot be appreciated if we hold on to the existing narrow definition of securitization.

The evolving map of stock market centres

The preceding section finished with translating the theory of stock market centres into a more general theory of securities market centres. This has an important practical implication. As hardly any firms operate solely within the stock market industry, such category does not exist in statistical datasets, making it impossible to map stock market centres systematically, other than just relying on proxies such as the value of stock trading on a stock exchange. Some comparable international data on the size of securities industry, however, can be assembled. Here we use data on employment in the securities industry in the world's six largest economies to get a glimpse of the map of stock market centres. The investigation of the map and its dynamic properties will substantiate the theory of stock market centres, adding to the evidence already presented in the book.

Table 8.1 presents employment in the securities industry and credit and insurance in the six largest economies in the world, in the leading financial centres in these economies, and change in employment over the last decade. Employment data are based on the location of establishments where people work, not the headquarters of the employer. Credit and insurance is defined simply as the rest of the financial sector (after deducting employment in the securities industry, and excluding real estate intermediation). Overall figures

Table 8.1. The number of employees in the financial sector (in 000s)

City/district/country	Securities industry		Credit and insurance	
	2008	1998	2008	1998
Hong Kong	69.5	54.5	137.2	113.6
Beijing	16.2	—	210.6	—
Shanghai	13.3	—	193.3	—
China	263.6	—	8363.5	—
Paris	33.8	25.7	263.3	275.9
France	64.4	37.9	653.4	617.7
Frankfurt am Main	9.8	8.7	58.4	61.5
Germany	140.5	87.0	862.8	964.4
Tokyo	62.3	77.4	295.5	392.3
Japan	111.5	168.2	1317.9	1807.5
Central London	106.3	62.4	174.6	167.8
Greater London	123.4	79.7	208.5	234.0
United Kingdom	324.1	206.3	738.9	825.2
Manhattan	173.1	163.8	140.4	176.1
New York	235.1	217.2	398.5	413.6
Boston	62.3	58.2	122.7	120.6
Chicago	58.9	43.2	217.4	224.3
The United States	942.1	724.2	5606.8	5046.0

Notes: Cities are defined as: Hong Kong – SAR; Beijing, Shanghai – municipality; Paris – Ile-de-France; Frankfurt am Main – Stadt; Tokyo – Prefecture (Tokyo-to); Central London – the boroughs of Camden, Islington, Kensington and Chelsea, Lambeth, Southwark, Westminster, City of London, and Tower Hamlets; Manhattan – New York County; New York – New York–Northern Jersey–Long Island Metropolitan Statistical Area (MSA); Boston – Boston–Cambridge–Quincy MSA; Chicago – Chicago–Naperville–Joliet MSA. Data for Germany is for 1999 and 2008; Japan – 1996 and 2006; the United States – 1998 and 2007; otherwise for 1998 and 2008. The definitions of securities industry and credit and insurance industry are not fully comparable between countries.

Sources: National Bureau of Statistics of China; Unistatis (France); Bundesagentur für Arbeit Statistik (Germany); Japanese Statistics Bureau; NOMIS, Office for National Statistics (the United Kingdom); County Business Patterns, US Census Bureau.

give us an idea of the size of the securities industry. In 2008, the securities industry employed approximately two million people, out of twenty million employed in the financial sector in the six largest economies of the world. With these countries accounting for 55 per cent of the global GDP, the total size of the securities industry could be estimated at three million people. While the two million figure includes much more than just the stock market industry, it does not really cover the whole of the securities or stock market industry as defined in our theory of stock market centres and securitization. The data do not include securities' lawyers, accountants, or investor relations experts, just to give some examples of missing categories. Although the definition of securities industry may differ from country to country, and so data are not perfectly comparable between countries, it is safe to say that the United States has by far the largest employment in the securities industry, although it has a much smaller financial sector employment than China. Second after the United States comes the United Kingdom, followed by China.

The recent boom in the securities industry is undisputable. With one exception – Japan – employment in the securities industry grew: by 28 per cent

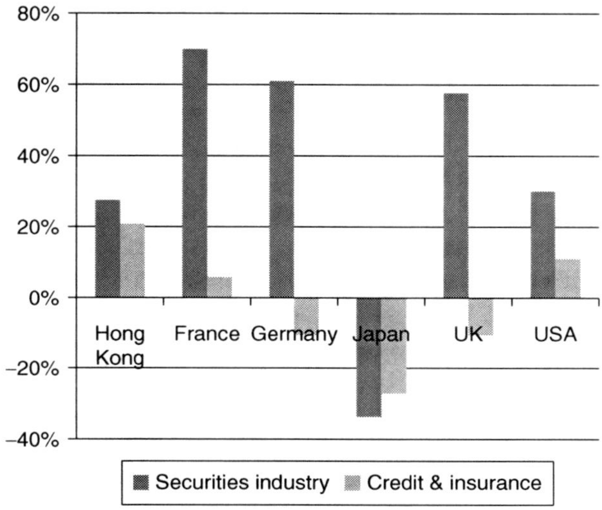

Figure 8.1. Change in employment between 1998 and 2008

Sources: Author, based on data from National Bureau of Statistics of China; Unistatis (France); Bundesagentur für Arbeit Statistik (Germany); Japanese Statistics Bureau; NOMIS, Office for National Statistics (the United Kingdom); County Business Patterns, US Census Bureau.

in Hong Kong (data for 1998 for Mainland China are unavailable) 57 per cent in the United Kingdom, 61 per cent in Germany, and 70 per cent in France (Figure 8.1). The year 1998, marking the end of the Asian financial crisis, may seem generous as a base of comparison, but remember that the decade under consideration includes years 2000–2, with falling stock market indices. While employment in the securities industry skyrocketed (with the exception of Japan), that in credit and insurance actually fell significantly in Japan, Germany, and the United Kingdom, and grew moderately in the United States and France. Only Hong Kong, serving the Chinese market, still far from saturated with basic financial products (such as bank cards, mortgages, or life insurance), recorded a large growth of employment in credit and insurance industry, only slightly lower than that in the securities industry. In the United States, Japan, Germany, and the United Kingdom combined, employment loss in credit and insurance was more than compensated by the employment gain in the securities industry. Financialization would clearly be a misnomer for the phenomenon illustrated in Figure 8.1 and Table 8.1. What has happened is securitization of the world economy, which has fed a tremendous growth in the securities industry. This supports proposition 2 of the theory of stock market (and securities market) centres.

Employment in the securities industry is highly concentrated. There are about as many people working in the securities industry in the New York metropolitan area as in the whole of Germany and Japan combined. Manhattan itself has a larger securities industry employment than Germany, Japan, or France. There are more securities industry professionals working in London than in Japan, Germany, or France. The concentration of the securities industry employment in the leading urban centre ranges from 7 per cent in Germany to 56 per cent in Japan. In the United Kingdom and France, no city has even a tenth of the securities industry employment of London or Paris, respectively. In Japan, Osaka follows Tokyo with only one-sixth of Tokyo's employment in the securities industry. In the United States, the advantage of New York over Boston and Chicago is approximately 4 to 1. In China, Hong Kong holds a similar advantage over Beijing and Shanghai. The only exception to this picture of very high concentration is Germany, where Munich and Berlin follow Frankfurt am Main very closely as leading securities market centres, with Hamburg, Stuttgart, and Cologne not far behind, illustrating a relatively decentralized geographical structure of German finance (Klagge and Martin 2005; Clark and Wójcik 2007).

In each of the countries analysed, the geographical concentration of the securities industry is higher than that for credit and insurance (Figure 8.2). This applies particularly to the continental size economies of China and the United States, where credit and insurance establishments seem to be spread

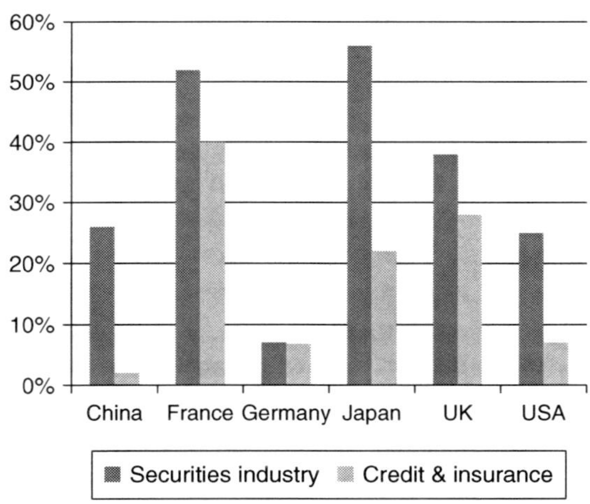

Figure 8.2. Concentration of employment in the leading city

Sources: Author, based on data from National Bureau of Statistics of China; Unistatis (France); Bundesagentur für Arbeit Statistik (Germany); Japanese Statistics Bureau; NOMIS, Office for National Statistics (the United Kingdom); County Business Patterns, US Census Bureau.

around the country close to their corporate and retail customers. The concentration in credit and insurance is particularly high in France and the United Kingdom, where the financial sector is strongly centralized, with few provincially headquartered banks or insurance companies. The high level of concentration in the securities industry could not be explained without acknowledging the benefits of co-location in this industry, which surpass those affecting the rest of the financial sector. Securities industry has mostly wholesale customers, large companies and very wealthy individuals, generating fewer but higher value, less routine transactions than the rest of the financial sector. Its customer base is likely to be more concentrated in space than the predominantly retail customer base of credit and insurance. Securities industry requires more skilled labour, found in fewer places. This supports proposition 3 of the theory of stock market (and securities market) centres.

In view of Figure 8.2, it makes more sense to talk about securities market centres rather than financial centres, even though the former term hardly exists in media and literature. Securities industry has a much stronger propensity to agglomerate and form centres than the rest of the financial sector. Since around the year of 2000, Manhattan has hosted more jobs in the securities industry than in the rest of the financial sector. Between 1998 and 2008, approximately 25,000 and 15,000 jobs in the credit and insurance industry migrated out of London and New York, respectively, but these losses were more than offset by the growth in the securities industry. While our data concerns concentration of employment, this is obviously accompanied by concentration of wealth and power. In 2007, average annual payroll per person in the US securities industry was 303 per cent of that in credit and insurance and 439 per cent of average for the whole economy. These percentages have risen since 1998 from 281 and 376 per cent, respectively (US Bureau of Labour Statistics).

To explore the relationship between the location of the securities industry and corporate headquarters, which is the subject of proposition 4 of the theory of stock market centres, we will use data for the United States (Wójcik 2011). Figure 8.3 shows the geographical concentration of employment at the state level for the securities industry in relation to credit and insurance and the concentration of corporate headquarters. The data covers fifty states plus District Columbia, but excludes Puerto Rico. Headquarters of only large corporations are included. They are defined as large if they satisfy one of the following conditions for year 2008: have operating revenue of at least $ 140m (€ 100m); total assets of at least $ 280m (€ 200m); at least 1000 employees are listed. Such criteria produce more than 35,000 corporations in 2008. Focus on large corporations is justified, as small and medium sized firms are much less likely to use the services of securities industry.

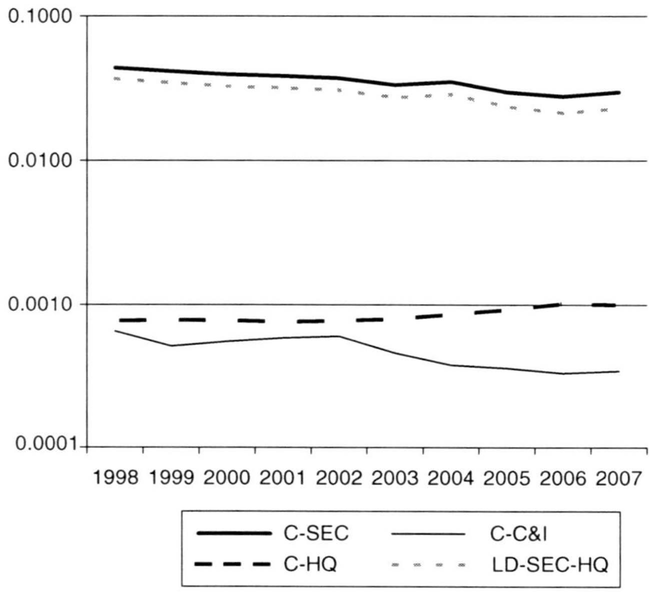

Figure 8.3. Geographical concentration and location difference in the United States

Notes: C-SEC – geographical concentration in the securities securities industry, C&I – geographical concentration in credit and insurance, HQ – geographical concentration in corporate headquarters; LD-SEC-HQ – location difference between securities industry and corporate headquarters. Logarithmic scale is used for indices.

Sources: Author's calculations based on data from the US Census County Business Patterns, and Orbis database from Bureau van Dijk.

The geographical concentration index is calculated as:

$$C = \sum_{i=1}^{N} (x_i - s_i)^2$$

where i stands for a given state; N for fifty-one geographical units; x is the fraction share of the state in employment in the securities industry (employment in credit and insurance or the number of corporate headquarters); and s is the fraction share of the state in total employment in the United States across all sectors. To compare the distribution of the securities industry and corporate headquarters, we use the location difference index, calculated with the same formula as that for geographical concentration, with x as the share of a given state in the total securities industry employment and s as its share in the total number of corporate headquarters.

Figure 8.3 confirms and extends the results from Figure 8.2. The distribution of securities industry is in a different category than that for credit and insurance, with incomparably higher concentration by state. There is nothing surprising in the difference, considering the wholesale nature of the securities industry, and the rather ubiquitous character of retail banking and insurance services. Over time, however, not only the concentration of credit and insurance fell from 0.0006 to 0.0003 but also the concentration of the securities industry fell from 0.044 to 0.030. The dispersion of the credit and insurance industry has been contributed to mostly by falling employment shares in New York, Illinois, Massachusetts, and Connecticut, traditionally strongholds of the sector. Major gains in employment took place in Texas, Florida, North Carolina, and Arizona. A declining share of New York, New Jersey, and Massachusetts, and the rise of Pennsylvania, Maryland, Arizona, North Carolina, and Utah underpinned the dispersion in the securities industry, which was also quite consistent over time. The boom of 1998–2007 has led to a more widespread distribution of securities industry employment across states. As we saw, employment grew in the hubs of the industry – New York City, Chicago, and Boston, but it also spilled over to other parts of the country, including the neighbour of New York City – the state of New Jersey.

As Figure 8.3 shows, corporate headquarters are far more dispersed across states than the securities industry, but far more concentrated than credit and insurance industry. With time, however, corporate headquarters became more concentrated, with the concentration index growing from 0.0008 to 0.0010. As the concentration of the securities industry declined, its distribution has become more similar to the distribution of headquarters, with the location difference index falling from 0.0369 to 0.0232. In short, there is evidence for increased co-location of securities industry and corporate headquarters. Consider the example of Boeing, which moved their headquarters from Seattle to Chicago in 2001 (Muellerleile 2009). On their website the company stressed that the principal focus of the new corporate headquarters would be on developing global growth opportunities and on creating shareholder value. Presence in a leading securities market centre could be seen as serving directly the latter focus. In other words, the Boeing case may be symptomatic of a larger trend. This evidence supports proposition 4 of the theory of stock market centres.

To be sure, for proposition 4 of the theory, we are only able to present detailed evidence from one country. Earlier we have studied six countries and found that for proposition 2 – Japan, with a shrinking securities industry – is a major exception; and for proposition 3 – Germany, with a relatively low concentration of securities industry. If exceptions can be found within a sample of six countries, there must be many more of them in the world. The Japanese case reminds us that the recent rise of the securities and stock market industry has not been ubiquitous. The German case suggests that the benefits of concentration in the securities industry can under certain circumstances be offset by the benefits of proximity to regional economic and political decision-making centres (Wójcik 2002*b*). These exceptions do not undermine the theory of stock market centres. Rather they serve as a call for further enquiry into the geographical footprint of the stock market and securities industry.

To complete the empirical elaboration of the theory, nothing illustrates the networked character of the securities industry and its centres, captured in proposition 5 of the theory, better than the worldwide office network of Goldman Sachs (GS), one of the largest, and arguably the most influential securities industry firm in the world. Presented in Table 8.2, the geographical structure of GS is testament not only to the theory of stock (and securities) market centres, but also to an array of empirical findings throughout this book. Stretched across the three major time zones, GS uses its hubs in New York, London, and Hong Kong as the central axis of the company. A considerable presence is maintained in the emerging markets, with focus on the BRICs (an acronym invented by an employee of GS) and the Persian Gulf states. Within the United States, GS have half of their offices in the Sun Belt, reflecting the strong position of the southern states in the US economic growth. It has an office in Jersey City, an extension of the securities market centre of New York, and a hub for the exchange industry. In India, it is present not only in the financial centre of Mumbai but also in the high-tech industry

Table 8.2. The worldwide office network of Goldman Sachs

Americas	Europe, Africa, and Middle East	Asia Pacific
New York, NY	London (UK)	Hong Kong (China)
Jersey City, NJ	Paris (France)	Beijing (China)
Boston, MA	Frankfurt (Germany)	Shanghai (China)
Philadelphia, PA	Geneva (Switzerland)	Singapore
Princeton, NJ	Zurich (Switzerland)	Tokyo (Japan)
Washington DC	Milan (Italy)	Seoul (Korea)
Chicago, IL	Monaco	Taipei (Taiwan)
Salt Lake City, UT	Madrid (Spain)	Mumbai (India)
Seattle, WA	Dublin (Ireland)	Bangalore (India)
San Francisco, CA	Stockholm (Sweden)	Bangkok (Thailand)
Los Angeles, CA	Moscow (Russia)	Melbourne (Australia)
Dallas, TX	Tel Aviv (Israel)	Sydney (Australia)
Houston, TX	Dubai (United Arab Emirates)	Auckland (New Zealand)
Atlanta. GA	Doha (Qatar)	
Miami, FL	Riyadh (Saudi Arabia)	
West Palm Beach, FL	Johannesburg (South Africa)	
Toronto (Canada)		
Calgary (Canada)		
Camana Bay (Cayman Is.)		
Mexico City (Mexico)		
São Paulo (Brazil)		
Buenos Aires (Argentina)		

Sources: Author, based on information from www2.goldmansachs.com/ (accessed on 29/07/10).

centre of Bangalore. In China, it covers Hong Kong as well as Beijing and Shanghai. Last but not least, its South African office is in Sandton, the new financial district of Johannesburg, and the new location of the stock exchange. Surely, if location and distance did not matter for the stock market, and securities industry in general, GS office would be in Cape Town.

The future of the global stock market

Despite the recent boom and internationalization in stock markets, potential for further growth and integration is large. As Chapter 2 has shown, an absolute majority of large firms, even in countries with the oldest and most developed stock markets, is still absent from stock markets. Potential for issuers tapping into foreign stock markets is large (Chapter 3), and so are opportunities for investors to diversify their portfolios by investing in foreign equity (Chapter 4). Significant capacity for future growth and integration exists in developed, emerging, and developing markets.

If potential for further growth exists in stock markets for large companies, the potential for small- and medium-sized companies (SMEs) entering stock markets is even larger. In developed economies, the spectacular growth of the secondary stock market does not seem to have stimulated much growth in the primary stock market. In fact, while stock market for young and dynamic companies experienced a boom in late 1990s, it has not been a part of securitization since 2001. In the United States, the number of listed companies declined considerably since the end of the Internet boom. In Europe, the new market model that flourished in late 1990s and collapsed in 2000–1 has not yet found a replacement. While the Alternative Investment Market in London succeeded in attracting companies from emerging markets (often via vehicles domiciled in tax heavens) as well as British small companies, it attracted hardly any companies from the Continental Europe. Its copies in Western Europe enjoyed little success either (in contrast to Poland). At the same time, the model of stock exchanges as pure trading platforms, in Europe operating as MTFs, while successful in attracting liquidity for large capitalization stocks, does not seem benefit the secondary stock market for SMEs. Optimists could claim that with a continued decline in trading, clearing, and settlement costs, trading SME stocks on MTFs and equivalents will become viable. Sceptics, however, would argue that if competition with MTFs leads to the dismantling of some incumbent exchanges, while others adopt the pure trading platform model, opportunities for SMEs to engage with public stock markets may become even more limited than they are. This may point to the need for identifying low cost options for trading SME stocks, if necessary, with government intervention. Interestingly, the European Venture

Capital Association, after a failed attempt in the 1990s, is still lobbying for a pan-European platform for listed SMEs. An MTF for SMEs might be an option.

As the book shows, however, access to stock markets is not just an issue of size; it is also an issue of geography. Provincial companies, away from large financial centres are less likely to engage with stock markets, even if they are large and come from dynamic economic sectors. This geographical bias holds even in the most developed stock markets. Indeed, while stock market bias against small companies is affected by fixed costs of participating in public stock markets, which is to some extent unavoidable, the fact that many large and dynamic provincial companies stay out of the stock market is much more difficult to justify from a policy perspective. The geographical bias has consequences not only for the size but also for the structure of the stock market. The bias implies a relatively low level of geographical diversification of corporate activity represented on the stock market. The French stock market, for example, is skewed towards representing the performance of the Parisian rather then the whole French economy. The British market biased towards the performance of firms from London and South East. If stock markets were better representations of underlying corporate economies, this could reduce the level of stock market volatility.

Stock market development of the last two decades has been accompanied by a spectacular growth of stock market intermediaries, being a part of the boom in the securities industry in general. Putting the issue of the financial and economic crisis aside at the moment, and focusing on the advancement of technology, should we expect future stock market development to be mirrored by the growth of the stock market industry? As we saw in Chapter 7, a firm employing forty people, using state-of-the-art technology, can do as much stock trading as a traditional exchange employing 1000 people. Technology clearly affects the nature of intermediation but does not eradicate it. Issuers, traders, and ultimate investors cannot connect directly without intermediaries – platforms are necessary and have to be provided by somebody. Even Internet requires telecommunication firms providing Internet services. Comparisons of different parts of the stock market in this book suggest that technology transforms secondary stock markets more than primary markets. Direct human interaction in primary markets remains crucial. In secondary markets, exchanges of the twenty-first century may employ few people, but by bringing the costs of trading down, they lead to the growth in the number of individual traders and specialized trading firms.

With the global financial crisis, economic downturn, and a wave of financial re-regulation, the future of the global stock market is uncertain. The most direct threat is that the depression in the corporate sector, accentuated risk-aversion of investors and limited credit will for a long time not allow a return to the level of stock market activity witnessed before 2007. Beyond this direct effect, the crisis also raises issues about the position of the stock market in financial markets and its structure. Regarding the relative position of stock markets, the threat is that large amounts of new government debt competing for limited amount of savings starve stock markets of capital. On the other hand, it did not go unnoticed by policymakers or the public, that while the crisis originated in Over-The-Counter (OTC) markets trading securitized mortgages and their derivatives, stock markets never shut down and continued to trade throughout the crisis. In addition, credit rating agencies were seen as failing in their role as reputational intermediaries evaluating the issuers and their securities. Hence, there are opinions that more of the securities trading should be shifted from the OTC markets to regulated exchanges, with the use of central clearing counterparties, in order to improve the transparency of transactions, lower the level of credit risk, and enhance the monitoring capacity of regulators.

The global financial crisis also raises issues with regard to the future structure and governance of the stock market industry. The crisis has highlighted the disastrous costs of myopia in the securities industry, including investment banks and credit rating agencies, where governance and incentives structures focused too much on short-term profit opportunities at the expense of the long-term development of the marketplace. The crisis has also proven that conflicts of interest within the securities industry had not been addressed adequately, as epitomized by the case of GS selling to their customers investment products, designed by a related hedge fund that was to benefit from the collapse of these products. Unless the development of primary stock markets is properly addressed, the revolution in the stock exchange industry, focused on trading large capitalization stocks, may yet prove to be myopic. Growing control of investment banks over the stock exchanges may exacerbate conflicts of interest within the stock market industry. Since the development of public securities markets rests on the quality of the securities traded, and hence corporate governance of their issuers, the corporate governance of companies organizing public securities markets should be spotless. As said before 'the corporate governance of the stock exchange should be like Caesar's wife, well above any suspicion' (Onado 1998: 240). The lawsuit against Richard Grasso, the former CEO of the NYSE, and the fraudulent activities of Bernard Madoff, the former chairman of NASDAQ did not help to fortify the reputation of exchanges. Policymakers, regulators, and researchers should watch this space carefully.

The future of cities

Throughout the book we have stressed the mutual constitution of cities and stock markets. Stock markets could not develop without cities and they play a significant part in the development of cities. The growth of stock markets, and securities markets in general, has contributed to the growth of London, New York, and Hong Kong in the last two decades, and lack of this growth added to the economic woes of Tokyo. The theory of stock (and securities) market centres presented in this book challenges the ideas of global city and creative city dominant in the debate on urban development in a globalized world. The global city theory creates an impression that cities should focus on attracting advanced services providers as those that need cities much more than other economic sectors. The creative city theory adds a focus on the creative class, including software engineers and artists, making it paramount for cities to be diverse and 'cool' to maintain and attract the creative class (Florida 2002). The theory of stock market centres reminds us that access to information critical to economic decision-making is highly uneven. Concentrations of corporate headquarters continue to matter to the development of cities, and are not replaced by the concentrations of advanced business services or bohemians.

A stock market centre does not necessarily have to have a stock exchange. Munich, with only a regional exchange, functions as a stock market and securities market centre by the virtue of its institutional investors (with insurance companies in the lead), wealthy individual investors and corporate headquarters. Boston is a stock market centre due to a concentration of corporate headquarters, institutional investors, and a large portfolio management industry. Beijing is a stock market centre due to a booming corporate sector, state-controlled institutional investors, and intermediaries benefiting from proximity to political institutions. Securities market centres can build their strength on other parts of the securities market than the stock market. Chicago's specialization, for example, is in derivatives trading. While a locally headquartered stock exchange is not a necessary condition for a stock market centre (and even less necessary for a securities market centre), cities and countries should not be complacent about losing their stock exchanges. At issue here is not so much nationality, but location of the stock exchanges, as the latter continue to contribute to the pool of expertise, infrastructure, and image of cities. This is particularly important for cities and countries where stock exchanges are active both in secondary and primary stock markets, in the absence of developed investment banking and venture capital industry. Take the case study of the Warsaw Stock Exchange from Chapter 6 as an example. If there was no active stock exchange focused on the Polish market, who would perform its functions? How long would it take to replace all the ways in which it connects issuers and investors in different parts of the country?

Predictions have often been made about the rise of stock market centres specialized in companies from specific industries on an international basis

(Young and Theys 1999; Walter and Smith 2000). Such specialization existed before, for example, with foreign electric tramway companies seeking capital via Brussels and listing on the Brussels exchange in early twentieth century (Michie 2006). While some degree of sectoral specialization in primary and secondary markets exists at present (as documented in Chapter 3), it is unlikely that exchanges should pay much attention to it in the future. An industrial sector does not seem to need or justify a separate trading platform. Issuers from a given industry do not lose when their stocks are traded with those of issuers from other sectors. Investors gain if one platform gives them access to trading stocks from diverse industries. If they want to focus on a specific industry, they can always use an index and analysts' reports for this industry. Thus far, MTFs in Europe show no interest in sector specialization. NASDAQ-OMX prides itself on its leadership in trading high-technology stocks, but since the end of the Internet boom in 2001 its annual reports project a drive towards diversifying its issuer base. Looking ahead, industrial specialization is much more of an option for primary rather than secondary market activities of stock market intermediaries and centres. Oslo, for example, has developed a reputation as a centre of expertise and stock market analysis focused on maritime and energy sectors. On secondary markets, in contrast, there is demand to extend stock trading platforms with other securities and create multi-asset trading platforms, offering a one-stop shop to investors.

The book confirms New York and London as the principal axis of the global stock market. New York's position is underwritten by the sheer size of the US stock market, for which New York continues to be the hub, and its role as the headquarter location for the world's largest international investment banks. Over the last decade, however, London has grown faster than New York as a securities industry centre. As illustrated in Chapters 3, 5, and 7, London is the centre of international primary stock markets, a major information exchange for multinational firms, and is consolidating its dominance in an integrating secondary stock market in Europe. In contrast to the global city theory, and in agreement with the Global Financial Centre Index (Z/Yen 2010), we argue that Hong Kong, not Tokyo is the leading stock (and securities) market centre in the Asia-Pacific region. This is due to the shrinking of Tokyo as a securities market centre and the continued growth of the Chinese stock market, for which Hong Kong acts as a central hub and interchange with foreign stock market centres, including New York and London. In this respect, Hong Kong has a huge lead within China over Beijing and Shanghai.

One important question for the future is the potential of Sovereign Wealth Funds (SWFs), particularly the largest of them from the Near and Far East, to redraw the map of the global stock market. Without investing or trading in domestic stocks SWFs would seem to contribute little to the development of stock market centres in the cities and countries they come from. In their foreign operations, they have focused on debt securities, and within corporate securities they have mostly pursued a strategy of acquiring large, often controlling, stakes rather than acting as diversified portfolio investors (Monk 2010). Some of the SWFs have acquired large stakes in the leading international investment banks, clearly seen as one of the strategic sectors by the governments behind the SWFs. The investment strategies of SWFs forge new connections between stock market centres in their home countries and those in the rest of the world. Indeed, the relationships between SWFs and global investment banks, as well as governments of their home countries will be one of the critical factors shaping the global network of stock market centres, and with it the future of financial markets, cities, and the global economy.

Appendix 1. Publicly Traded Companies by Country at the End of September 2006

Austria	109	Prime and Standard segment of the Wiener Börse
Belgium	159	Eurolist and Marché Libre of the Euronext Brussels
Bulgaria	341	All companies listed on the Official and Unofficial Market of the Bulgarian Stock Exchange
Cyprus	142	All companies listed on the Cyprus Stock Exchange
Czech Republic	37	All companies listed on the Prague Stock Exchange
Denmark	178	All companies listed on the OMX Copenhagen and the First North Exchange
Estonia	16	All companies listed on the OMX Tallin
Finland	134	All companies listed on OMX Helsinki
France	946	Eurolist, Alternext, and Marché Libre of the Euronext Paris
Germany	1014	Official Market and the Open Market (Freiverkehr, i.e. the Regulated Unofficial market) of the Deutsche Börse
Greece	336	Big cap, mid cap, and small cap, special financial character, and under surveillance companies at the Athens Stock Echange, but not suspended listed companies
Hungary	37	All companies with equities category A or B traded on the Budapest Stock Exchange
Iceland	22	All companies listed on the Iceland Stock Exchange
Ireland	114	The Official List and the Irish Enterprise Exchange (IEX) of the Irish Stock Exchange
Italy	292	All segments of the Borsa Italiana, that is, Blue Chip, Star, Standard, and Mercato Expandi
Latvia	39	All companies listed on the OMX Riga
Liechtenstein	2	Liechtenstein domiciled companies listed on the SWX Swiss Exchange
Lithuania	43	All companies listed on the OMX Vilnius
Luxembourg	49	All companies listed on the Luxembourg Stock Exchange
Malta	11	All companies listed on the official list of the Malta Stock Exchange
The Netherlands	224	All companies listed at Euronext Amsterdam

(*Continued*)

Appendix 1. Continued

Norway	277	All segments of the Oslo Stock Exchange, that is, OBX, OB Match, OB Standard, and OB New
Poland	241	All companies listed on the Main and the Parallel Market of the Warsaw Stock Exchange
Portugal	73	All companies listed on the Euronext Lisbon
Romania	69	All companies listed on the Bucharest Stock Exchange
Slovakia	251	All companies with shares traded on the Bratislava Stock Exchange
Slovenia	81	All companies on the Official and Semi-Official Market of the Ljubljana Stock Exchange
Spain	198	Companies traded on the Continuous Market and the Floor of the Bolsas y Mercados Españoles (BME-X). SICAVs and SIMs are not included
Sweden	395	All companies listed on the OMX Stockholm, the Nordic Growth Market, and the First North Exchange
Switzerland	274	Main Market, Local Caps, Real Estate Companies, and Investment Companies of the SWX Swiss Exchange
The United Kingdom	2542	All companies listed on the London Stock Exchange, including the AIM
Japan	3858	All companies traded on the Tokyo Stock Exchange, the JASDAQ, the Nagoya SE, the Osaka Securities Exchange, the Sapporo Stock Exchange, and the OTC Japan
The United States	8861	The New York Stock Exchange, the NASDAQ National Market, the NASDAQ Bulletin Board, the American Stock Exchange, and other OTC markets

Note: For each country the Appendix gives the total number of publicly traded companies, and a description of stock market segments included. The data were obtained from ORBIS by the BVDEP, and their consistency was tested by comparison to data from the World Federation of Exchanges, the Federation of European Stock Exchanges, and the websites of individual stock exchanges. In addition to the domestic segments stated, for each country the numbers include companies that are publicly traded only on a foreign exchange (e.g. the Irish companies traded on the Alternative Investment Market (AIM) of the London Stock Exchange, but not traded on the Irish Stock Exchange).

Appendix 2. Financial Centres and Other Cities Analysed and their Spatial Scope

Austria	Vienna	The State of Vienna
Belgium	Brussels	The Brussels Capital Region
Bulgaria	Sofia	The Capital Municipality of Sofia
Cyprus	Nicosia	Nicosia Municipality
Czech Republic	Prague	The Capital City of Prague
Denmark	Copenhagen	Metropolitan Copenhagen – Storkøbenhavn
Estonia	Tallinn	Tallinn Municipality
Finland	Helsinki	Helsinki Metropolitan Area
France	Paris	Île-de-France
Germany	Berlin	The State of Berlin
	Düsseldorf	The Urban District (Stadkreise) of Düsseldorf
	Frankfurt am Main	The Urban District of Frankfurt am Main
	Munich	The Urban District of Munich
Greece	Athens	Athens–Piraeus Super–Prefecture
Hungary	Budapest	The Capital City of Budapest
Iceland	Reykjavik	The Capital Region of Reykjavík
Ireland	Dublin	County Dublin
Italy	Milan	The Province of Milan
	Rome	The Province of Rome
	Turin	The Province of Turin
Latvia	Riga	Riga District
Lithuania	Vilnius	The Vilnius City Municipality
Luxembourg	Luxembourg	Luxembourg City
Malta	Valetta	The Municipality of Valletta
The Netherlands	Amsterdam	The Municipality of Amsterdam
	Rotterdam	The Municipality of Rotterdam
Norway	Oslo	Greater Oslo Region
Poland	Warsaw	The Capital Municipality of Warsaw
Portugal	Lisbon	Greater Lisbon
	Porto	Greater Porto
Romania	Bucharest	The Municipality of Bucharest
Slovakia	Bratislava	The Municipality of Bratislava
Slovenia	Ljubljana	The Municipality of Ljubljana
Spain	Barcelona	The County of Barcelona – Comarca el Barcelonès
	Madrid	The Autonomous Community of Madrid

(Continued)

Appendix 2. Continued

Sweden	Stockholm	Greater Stockholm – Storstockholm
Switzerland	Basel	The Cantons of Basel City and Basel-Land
	Geneva	The Canton of Geneva
	Zürich	The Canton of Zürich
The United Kingdom	London	Greater London
Japan	Tokyo	Tokyo Prefecture
The United States	New York	New York–Northern New Jersey–Long Island MSA
	Los Angeles	Los Angeles–Long Beach–Santa Ana MSA
	Chicago	Chicago–Naperville–Joliet MSA
	Philadelphia	Philadelphia–Camden–Wilmington MSA
	Boston	Boston–Cambridge–Quincy MSA
	San Francisco	San Francisco–Oakland–Fremont MSA

References

Agarwal, S., Liu, C., and Rhee, S. G. (2007). Where does price discovery occur for stocks traded in multiple markets? Evidence from Hong Kong and London. *Journal of International Money and Finance*, 26, 46–63.

Aglietta, M. and Reberioux, A. (2005). *Corporate Governance Adrift: A Critique of Shareholder Value*. Cheltenham: Edward Elgar.

Akerlof, G. and Shiller, R. (2009). *Animal Spirits: How Human Psychology Drives the Economy and Why It Matters For Global Capitalism*. Princeton: Princeton University Press.

Albuquerque, R., Bauer, G. H., and Schneider, M. (2009). Global private information in international equity markets. *Journal of Financial Economics*, 94, 18–46.

Amin, A. and Thrift, N. (1992). Neo-Marshallian nodes in global networks. *International Journal of Urban and Regional Research*, 16, 571–87.

Anand, A., and Subrahmanyam, A. (2008). Information and the intermediary: Are market intermediaries informed traders in electronic markets? *Journal of Financial and Quantitative Analysis*, 43(1), 1–28.

—— Gatchev, V. A., Madureira, L., Pirinsky, C. A., and Underwood, S. (2008). Geographic proximity and price discovery: Evidence from Nasdaq. Available at SSRN: http://ssrn.com/abstract=1032633

Authers, J. (2007). Nationalism bites the dust. *Financial Times Special Report on World Financial Centres and Exchanges*, 19 November, 1.

Bae, K.-H., Stulz, R. M., and Tan, H. (2008). Do local analysts know more? A cross-country study of the performance of local analysts and foreign analysts. *Journal of Financial Economics*, 88, 581–606.

Baibakov, A. (2004). NASDAQ to attract Russian clients by native language. *Komersant*, 23 June, 6.

Bancel, F. and Mittoo, U. R. (2008). Why European firms go public? Working Paper. Available at SSRN: http://papers.ssrn.com/sol3/papers.cfm?abstract_id=1034164

Bank for International Settlements (2010). *Triennial Central Bank Survey of Foreign Exchange and Derivatives Market Activity in 2007 – Final Results*. Available at: http://www.bis.org/publ/rpfxf07t.htm

Bank of England (2007). *Financial Stability Report*. April 2007, Issue No. 21. Available at: http://www.bankofengland.co.uk/publications/fsr/2007/fsrfull0704.pdf

Barber, B. M. and Odean, T. (2008). All that glitters: The effect of attention and news on the buying behavior of individual and institutional investors. *Review of Financial Studies*, 21, 785–815.

Barclay, M. J. and Warner, J. B. (1993). Stealth trading and volatility. Which trades moves prices? *Journal of Financial Economics*, 34, 281–305.

Bathelt, H., Malmberg, A., and Maskell, P. (2004). Clusters and knowledge: Local buzz, global pipelines and the process of knowledge creation. *Progress in Human Geography*, 28(1), 31–56.

Beaverstock, J. V., Holyer, M., Pain, K., and Taylor, P. J. (2003). London and Frankfurt: Competition or synergy? In P. Shearlock (ed.), *International Investor* (pp. 223–8). London: Sovereign Publications.

Bebchuk, L. and Fried, J. (2004). *Pay Without Performance: The Unfulfilled Promise of Executive Compensation*. Cambridge, MA: Harvard University Press.

Becht, M., Bolton, P., and Röell, A. A. (2003). Corporate governance and control. In G. M. Constantinides, M. Harris, and R. Stulz (eds.), *Handbook of the Economics of Finance* (pp. 1–109). Amsterdam: North Holland.

Bekaert, G. and Wang, X. (2009). Home bias revisited. Available at SSRN: http://papers.ssrn.com/sol3/papers.cfm?abstract_id=1344880

Berger, A. N., Miller, N. H., Petersen, M. A., Rajan, R. G., and Stein, J. C. (2005). Does function follow organizational form? Evidence from the lending practices of large and small banks. *Journal of Financial Economics*, 76, 237–69.

Bhattacharya, U. and Groznik, P. (2008). Melting pot or salad bowl: Some evidence from US investments abroad. *Journal of Financial Markets*, 11, 228–58.

Biglari, H. (2007). Exchanges seek a new model. *Financial Times Special Report on World Financial Centres and Exchanges*, 19 November, 5.

BNYM (Bank of New York Mellon) (2007). *The Depositary Receipts Markets: The Year in Review 2007*. Available at: www.adrbnymellon.com/dr_pub_statistics.jsp

—— (2008). *Depositary Receipts: The Year in Review 2008*. Available at: www.adrbnymellon.com/dr_pub_statistics.jsp

Bodnaruk, A. (2004). Proximity Always Matters: Evidence from Swedish Data. EFA 2004 Maastricht Meetings Paper No. 3765, July 29, 2004. Available at SSRN: http://ssrn.com/abstract=565345

—— Massa, M., and Simonov, A. (2007). Investment banks as insiders and the market for corporate control. CEPR Discussion Paper 6953. Available at SSRN: http://papers.ssrn.com/sol3/papers.cfm?abstract_id=966202

Boschma, R. A. (2005). Proximity and innovation: A critical assessment. *Regional Studies*, 39(1), 61–74.

Braithwaite, J. and Drahos, P. (2000). *Global Business Regulation*. Cambridge: Cambridge University Press.

Brau, J. and Fawcett, S. (2006). Initial public offerings: An analysis of theory and practice. *Journal of Finance*, 61, 399–436.

Brown-Humes, C. and Chung, J. (2006). Russian watchdog acts to stop companies from listing abroad. *Financial Times*, 9 February, 17.

Budd, L. (1995). Globalisation, territory and strategic alliances in different financial centres. *Urban Studies*, 32, 345–60.

Burton, B., Helliar, C., and Power, D. (2004). The role of corporate governance in the IPO process: A note. *Corporate Governance: An International Review*, 12, 353–60.

—— —— ——. (2006). Practitioners' perspectives on the IPO process and the perils of flotation. *European Journal of Finance*, 12, 671–92.

Capaldo, A., Härle, P., and Marrs, A. (2008). What's next for exchanges. *McKinsey Quarterly*, March.

Casey, J.-P. and Lannoo, K. (2009). *The MiFID Revolution*. Cambridge: Cambridge University Press.

Cashman, G. D. and Deli, D. N. (2009). Locating decision rights: Evidence from the mutual fund industry. *Journal of Financial Markets*, 12, 645–71.

Cassis, Y. (2006). *Capitals of Capital: A History of International Financial Centres, 1780–2005*. Cambridge: Cambridge University Press.

Chan, K., Menkveld, A. J., and Yang, Z. (2007). The informativeness of domestic and foreign investors' trades: Evidence from the perfectly segmented Chinese market. *Journal of Financial Markets*, 10, 391–415.

Chen, J., Hong, H., Huang, M., and Kubik, J. D. (2004). Does fund size erode mutual fund performance? The role of liquidity and organization. *American Economic Review*, 94(5), 1276–302.

Christoffersen, S. E. K. and Sarkissian, S. (2009). City size and fund performance. *Journal of Financial Economics*, 92, 252–75.

Citibank (2007). *The Role of Depositary Bank: A Resource for Issuers in the US and Global Securities Markets*. Available at: wwss.citissb.com/adr

Claessens, S., Lee, R., and Zechner, J. (2003). *The Future of Stock Exchanges in European Union Accession Countries. Report commissioned by the Corporation of London*. Available at: www.cepr.org/pubs/fse

Clark, G. L. (2000). *Pension Fund Capitalism*. Oxford: Oxford University Press.

—— (2002). London in the European financial services industry: Locational advantages and product complementarities. *Journal of Economic Geography*, 2, 433–54.

—— (2005). Money flows like mercury: The geography of global finance. *Geografiska Annaler B*, 87, 99–112.

—— Thrift, N. (2005). The return of bureaucracy: Managing dispersed knowledge in global finance. In K. Knorr Cetina and A. Preda (eds.), *The Sociology of Financial Markets* (pp. 229–49). Oxford: Oxford University Press.

—— Wójcik, D. (2001). The city of London in the Asian crisis. *Journal of Economic Geography*, 1, 107–30.

—— —— (2007). *The Geography of Finance: Corporate Governance in the Global Marketplace*. Oxford: Oxford University Press.

—— Dixon, A. D., and Monk, A. H. B. (2009). *Managing Financial Risks: From Global to Local*. Oxford: Oxford University Press.

—— Wójcik, D., and Bauer, R. (2006). Geographically dispersed ownership and intermarket stock price arbitrage: Ahold's crisis of corporate governance and its implications for global standards. *Journal of Economic Geography*, 6, 639–60.

Clayton, M. J., Jorgensen, B. N., and Kavajecz, K. A. (2006). On the presence and market structure of exchanges around the world. *Journal of Financial Markets*, 9, 27–48.

Cohen, L., Frazzini, A., and Malloy, C. (2008). The small world of investing: Board connections and mutual fund returns. *Journal of Political Economy*, 116(5), 951–79.

Conway, E. (2009). Treasury admits 'intellectual failure' behind credit crisis. *Daily Telegraph*, 8 July, 1.

Corbridge, S., Thrift, N., and Martin, R. (eds.) (1994). *Money, Power and Space*. Oxford: Blackwell.

Corwin, S. and Schultz, P. (2005). The role of IPO underwriting syndicates: Pricing, information production, and underwriter competition. *Journal of Finance*, 60, 443–86.

Coval, J. D. and Moskowitz, T. J. (1999). Home bias at Home: Local equity preference in domestic portfolios. *Journal of Finance*, 54(6), 2045–73.

——— (2001). The geography of investment: Informed trading and asset prices. *Journal of Political Economy*, 109(4), 811–41.

Crotty, J. (2008). If financial market competition is intense, why are financial firm profits so high? Reflections on the current 'Golden Age' of finance. *Competition and Change*, 12(2), 167–83.

Crouch, C. and Streeck, W. (eds.) (1997). *Political Economy of Modern Capitalism: Mapping Convergence and Diversity*. London: Sage.

Dahlquist, M., Pinkowitz, L., Stulz, R. M., and Wiliamson, R. (2003). Corporate governance and the home bias. *Journal of Financial and Quantitative Analysis*, 38(1), 87–110.

Dass, N. and Massa, M. (2008). The bank-firm relationship: A trade-off between better governance and greater information asymmetry. Working Paper. Available at: http://siteresources.worldbank.org/INTFR/Resources/The_Bank_Firm_Relationship_A_Trade_off_between_Better_Governance.pdf

Davies, J. (1961). *Corporations: A Study of the Origin and Development of Great Business Combinations and their Relation to the Authority of the State*. New York: Capricorn Books.

Davies, R. J. (2008). MiFID and a changing competitive landscape. Working Paper. Available at SSRN: http://papers.ssrn.com/sol3/papers.cfm?abstract_id=1117232

Davis, E. P. (1990). International financial centres – An industrial analysis. Discussion Paper 51, Bank of England.

DeMarzo, P. M., Kaniel, R., and Kremer, I. (2004). Diversification as public good: Community effects in portfolio choice. *Journal of Finance*, 59(4), 1677–715.

Dicken, P. (2004). Geographers and 'globalization': (Yet) another missed boat? *Transactions of the Institute of British Geographers*, 29(1), 5–26.

Dimson, E., Marsh, P., and Staunton, M. (2002). *Triumph of the Optimists: 101 Years of Global Investment Returns*. Princeton: Princeton University Press.

Doidge, C., Karolyi, G. A., and Stulz, R. M. (2004). Why are foreign firms that are listed in the US worth more? *Journal of Financial Economics*, 71, 205–38.

————— (2009). Has New York become less competitive than London in global markets? Evaluating foreign listing choices over time. *Journal of Financial Economics*, 91, 253–77.

Dore, R. (2000). *Stock Market Capitalism: Welfare Capitalism. Japan and Germany versus the Anglo-Saxons*. Oxford: Oxford University Press.

—— (2008). Financialization of the global economy. *Industrial and Corporate Change*, 17(6), 1097–112.

Doremus, P. N., Keller, W. W., Pauly, L. W., and Reich, S. (1998). *The Myth of the Global Corporation*. Princeton: Princeton University Press.

Dyck, A. and Zingales, L. (2004). Private benefits of control: An international comparison. *Journal of Finance*, 59, 537–600.

Economist (2009). The other-worldly philosophers. 18 July, 70–2.

Edison, H. J. and Warnock, F. E. (2008). Cross-border listings, capital controls, and equity flows to emerging markets. *Journal of International Money and Finance*, 27, 1013–27.

Eisenmann, T. R., Parker, G., and Van Alstyne, M. (2006). Strategies for two-sided markets. *Harvard Business Review*, 84(10), 92–101.

——————— (2009). Opening platforms: How, when and why? Harvard Business School Working Paper No. 09-030.

Ellis, K., Michaely, R., and O'Hara, M. (1999). A guide to the initial public offering process. *Corporate Finance Review*, 3, 14–18.

Engelen, E. (2003). The logic of funding European pension restructuring and the dangers of financialisation. *Environment and Planning A*, 35(8), 1357–72.

—— Grote, M. H. (2009). Stock exchange virtualisation and the decline of second-tier financial centres – The cases of Amsterdam and Frankfurt. *Journal of Economic Geography*, 9, 679–96.

Evans, D. S. and Schmalensee, R. (2007). The industrial organization of markets with two-sided platforms. *Competition Policy International*, 3(1), 151–79.

Faulconbridge, J. R. (2004). London and Frankfurt in Europe's evolving financial centre network. *Area*, 36, 235–44.

—— (2008). Negotiating cultures of work in transnational law firms. *Journal of Economic Geography*, 8, 497–517.

—— Hall, S., and Beaverstock, J. (2008). New insights into the internationalization of producer services: Organizational strategies and spatial economies for global headhunting firms. *Environment and Planning A*, 40(1), 210–34.

Feng, L. and Seasholes, M. S. (2004). Correlated trading and location. *Journal of Finance*, 59(5), 2117–44.

Ferguson, N. (2008). *The Ascent of Money*. New York: Penguin.

Fernandes, N. and Giannetti, M. (2009). On the fortunes of stock exchanges and their reversals: Evidence from foreign listings. Available at SSRN: http://papers.ssrn.com/sol3/papers.cfm?abstract_id=1201643

Ferrarini, G. (ed.) (1998). *European Securities Markets: The Investment Services Directive and Beyond*. London: Kluwer Law International.

Florida, R. (2002). *The Rise of the Creative Class: And How It's Transforming Work, Leisure, Community and Everyday Life*. New York: Basic Books.

Francis, B., Hasan, I., and Waisman, M. (2007). Does geography matter to bondholders? FRB of Atlanta Working Paper No. 2007-2. Available at SSRN: http://ssrn.com/abstract=962888

Franks, J., Mayer, C., and Rossi, S. (2009). Ownership: Evolution and regulation. *Review of Financial Studies*, 22(10), 4009–56.

Froud, J., Johal, S., Leaver, A., and Williams, K. (2006). *Financialization and Strategy: Narrative and Numbers*. London: Routledge.

Gaspar, J. and Glaeser. E. (1998). Information technology and the future of cities. *Journal of Urban Economics*, 43, 136–56.

Gaspar, J.-M. and Massa, M. (2007). Local ownership as private information: Evidence on the monitoring-liquidity trade-off. *Journal of Financial Economics*, 83, 751–92.

Gehrig, T. (2000). Cities and the Geography of Financial Centers. In J. Thisse and J.-M. Huriot (eds.), *The Economics of Cities* (pp. 415–45). Cambridge: Cambridge University Press.

Germain, R. D. (1997). *The International Organization of Credit: States and Global Finance in the World Economy*. Cambridge: Cambridge University Press.

Gertler, M. S. (2003). Tacit knowledge and the economic geography of context, or the undefinable tacitness of being (there). *Journal of Economic Geography*, 3(1), 75–100.

Glaeser, E., Johnson, S., and Shleifer, A. (2001). Coase versus the Coasians. *Quaterly Journal of Economics*, 116(3), 853–99.

Grinblatt, M. and Keloharju, M. (2001). How distance, language, and culture influence stockholdings and trades. *Journal of Finance*, 56(3), 1053–73.

Gritsai, O. (2004). Global business services in Moscow: Patterns of involvement. *Urban Studies*, 41, 2001–24.

Grossman, S. and Stiglitz, J. E. (1976). Information and competitive price systems. *American Economic Review*, 66(2), 246–53.

—— —— (1980). On the impossibility of informationally efficient markets. *American Economic Review*, 70(3), 393–408.

Grote, M. H. (2007). Mobile marketplaces – Consequences of the changing governance of European stock exchanges. *Growth and Change*, 38(2), 260–78.

Guiso, L., Haliassos, M., and Jappelli, T. (2003). Equity culture: Theory and cross-country evidence. *Economic Policy*, 18(36), 123–70.

Hall, P. and Soskice, D. (2001). *Varieties of Capitalism: The Institutional Foundations of Comparative Advantaage*. Oxford: Oxford University Press.

Halling, M., Pagano, M., Randl, O., and Zechner, J. (2008). Where is the market? Evidence from cross-listings in the United States. *Review of Financial Studies*, 21, 725–61.

Harris, L. (2003). *Trading and Exchanges. Market Microstructure for Practitioners*. Oxford: Oxford University Press.

Hasan, I. and Malkamäki, M. (2000). Are expansions cost effective for stock exchanges? A global perspective. Bank of Finland Discussion Paper 20/2000, Helsinki.

Hau, H. (2001). Location matters: An examination of trading profits. *Journal of Finance*, 56(5), 1959–83.

Held, D., McGrew, A. G., Goldblatt, D., and Perraton, J. (1999). *Global Transformations: Politics, Economics and Culture*. Cambridge: Polity.

Hengelbrock, J. and Theissen, E. (2009). Fourteen at one blow: The market entry of Turquoise. Available at SSRN: http://papers.ssrn.com/sol3/papers.cfm?abstract_id=1570646

Holmén, M. and Högfeldt, P. (2004). A law and finance analysis of initial public offerings. *Journal of Financial Intermediation*, 13, 324–58.

Hong, H., Kubik, J. D., and Stein, J. C. (2004). Social interaction and stock-market participation. *Journal of Finance*, 59(10), 137–63.

Huberman, G. (2001). Familiarity breeds investment. *Review of Financial Studies*, 14(3), 659–80.

Hung, M., Wong, T. J. and Zhang, T. (2008). Political relations and overseas stock exchange listing: Evidence from Chinese state-owned enterprises. Available at SSRN: http://papers.ssrn.com/sol3/papers.cfm?abstract_id=1224162

Hupperets, E. C. J. and Menkveld, A. J. (2002). Intraday analysis of market integration: Dutch blue chips traded in Amsterdam and New York. *Journal of Financial Markets*, 5, 57–82.

Ivković, Z. and Weisbrenner, S. (2005). Local does as local is: Information content of the geography of individual investors common stock investments. *Journal of Finance*, 60(1), 267–306.

Jenkinson, T. and Ljungqvist, A. (2001). *Going Public: The Theory and Evidence on How Companies Raise Equity Finance*. Oxford: Oxford University Press.

Jones, A. (2002). The 'global city' misconceived: The myth of 'global management' in transnational service firms. *Geoforum*, 33, 335–50.

JP Morgan (2009). *Depositary Receipts: Reference Guide*. Available at: www.adr.com/Reference/Reference.aspx

Kahneman, D. and Tversky, A. (1979). Prospect theory: An analysis of decision under risk. *Econometrica*, 47, 263–91.

Kalev, P. S., Nguyen, A. H., and Oh, N. Y. (2008). Foreign versus local investors: Who knows more? Who makes more? *Journal of Banking and Finance*, 32, 2376–89.

Kaminsky, G. and Schmuckler, S. (2003). Short-run pain, long-run gain: The effects of financial liberalization. NBER Working Paper No. 9787, Cambridge, MA.

Kang, J.-K. and Kim, J-K. (2008). The geography of block acquisitions. *Journal of Finance*, 63(6), 2817–58.

Karlsson, A. and Nordén, L. (2007). Home sweet home: Home bias and international diversification among individual investors. *Journal of Banking and Finance*, 31, 317–33.

Karmel, R. S. (2006). The Brazilian securities market: Brazil finds favour among foreign securities investors. *New Jersey Law Journal*, 13 November, 23.

Karolyi, G. A. (2003). DaimlerChrysler AG, the first truly global share. *Journal of Corporate Finance*, 9, 409–30.

—— (2004). The role of American depositary receipts in the development of emerging equity markets. *Review of Economics and Statistics*, 86, 670–90.

—— (2006). The world of cross-listings and cross-listings of the world: Challenging conventional wisdom. *Review of Finance*, 10(1), 99–152.

Kindleberger, C. P. (1974). *The Formation of Financial Centres: A Study in Comparative Economic History*. Princeton Studies in International Finance 36. Princeton University.

—— Aliber, R. Z. (2005). *Manias, Panics and Crashes: A History of Financial Crises*. Princeton Studies in International Finance 36. New York and Basingstoke: Palgrave Macmillan.

Klagge, B. and Martin, R. (2005). Decentralized versus centralized financial systems: Is there a case for local capital markets? *Journal of Economic Geography*, 5(4), 387–422.

Knorr Cetina, K. and Preda, A. (eds.) (2005). *The Sociology of Financial Markets*. Oxford: Oxford University Press.

Landier, A., Nair, V. B., and Wulf, J. (2009). Trade-offs in staying close: Corporate decision making and geographic dispersion. *Review of Financial Studies*, 22(3), 1119–48.

Langley, P. (2008). *The Everyday Life of Global Finance: Saving and Borrowing in Anglo-America*. Oxford: Oxford University Press.

Lannoo, K. (2007). The future of Europe's financial centres. European Capital Markets Institute Policy Brief No. 10. Available at: www.ceps.be/ceps/download/1405

La Porta, R., Lopez-de-Silanes, F., and Shleifer, A. (1999). Corporate ownership around the world. *Journal of Finance*, 54, 471–517.

—— —— —— Vishny, R. W. (1998). Law and finance. *Journal of Political Economy*, 106(6), 1113–55.

Laulajainen, R. (2001). End of geography at exchanges? *Zeitschrift für Wirtschaftsgeographie*, 45, 1–14.

—— (2003). *Financial Geography – A Banker's View*. London: Routledge.

Lazonick, W. and O'Sullivan, M. (2000). Maximizing shareholder value: A new ideology for corporate governance. *Economy and Society*, 29(1), 13–35.

Lee, R. (1998). *What is an Exchange? The Automation, Management and Regulation of Financial Markets*. Oxford: Oxford University Press.

—— Schmidt-Marwede, U. (1993). Interurban competition? Financial centres and the geography of financial production. *International Journal of Urban and Regional Research*, 17, 492–515.

Lerner, J. (2001). Where does *State Street* lead? A first look at finance patents, 1971–2000. Working Paper. Available at: http://www.hbs.edu/research/facpubs/workingpapers/papers2/0001/01-005.pdf

Levine, R. (2005). Finance and growth: Theory and evidence. In P. Aghion and S. Durlauf (eds.), *Handbook of Economic Growth*, edn.1, vol. 1A (pp. 865–934). Amsterdam: Elsevier.

Leyshon, A. (1995). Geographies of money and finance I. *Progress in Human Geography*, 19, 531–43.

—— (1997). Geographies of money and finance II. *Progress in Human Geography*, 21, 381–92.

—— Thrift, N. (1997). *Money/Space. Geographies of Monetary Transformation*. London: Routledge.

—— —— Justice, M. (1993). *A Reversal of Fortune? Financial Services and South East of England*. Stevenage: South East Economic Development Strategy.

Ling, T. H. (2005). Chinese firms face overseas listing blues. *Business Times Singapore*, 3 May, 4.

Lo, V. and Grote, M. H. (2002). Where traders go when stock markets go virtual – Concentration, dissemination or persistence? In M. Balling, F. Lierman, and A. Mullineux (eds.), *Technology and Finance: Challenges for Financial Markets Business Strategies and Policy Makers* (pp. 190–203). London: Routledge.

Loughran, T. (2008). The impact of firm location on equity issuance. *Financial Management*, Spring, 1–21.

—— Schultz, P. (2004). Weather, stock returns, and the impact of localized trading behavior. *Journal of Financial and Quantitative Analysis*, 39(2), 343–64.

—— —— (2005). Liquidity: Urban versus rural firms. *Journal of Financial Economics*, 78, 341–74.

Macey, J. R. and O'Hara, M. (2002). The economics of stock exchange listing fees and listing requirements. *Journal of Financial Intermediation*, 11, 297–319.

MacKenzie, D. (2006). *An Engine, Not a Camera: How Financial Models shape Markets*. Cambridge, MA: The MIT Press.

Majury, N. (2005). Technology and the architecture of markets: The re-configuration of the Canadian equity market. Unpublished manuscript, n.majury@qub.ac.uk

Malkamäki, M. (2000). Economies of scale and implicit mergers in stock exchange activities? Unpublished paper available at: www2.lse.ac.uk/fmg/documents/events/conferences/.../40_malkamaki.pdf

Malloy, C. J. (2005). The geography of equity analysis. *Journal of Finance*, 60(2), 719–55.

Markwat, T., Kole, E., and van Dijk, D. (2009). Contagion as a domino effect in global stock markets. *Journal of Banking and Finance*, 33, 1996–2012.

Martin, R. (ed.) (1999). *Money and the Space Economy*. Chichester: J Wiley & Sons.

——— (2000). Institutional approaches in economic geography. In E. Sheppard and T. Barnes (eds.), *A Companion to Economic Geography* (pp. 77–94). Oxford: Blackwell.

Martin, R. (2002). *The Financialization of Daily Life*. Philadelphia: Temple University Press.

Massa, M. and Simonov, A. (2006). Hedging, familiarity and portfolio choice. *Review of Financial Studies*, 19(2), 633–85.

McKinsey (2007). *Sustaining New York's and the US' Global Financial Services Leadership*. Available at: www.nyc.gov:80/html/om/pdf/ny_report_final.pdf

Menkveld, A. J., Koopman, S. J., and Lucas, A. (2007). Modeling around the clock price discovery for cross-listed stocks using state space methods. *Journal of Business & Economic Statistics*, 25, 213–25.

Merton, R. C. and Bodie, Z. (2004). The design of financial systems: Towards a synthesis of function and structure. NBER Working Paper No. 10620, Cambridge, MA.

Michie, R. C. (1999). *The London Stock Exchange: A History*. Oxford: Oxford University Press.

—— (2006). *The Global Securities Market: A History*. Oxford: Oxford University Press.

—— (2008). Reversal or change? The global securities market in the 20th century. *New Global Studies*, 2(1), 1–40.

Mishkin, F. S. (2007). *The Economics of Money, Banking, and Financial Markets*. Boston, MA: Pearson.

Moel, A., Rigobon, R., and Karolyi, G. A. (2001). The role of American depositary receipts in the development of emerging markets. *Economia*, 2, 209–73.

Moles, P. and Terry, N. (1999). *The Handbook of International Financial Terms*. Oxford: Oxford University Press.

Monk, A. H. B. (2010). Sovereignty in the era of global capitalism: The rise of sovereign wealth funds and the power of finance. Available at SSRN: http://papers.ssrn.com/sol3/papers.cfm?abstract_id=1587327

Morck, R. and Nakamura, M. (1999). Banks and corporate control in Japan. *Journal of Finance*, 54, 319–40.

Moyer, L. and Lambert, E. (2009). The new masters of Wall Street. *Forbes Magazine*, 21 September. Available at: www.forbes.com

Muellerleile, C. M. (2009). Financialisation takes off at Boeing. *Journal of Economic Geography*, 9, 663–77.

Neumark, D., Tinsley, P. A., and Tosini, S. (1991). After hours stock prices and post-crash hangovers. *Journal of Finance*, 46(1), 159–78.

Nielsson, U. (2009). Stock exchange merger and liquidity: The case of Euronext. *Journal of Financial Markets*, 12, 229–67.

O'Brien, R. (1992). *Global Financial Integration: The End of Geography*. London: Chatham House.

OECD (2006). *Purchasing Power Parities*. Report available at: www.oecd.org/std/ppp

Onado, M. (1998). Competition between exchanges or financial systems? In G. Frrerrarini (ed.), *European Securities Markets: The Investment Services Directive and Beyond* (pp. 225–44). London: Kluwer Law International.

Oxera (2006). *The Cost of Capital: An International Comparison*. Available at: www.oxera.com

Oxford Metrica (2009). *Depositary Receipts: Investing in a World Asset Class*. Available at: www.adrbnymellon.com/files/OxfordMetrica.pdf

Pagano, M. (1998). The changing microstructure of European equity markets. In Ferrarini, G. (ed.), *European Securities Markets: The Investment Services Directive and Beyond* (pp. 177–204). London: Kluwer Law International.

—— Panetta, F., and Zingales, L. (1998). Why do companies go public? An empirical analysis. *Journal of Finance*, 53, 27–64.

—— Röell, A. A., and Zechner, J. (2002). The geography of equity listing: Why do companies list abroad? *Journal of Finance*, 57, 2651–94.

Parwada, J. T. (2008). The genesis of home bias? The location and portfolio choices of investment company start-ups. *Journal of Financial and Quantitative Analysis*, 43(1), 245–66.

Pascual, R., Pascual-Fuster, B., and Climent, F. (2006). Cross-listing, price discovery and the informativeness of the trading process. *Journal of Financial Markets*, 9, 144–61.

Peck, J. and Theodore, N. (2007). Variegated capitalism. *Progress in Human Geography*, 31(6), 731–72.

Perotti, E. C. and Oijen van, P. (2001). Privatization, market development and political risk in emerging economies. *Journal of International Money and Finance*, 20, 43–69.

Piotroski, J. D. and Srinivasan, S. (2008). Regulation and bonding: The Sarbanes-Oxley Act and the flow of international listings. *Journal of Accounting Research*, 46, 383–425.

Pirrong, C. (1999). The organization of financial exchange markets: Theory and evidence. *Journal of Financial Markets*, 2, 329–57.

Porteous, D. (1999). The development of financial centres: Location, information externalities and path dependence. In R. Martin (ed.), *Money and the Space Economy* (pp. 95–114). Chichester: John Wiley.

Portes, R. and Rey, H. (2005). The determinants of cross-border equity flows. *Journal of International Economics*, 65, 269–96.

Posner, E. (2005). Sources of institutional change: The supranational origins of Europe's new stock markets. *World Politics*, 58, 1–40.

—— (2009). *The Origins of Europe's New Stock Markets*. Cambridge, MA: Harvard University Press.

Prinsky, C. and Wang, Q. (2006). Does corporate headquarters location matter for stock returns. *Journal of Finance*, 61(4), 1991–2015.

Rajan, R. and Zingales, L. (2003a). *Saving Capitalism from the Capitalists*. New York: Crown Business.

—— —— (2003b). The great reversals: the politics of financial development in the 20th century. *Journal of Financial Economics*, 69(1), 5–50.

Research Republic (2008). *The Future of Asian Financial Centres – Challenges and Opportunities for the City of London*. Available at: www.cityoflondon.gov.uk/Corporation/LGNL_Services/Business/Business_support_and_advice/Economic_information_and_analysis/Research_publications/

Ritter, J. (2003). Differences between European and American IPO markets. *European Financial Management*, 9, 421–34.

—— Welch, I. (2002). A review of IPO activity, pricing, and allocations. *Journal of Finance*, 57, 1795–1828.

Röell, A. (1996). The decision to go public: An overview. *European Economic Review*, 40, 1071–81.

Rogowski, W. (2005). Corporate governance in banking sector, the evidence from pre-accession Member States of the EU. Unpublished manuscript, Wojciech.Rogowski@mail.nbp.pl

Rossi, E. C. and Taylor, P. J. (2005). Banking networks across Brazilian cities: Interlocking cities within and beyond Brazil. *Cities*, 22, 381–93.

—— —— (2006). 'Gateway Cities' in economic globalization: How banks are using Brazilian cities. *Tijdschrift voor Economische en Sociale Geografie*, 97, 515–34.

Roxburgh, C., Lund, S., Atkins, C., Belot, S., Hu, W. W., and Pierce, M. S. (2009). *Global Capital Markets: Entering a New Era*. McKinsey Global Institute, September. Available at: http://www.mckinsey.com/mgi/publications

SAMI Consulting (2009). *An Assessment of the City's ICT Infrastructure*. Available at: http://www.cityoflondon.gov.uk/NR/rdonlyres/BD28AC92-B6DE-45AF-8690-9ACE76E09D2B/0/RS_BC_assessingICT.pdf

Sarkissian, S. and Schill, M. J. (2004). The overseas listing decision: New evidence of proximity preference. *Review of Financial Studies*, 17, 769–809.

—— —— (2008). Cross listing waves. Available at SSRN: http://papers.ssrn.com/sol3/papers.cfm?abstract_id=1244042

Sarre, P. (2007). Understanding the geography of international finance. *Geography Compass*, 1(5), 1076–96.

Sassen, S. (2001). *The Global City: New York, London, Tokyo*. Princeton: Princeton University Press.

—— (2005). The embeddedness of electronic markets: The case of global capital markets. In K. Knorr Cetina and A. Preda (eds.), *The Sociology of Financial Markets* (pp. 17–37). Oxford: Oxford University Press.

Scottish Enterprise (2005). *Pan-European Perspectives: Financial Services International Benchmarking Report*. Available at: http://www.scottish-enterprise.com/about-us/se-whatwedo/public-sector-info/search-iar/Pan-European-Perspectives—Financial-Services-International-Benchmarking-Report.aspx

Shiller, R. (2005). *Irrational Exuberance*. Princeton: Princeton University Press.

Shleifer, A. and Summers, L. (1988). Breach of trust in hostile takeovers. In A. Auerbach (ed.), *Corporate Takeovers: Causes and Consequences* (pp. 33–56). Chicago: University of Chicago Press.

—— Vishny, R. (1997). A survey of corporate governance. *Journal of Finance*, 52, 737–83.

Shukla, R. K. and van Inwegen, G. B. (1995). Do locals perform better than foreigners? An analysis of UK and US mutual fund managers. *Journal of Economics and Business*, 47, 541–54.

Sidaway, J. and Bryson, J. (2002). Constructing knowledges of 'emerging markets'. UK based fund managers and their overseas connections. *Environment and Planning A*, 34, 401–16.

Solnik, B. (1999). *International Investments*. New York: Longman.

Sonney, F. (2009). Financial analysts' performance: Sector versus country specialization. *Review of Financial Studies*, 22(5), 2087–131.

Steil, B. (2001). Creating securities markets in developing countries: A new approach for the age of automated trading. *International Finance*, 4, 257–78.

Stein, J. C. (2002). Information production and capital allocation: Decentralized versus hierarchical forms. *Journal of Finance*, 57(5), 1891–921.

Storper, M. and Venables, A. (2004). Buzz: Face-to-face contact and the urban economy. *Journal of Economic Geography*, 4, 351–70.

Story, J. and Walter, I. (1997). *Political Economy of Financial Integration in Europe*. Manchester: Manchester University Press.

Strange, S. (1997). *Casino Capitalism*. Manchester: Manchester University Press.

Stulz, R. M. (1999). Globalization, corporate finance, and the cost of capital. *Journal of Applied Corporate Finance*, 12, 8–25.

—— (2005). Presidential address: The limits of financial globalization. *Journal of Finance*, 60(4), 1595–638.

Subrahmanyam, A. and Titman, S. (1999). The going-public decision and the development of financial markets. *Journal of Finance*, 54, 1045–82.

Taylor, P. J. (2004). *World City Network: A Global Urban Analysis*. London and New York: Routledge.

—— Walker, D. R. F., and Beaverstock, J. V. (2002). Firms and their global service networks. In S. Sassen (ed.), *Global Networks, Linked Cities* (pp. 93–116). London: Routledge.

—— Ni, P., Derudder, B., Hoyler, M., Huang, J., Lu, F., Pain, K., Wiltox, F., Yang, X., Bassens, D., and Shen, W. (2009). The way we were: Command and control centres in the global space-economy on the eve of the 2008 geoeconomic transition. *Environment and Planning A*, 41, 7–12.

Teo, M. (2009). The geography of hedge funds. *Review of Financial Studies*, 22(9), 3531–61.

Tesar, L. and Werner, I. M. (1995). Home Bias and High Turnover. *Journal of International Money and Finance*, 14, 467–93.

Thrift, N. (1994). On the social and cultural determinants of international financial centres: The case of the city of London. In S. Corbridge, N. Thrift, and R. Martin (eds.), *Money, Power and Space* (pp. 327–55). Oxford: Blackwell.

Tickell, A. T. (2000). Unstable futures: creating risk in international finance. *Geoforum*, 3, 87–99.

Verdier, D. (2002). *Moving Money: Banking and Finance in the Industrialized World*. Cambridge: Cambridge University Press.

Walter, I. and Smith, R. C. (2000). *High Finance in the €uro-Zone: Competing in the New European Capital Market*. London: Financial Times.

Wang, J., Gulser, M., Liu, Z., and Meric, I. (2009). Stock market crashes, firm characteristics, and stock returns. *Journal of Banking and Finance*, 33, 1563–74.

Warsaw Stock Exchange (2009). *Factbook 2009*. Available at: www.gpw.com.pl

Weber, K., Davis, G. F., and Lounsbury, M. (2009). Policy as myth and ceremony? The global spread of stock exchanges, 1980–2005. *The Academy of Management Journal*, 52(6), 1319–47.

Wenger, E. and Kaserer, C. (1998). The German system of corporate governance: A model which should not be imitated. In S. W. Black and M. Moersch (eds.), *Competition and Convergence in Financial Markets: The German and Anglo-American Models* (pp. 41–78). New York: North Holland.

Werner, I. M. and Kleidon, A. W. (1996). UK and US trading of British cross-listed stocks: An intraday analysis of market integration. *Review of Financial Studies*, 9, 619–64.

Wójcik, D. (2002a). Cross-border corporate ownership and capital market integration in Europe: Evidence from portfolio and industrial holdings. *Journal of Economic Geography*, 2(4), 455–92.

—— (2002b). The Länder are the building blocks of the German capital market. *Regional Studies*, 36, 877–95.

—— (2003). Change in the German model of corporate governance: Evidence from blockholdings 1997–2001. *Environment and Planning A*, 35, 1431–58.

—— (2006). Convergence in corporate governance: Evidence from Europe and the challenge for economic geography. *Journal of Economic Geography*, 6(5), 639–60.

—— (2007). Do stock markets represent economies? Available at SSRN: http://papers.ssrn.com/sol3/papers.cfm?abstract_id=998814

—— (2008). Innovation and stock markets: International evidence on manufacturing and services. Available at SSRN: http://papers.ssrn.com/sol3/papers.cfm?abstract_id=1275384

—— (2009). Governance, corporate. In R. Kitchin and N. Thrift (eds.), *International Encyclopedia of Human Geography*, vol. 1 (pp. 600–5). Oxford: Elsevier.

—— (2011). Securitisation and its footprint: the rise of the US securities industry centres 1998–2008. *Journal of Economic Geography*. Available at: http://joeg.oxfordjournals.org/content/early/2011/01/03/jeg.lbq045.full/

Wood, P. (ed.) (2002). *Consultancy and Innovation: The Business Service Revolution in Europe*. Edinburgh: Pearson.

World Federation of Exchanges (2003). *The Significance of the Exchange Industry*. Available at:www.world-exchanges.org, secretariat@world-exchanges.org

—— (2010). *10 Years in Review*. Available at: www.world-exchanges.org/files/file/10%20Year%20Review.doc

Young, P. and Theys, T. (1999). *Capital Market Revolution: The Future of Markets in an Online World*. Edinburgh: Pearson.

Z/Yen (2010). *Global Financial Centres 7*. Available at: http://www.cityoflondon.gov.uk/Corporation/LGNL_Services/Business/Business_support_and_advice/Economic_information_and_analysis/Research_publications/

Index

Lightning Source UK Ltd.
Milton Keynes UK
UKOW030725191012

200847UK00001B/39/P